My name is NOT ME

Copyright © 2013 by Nami Ha All rights reserved.

Scripture quotations marked (NIV) are taken from the Holy Bible, New International Version®, NIV®. Copyright © 1973, 1978, 1984, 2011 by Biblica, Inc.™ Used by permission of Zondervan. All rights reserved worldwide. www.zondervan.com The "NIV" and "New International Version" are trademarks registered in the United States Patent and Trademark Office by Biblica, Inc.™

Cover Ilustration: Illustrator Chul Min Choi (www.illustmin.com)
Cover and Interior Book Design: Nami Ha
EPUB: Nami Ha
Contact: namiha@yahoo.com
Mail: P.O. Box 15654, Minneapolis, MN 55415-0654

Library of Congress Control Number: 2013905464

ISBN 9780989222204 (print version)
ISBN 9780989222211 (ebook)

Printed in the U.S.A.

My name is NOT ME

Dear God,

I have finally completed the homework that You gave me. It seemed to be an impossible dream at the beginning but I did it because of You. Now I realize that my language barrier or my lack of writing experience could not be an excuse. All I had to do was just to trust You and be obedient.

Here is the book. I was afraid of revealing my personal stories and the sinful life I had lived in the past. But in the process of writing I realized how much unconditional love You had shown me in every situation then I was called to be a righteous one through the blood of Jesus Christ. Thank you for forgiving my sins and bringing me back to You.

Being obedient to You is not that we lose our freedom. Surrendering our lives to You is not that we become a slave with no hope. It is breaking our chains of slavery and getting rid of our old habits in order to become a citizen of the Kingdom of God through our Lord Jesus Christ.

Thank you for this invaluable opportunity to share my stories. This book belongs to You. Please use it for Your will. May Your grace and mercy be with the readers wherever they are and whatever they may face right now.

In Jesus,
Amen

Contents

My name is NOT ME

Nami Ha

1

God's Alarm Clock

I did not know how long I had been sleeping. I did not hear the alarm go off. I was not sure if I was sleeping or half awake. I kept telling myself I should not miss the flight. *What time is it now?*

It must have been really windy outside. I thought I was still sleeping but somehow I was able to hear a rattling noise caused by a couple of small pebbles in an empty can rolling from side to side. I thought I was dreaming but the constant rattling noise became irritating and I could not sleep any more.

I slowly opened my eyes and felt my own body was so heavy like soaked cotton. I felt sick. I barely got up and dragged myself to the shower room at the Youth Hostel where I stayed. It was a little after five o'clock in the morning. I was glad that I heard the annoying can noise. If it was not there, I probably was not able to get up. I did not know what happened to the alarm. I did not hear it or maybe I was unable to set the alarm properly the night before. I wondered how the can ended up tossed right under my window with the pebbles in it. I believed God woke me up that morning.

I called a cab and headed to the airport. I was so sick and could not sit up. I was lying on the back seat. Then all of sudden, I wanted to check if I brought my old passport. Although I was going to get a new one, I still needed to show it at the airport in Canada. I was a foreigner there. I realized that I forgot to bring my old passport. I felt so dumb and stupid. I did not know how to apologize to the taxi driver.

"I am soooooo sorry. I did not bring my passport. Would you please go back to the Youth Hostel? I need to grab my passport. I am really sorry. I made a terrible mistake. I had too much to drink last night."

The female driver said, "Not a problem. I understand. We all make mistakes sometimes."

She could have thought that I was a stupid drunk girl but at least she did not show any unpleasant manner to me. I ran into the room and found my passport then ran back to the taxi.

"Thank you so much for waiting. Thank you."

When I was checking in to get my boarding pass, the airline ticket agent kindly asked me, "Excuse me. Are you okay? You look so pale."

I was hardly able to stand up. The lack of food all day long the day before and drinking too much made me sick. My head was spinning and I collapsed right in front of the check-in counter. I was so cold and shivering. I just wanted to sleep forever. I did not want to go anywhere. I was not sure why I had that much to drink the night before. I drank more than usual and it was too late for regret.

The ticket agent asked me if I could travel in that condition. I said I must go. Soon a wheelchair was brought and they put me on the wheelchair. While I was being pushed on the wheelchair to the gate, I felt people were staring at me. I was ashamed of myself that I was sick because I had a hangover. So I had my head down and pretended that I was really sick.

As soon as I was seated in the airplane I covered myself with a blanket but a thin blanket was not nearly enough. I was still cold. I asked for another blanket. The flight attendant brought me two more blankets. I felt like vomiting. I had the sick bag ready but since I had no food, nothing came out. I was glad that no one was sitting next to me. I laid down on the three seats and closed my eyes to get some sleep. I was exhausted and didn't want to wake up. My thoughts were all mixed up.

How have I come to this point? Who am I? Where am I going? What's going to happen next? Oh boy….I am just freaking tired of this life...

Sunflowers

It was just a small one bedroom house. The narrow kitchen had a charcoal block heating furnace with pipes that ran under the bedroom for heating the floor. I was about seven years old and I had two younger brothers; two years younger and five years younger than me. My parents and the three of us all slept in the single bedroom. The room was our bedroom, study room and living room. Although the house was tiny, we had a large empty front yard. My mother planted lots of sunflowers and they became very tall. The stems were thick and the yellow flowers were huge. She wanted to have sunflower oil later but one night she was frightened by the sunflowers. She thought some people were standing there in the middle of the night and staring at her, so before she had the sunflower oil, she had them all cut down right away.

A couple of years later my father, who was a carpenter, built a three bedroom house on the empty lot where the sunflowers were. The main bedroom had four sliding doors. It looked like two rooms from outside but it was actually one large room. He put large sliding partitions in the middle of the room. We could push the partitions to one side and make it as one room or spread them to make it two rooms instantly, though I never understood why he did not put a regular wall in the middle of the room to make it as two. The floor was heated by a charcoal block furnace in the kitchen which was also used for cooking, much like the arrangement in our smaller house. Only the area close to the furnace was warm. The far end of the room was always cold so we stayed closer to the furnace in winter.

We did not have a television or a refrigerator like many other people back then. Not many people owned private automobiles or telephones. People never heard of personal computers. There was only one household in the entire neighborhood who owned a black and white television that had accordion style doors to open and close and four legs under the television. Some neighbors went to the house after having dinner to watch television. My parents never went to that house. I went there once out of curiosity. The owner opened his bedroom door wide where the television was and people stood outside on the ground. They shouted and clapped when they were watching a wrestling match. When I came home my mother told me not to go there anymore. "Stay home and study," she would tell me.

My family, like many others, relied on public transportation. Public buses cost 30 Korean won which was about a quarter U.S. dollar. Each bus was run by a driver and a bus stewardess. When the bus was not packed the bus stewardess walked in the running bus and collected bus fare from the passengers but when it was packed, we paid to the stewardess at the rear door right before we got off the bus. Most of the roads were unpaved dirt roads. When the buses left after passengers got off, people closed their eyes and mouths or looked in different directions not to breathe the dust clouds.

Spring was always short. Yellow Forsythia and pink Azalea flowers were all over the hills and the mountains. Sometimes my mother worked at a peach farm. Her job was to wrap each peach with cut off newspapers to protect them from fruit bugs. My brothers and I did our chores while she was away at work.

I was taught how to take care of myself. My mother once showed me how to sew a patch that was cut from an older sock to repair holes in the heels of my better socks. When I completed other chores such as washing dishes or wiping the floors, sewing socks with patches was the next thing I did in my spare time. I did not play with the neighborhood children at all. It was not allowed by my mother. Their parents were uneducated and the kids spoke with foul language. So I thought I was different and special from other kids in the neighborhood.

Summer was hot, dusty and humid. Small convenient stores had several long wooden boxes in front of them. Each box had a lid on top and a cold rubber pouch that had a big chunk of dry ice in it to keep sweet bean ice bars cold in the humid hot summer. My mother hardly bought us those sweet ice bars. But she had several different kinds of beans roasted and ground them to make them like fine powder. It smelled really good. Instead of buying the sweet bean ice bars, she mixed the ground bean powder in water and we drank it. When we could we would add some ice cubes and sugar that we bought at a store. It became a fantastic summer drink. We also enjoyed lots of water melons and tomatoes during the summer time.

Some women in the neighborhood sat under a Zelkova Serrata tree to enjoy the cool breeze and let their children lay down on their laps to catch lice falling from their hair. I remember being able to recognize the kids who had lice because they were constantly scratching their heads. Sometimes I envied those kids who were lying down on their mothers' laps. They were laughing and giggling even though their mothers were scolding them because of the lice, though they seemed to be happy together. When I had lice once, my mother scolded me harshly and questioned what kind of bad kids I hung out with to get the lice from. Then she had me lay down on her lap and started squeezing my head with her two thumb nails to catch the lice. When it was done, I felt my head was burning from the squeezing.

Autumn was short, like spring. The mountains were covered with colorful maple trees. Choo-Suk, the Korean Thanksgiving, was one of the biggest Korean holidays. Every train station and bus station was jam packed with people who wanted to go visit their hometowns. Children were especially excited because parents bought them new pairs of shoes, socks and clothes. My family always visited grandparents on Choo-Suk. First my father's parents, then my mother's.

My family, like many other families back then never celebrated Christmas or had gifts from Santa on Christmas day. The very first time I went to church was when I was about five years old. My mother told me that the church nearby our old house that we use to rent gave away candies to children in the neighborhood on Sunday. So I went to the church to get the free candy. That was how I started going to church. I did not know what church meant. To me it was just a nice place where I could get some free candy and hear some interesting old stories. I still remember that I heard about how King David defeated Goliath with three sling stones. I did not know it was a story from the Bible. I just thought the old man at the church told the neighborhood children some interesting stories. That was a church to me—free candies and interesting stories. I learned gospel songs, prayed in the name of Jesus and said Amen along with other children at the church. So I learned that there was God.

"Before I formed you in the womb I knew you, before you were born I set you apart;"

—Jeremiah 1:5

I want to be an orphan

The first day at school we were not wearing school uniforms yet but I still remember that all of the first grade students lined up at the school track field in front of their teachers. We were all wearing our name tags and white hankies together. Our school uniform was a white sailor's uniform with green stripes for summer and black with white stripe for winter. We all wore blue cloth shoes.

Ever since I started school my mother demanded that I do exactly what she said and expected me to do exactly as she was thinking. I remember the days when my mother taught me how to write the Korean alphabet. I had a notebook that had grid lines and I wrote each Korean character in each square. When I finished writing my mother told me to erase them all and do it again because the letters didn't exactly look like the printed sample. If they looked crooked or had too much empty space she told me to rewrite the characters again and again until the characters looked perfect to her. When I brought the notebook to school to show my homework my teacher couldn't believe how many times I practiced writing. My notebook pages became ragged. It was made that way from my tears and sweat.

Gradually I found myself being afraid of my mother. No matter what I did it was nearly impossible to satisfy her expectations and I was punished for that. When I came near our house after school I was reluctant to go in, so I walked around the house several times to see if there was any sign that my mother was happy or angry. She would probably be upset as usual and wait for me to complain about something and then beat me. I was scared and hated going home. Another miserable day was waiting for me in the hell house. It happened pretty much every day.

On Sundays sometimes I would sneak out of the house and go to church. My prayer was only one—Dear God, please don't let my mother beat me anymore. Once in a while God answered my prayer and I thanked Him but most of the time it didn't work that way. I could not recall when my mother was happy or laughed out loud. She often argued with my father or they hardly talked to each other at all.

My mother poured out her anger and stress on my brothers and I. When she beat my younger brothers I could not do anything but watch them helplessly being in awful pain and shock. She also beat us if we made any crying sound. She said neighbors could hear us so we had to cry without making any sound no matter how painful it was. She cursed and beat us to death with a leather belt, water hose, wooden laundry bat, sewing needles to poke our heads and just about anything she could get her hands on. She beat us until we were covered with sweat, numb and could not move our fingers or legs freely. Our hands were often shaky and trembled from the pain and the horror. Sometimes she even bit us with her own teeth. I used to have a hard dried wart on my right hand on top of my index finger. When she bit me one day the hard dried wart got soften from the sweat and her teeth cut it off. Blood was all over my hand. At first I thought I lost a finger because of the pain and the blood. If there was any place that I hated the most on the earth, it was the place where my mother was. She abused me and my brothers verbally, physically, emotionally and mentally.

Her strange personality was getting worse and worse every day. I had no memory of when she was kind and gentle to us. She was always unhappy with something. If there was nothing to complain about, then she imagined and created her own things.

She said, "You could have said so. You could have done so." Then she said terrible things to me.

"But I did not do it and I did not say it."

Then, she insisted and said, "If it ever happened for real, you would surely say such things and do such things. I have no doubt. Admit it that you would do just as what I said. ADMIT IT!"

If I did not say anything, she ran to me to beat me again so I had to falsely admit immediately as if I would do it.

"Yes, you are right, Mom. I would say as what you just said. You are right."

Then she walked away from me. I was so upset but could not stop her. I just had to be quiet and swallow my tears. She manipulated and brainwashed me with her own imagination. She made me think and believe what she said. It drove me nuts. I hated being accused for something I never even dreamt of.

I loved rainy days. When it rained, my father did not have to go to work early in the morning. He slept late. Then my mother couldn't do anything to us. But he did not stay home all day long unless it was pouring rain with thunder and lightning. He would often go out and came home late after getting drunk. Whether he was drunk or not, as long as he was with us at home, he was protecting us from our mother. My happy days were gloomy rainy days with thunder and lightning. I felt I had some relief and protection. My father probably didn't like rain as much as I did because people complained that their houses my father built were leaking from the rain. It was not just the houses he built. I saw other houses and even my school and church had the same problems when it rained. But my mother complained that my father was incapable and said disrespectful things about him in front of us.

After she beat me to death one day my legs turned black and blue. So she told me to wear winter stockings in the hot summer. My father thought it was awkward to see me wearing thick long winter stockings in summer time. He told me to take them off and saw my brutally beat up legs. He became so mad but she could not say a word to defend herself. I pretended that I was protecting her so I said it was my fault and I deserved to be punished. I thought she would not beat me much in the future as a favor if I defended her like that. But deep inside of me, I wished he would slap her cheeks left and right really hard like she did to me and kick her or maybe kill her if he ever could. My lips were torn and bleeding when she slapped my cheeks. I wanted my father to do the exact same thing to her. The more he raised his voice, the more I felt comforted inside. I thought it would be fair for her to be treated like that.

I witnessed a couple of occasions when my father finally lost his control. My mother complained about not having enough money for groceries. She kept complaining and aggravating him.

The dinner table was upside down and food was scattered all over. But my mother talked back and didn't stop arguing with him. So he kicked her, grabbed her by the hair and slapped her cheeks. She cried out and complained about her poor unhappy life. She said she wanted to die and my father said, "Let's die all together tonight."

He finally punched on the floor so hard several times. His knuckles were bleeding. My brothers and I crouched in the corner of the room and cried with fear. Then he left the house for a drink and came home heavily drunk after midnight. After cleaning the chaotic room, we didn't say a word. We all laid down under the blanket when he came home. He mumbled but my mother lay on her side and didn't say a word. We all pretended we were sleeping but I knew we were all nervous and wide awake. Deep inside of me I blamed God that He let my brothers and I be born into such a miserable, unhappy family.

My parents often said that they should get divorced. I really wished that they would do so. The sooner the better. My decision was already made. I wanted to go live with my father. Of course, it never happened. One day my mother told us that he decided to go to Saudi Arabia for a year to get a job working on a construction site. When I heard that news the first time I thought my life was over. She was probably happy about a fixed monthly salary from him and her own life without him but I was miserable and depressed. The fear of being with her without my father's protection overwhelmed me. I just couldn't help but sob quietly. He would be gone for a whole year!!! I didn't know how to survive at the hell house even a day without him. A week, a month, a whole year!!! It was just too long. It was out of my control. There was nothing I could do to protect myself from her. I was just a defenseless little girl.

After my father was gone to Saudi Arabia, my mother forced me to learn using the abacus. I was in the fourth grade. She taught me the basics first then she sent me to an abacus learning school after my regular school. She said just in case if my father died by accident, then I had to go get a job as a clerk, so I should have the abacus skill. Back then abacus was commonly used for business and there were no personal computers. Abacus skills were graded and certificates were given to students who passed each level test. The more fast and accurate abacus skills they had the better jobs they got right after high school as office clerks.

I had several practice books that were full of numbers. My mother gave me large old calendars to use the blank backsides as scratch paper. I calculated the numbers with my abacus then wrote down the answers on the calendar scratch papers. She was timing me to see how fast I could calculate and I gave her my answers once I practiced page by page. When I did well I went to sleep early but when I gave her wrong answers, she beat my hands with the laundry bat. My hands were shaky and could no longer practice. Sometimes she smacked my head or hit the floor with my abacus. She broke several abacuses. I collected the scattered abacus beads with tears. I cried and begged for her mercy. She went to sleep but I had to continue my practice. I was worried that I might not be able to finish the assignments she gave me in time. It was getting really late, almost midnight or even later. So I secretly started copying the answers from the answer sheets. I wrote some wrong answers on purpose so it would look more natural instead of copying perfect answers.

When I was a beginner I calculated line by line but when I reached the advanced level, instead of doing line by line, I was able to calculate two lines in memory then plugged the numbers in the abacus. I heard a few high school students who were way more advanced than me calculated three lines at once in memory then put the numbers in the abacus. That kind of speed was a whole different world compared to others who did it line by line. I learned the abacus from the fourth grade to the sixth grade. At school, some teachers called me to help them with their students' grades. When I went home late after helping the teachers I told my mother what I had been doing then she didn't say much on that particular day.

My life without my father was just unthinkable day by day. One time my mother pushed me to the corner of the room and kept banging my head against the wall. The skin on my head was torn and started bleeding. I ended up going to a hospital to have the wound stitched. I still have the scar on the left side of my head. Another day she pulled my arm so hard that my shoulder was dislocated. She took me to a place where a big sign said "BONE" which turned out to be a quasi orthopedic therapy office. When we came out of the bone place, she bought me sugar sprinkled twisted donuts on the street. It was probably the very first time that I had a donut. It may have been one of the few times she showed some remorse for her abusive behavior.

She also went through a phase where she would not let me sleep. She heard a strange story from someone one day. She heard a successful man talking about how he became very successful. The man said he worked hard and slept only four hours a day. She told me that I had to sleep for four hours from now on and she forced me to memorize certain portions of text books exactly as they were written. Telling her a summary was not what she wanted. She wanted me to recite them line by line. She was not herself anymore. She was definitely a psychotic woman to me. When I was dozing off she got up from her sleep and demanded to know how much I memorized of the assignment she gave to me.

If I did not do well then she brought the laundry bat or the water hose to beat me. Sometimes she put me outside of the bedroom in cold winter where there was no heater. My whole body shivered. My hands and feet got so cold. My teeth were hitting against each other. I remembered a prisoner's story that I once heard. He was so cold in his prison cell so he started reading the Bible that his mother gave him. He tried to find the word "Fire" in the Bible. He desperately read the Bible and as soon as he found the word "Fire" in the Bible, all of a sudden he felt the cold prison cell was getting warm and his body was also warming up. I wished I would have that kind of miracle happened to me too but I thought I was nobody to have such kind of a miracle from God. I wondered if God ever knew about my miserable life.

"And even the very hairs of your head are all numbered."

—Matthew 10:30

One night my mother turned the light off while I was still doing my homework. She said I was wasting electricity and I should have finished my homework earlier. She did not care that I had to do the abacus practice she told me to do and that I did not have time for my assigned homework from school. I hated her being so unfair but could not say a word to her. I was sitting on the wooden floor outside the bedroom. I couldn't read my book so I took out a magnifying glass that my brothers and I had used for burning paper on sunny days. I needed to use the moon beam to do my homework. It was ridiculous that I had to use a magnifying glass to read and write because of my crazy mother.

Early in the morning she gave me several oral questions to answer right before I headed out the door to go to school. If I did not give her the right answers then she did not let me go to school. She gave me another question to answer. I was getting late for school.

I cried and begged, "Please, let me go to school. I am already late. I will be punished by the teacher. Please let me go. Please."

She ignored my pleas. School started at 9:00 A.M. but she let me leave the house around 8:55 A.M. It took almost twenty minutes to walk to the school. Then I had to hastily run all the way to the school, wiping tears from my eyes the entire way. I was worried what my teacher was going to say or how she may punish me in front of the other students. When I arrived at the classroom I quietly walked to my seat. I was sweating and my face was red. When my teacher asked me why I was late I just said that I slept late. I never said any bad things about my mother.

We used to have dogs. All of them died one by one because of my mother. Indeed they were killed by her mistakes. She wanted to catch rats around the house, so she put poison here and there. Instead of catching the rats, our dogs ate the poison and died right in front of her eyes. She saw the dogs struggling with rolled eyes and white foam in their mouths in such pain for hours before they died. She said she was so sorry but they were just dogs after all and she forgot about them. She repeated the same stupid mistake again and again. I thought she was a true devil to kill these innocent dogs. I thought if I were one of the dogs I was surely killed by now too. She never hesitated threatening me to die. She brought some white powder to me once and told me to eat the poison and die. It looked like white sugar to me but I was so disgusted that she demanded me to eat the poison and die there. I doubted if she was truly my mother who birthed me into this world. I wanted to rub her face with real poison if I could. But I COULD NOT DO ANYTHING! I could do nothing but cry and beg for her mercy.

Back then dogs ate whatever we left after we had meals. We boiled the leftover food to make soup and fed them. When we did not have much food left then we added some vegetables and boiled them. One day she told me to feed the dog and I brought the food container to the dog. She came after me a few minutes later and screamed at me that I gave the dog uncooked food. She said the radish was still raw and brought the food container and shoved it under my eyes. She said, "Look at this. Is this fully cooked in your eyes? Why don't you eat it and tell me!"

I refused to eat the dog food. She cursed at me and demanded, "Eat it! And tell me if it's cooked!"

I picked up one slice of the half cooked radish and chewed it. I shed tears and said, "It is not fully cooked yet. I thought it was but please forgive me. I am so sorry."

Although the food was boiling, usually radish took a long time to be fully cooked unless it was thinly sliced. I didn't know that at the time.

When she was beating me one day, I told her that I didn't think she was my real mother and I was going out to find my real mother or was going to an orphanage. She did not take it seriously and said to leave. I did not pack anything but started walking toward the house entrance door. She said she was going to kill me if I really left the house. I did not stop then she actually grabbed our big kitchen knife. She thought I would stop if I saw her grabbing the knife but I ran away. She wrapped the kitchen knife in a towel and followed me. I walked and walked in the rain. I did not know where I was going but I had a long walk along the river. I started thinking if I did not turn and go back home by now, she might either really kill me or beat me to death. So I reluctantly turned around and came back home. Surprisingly she did not talk to me much or beat me that night.

When my father finally came back home after a year of working in Saudi Arabia I could not describe how happy I was. It was the first time seeing him in a year. My father brought us some cookies made in Saudi Arabia as well as pencils and a pencil sharpener made in the U.S.A. He also brought a SONY radio and cassette player made in Japan. I was excited to have those gifts made in foreign countries but I was more excited that he was not going anywhere but may stay with us forever. I was going to have a brand new life now. I felt that my misery was over, finally, or at least while he was at home with us.

Though it was great to have my father home again, some of his behavior often made me worried. He used to ride bicycles in the past but he purchased a motor cycle. I loved the loud engine noise when he was coming home. I knew I was free from my mother. I got really excited especially when the loud engine noise was getting closer and louder. But when it turned out to be someone else who was just passing by my heart sank so deep and I was so disappointed and wanted to cry. But when it was him my brothers and I all rushed to the door to greet him. He had several serious motor cycle accidents from driving drunk. I remember seeing him with blood all over himself. I saw his elbows and knees hurt severely. He could not sleep well because of the pain. Sometimes the pain from the injuries caused him to miss work. A guy helped my father one time and brought him home. He said my father fell off after hitting against the back of a truck and slid several meters away. If he did not wear his helmet he could have killed himself. I saw his damaged helmet. He was very lucky. My mother didn't like him drinking at all and it was one of their arguing subjects but he said he had to drink because of his job. He was with his construction crew and they drank pretty much every day after their long hours of work. He could not refuse to drink when they offered a So-Ju (distilled rice wine) cup to him.

One night my father told me to bring him a glass of cold water. I went to the kitchen but wanted to sleep just for two minutes. I was exhausted because my mother had me stay up late for the abacus training and then would get up early in the morning.

"No more than two minutes," I said to myself.

One minute was too short and three minutes were too long. So I decided to close my eyes for two minutes only. I curled up my body and laid down on the cold tile floor in the kitchen and closed my eyes. I counted one, two, three, four to count two minutes. The total lack of sleep for night after night put me in an unconscious sleep instantly. I had no idea how I ended up in the bedroom and woke up the next day.

My mother took me to an oriental medicine doctor as soon as I came home from school that next day. He checked my pulse and told her that I needed to avoid any stress from now on. I became very weak and pale. He asked what extra activities I was involved with besides school. I said Abacus practice. He said I needed to pause from that kind of practice for a while I needed to relax. I thought the doctor was very gracious to say that. Maybe God sent him! *Oh, thank you God for telling my mother through this doctor.* Since then, my mother did not tell me to do the abacus practice anymore.

After I quit doing the abacus I didn't do anything for a while after school. I didn't know what to do with my spare time all of a sudden. She didn't like me doing nothing either so she took me to a Piano Hak-One which was a private teaching school. I saw some piano books in one of the rooms while my mother was talking with a teacher and the complicated music notes were not appealing to me at all. After visiting the Piano Hak-One she suggested fine art. So we went to a fine art school in downtown. When we were entering the art school I smelled pine trees. I really liked it. It reminded me of visiting my grandmother's house in the deep country. It was coming from oil paintings. I saw a lot of white statues for charcoal drawings lined up on a long shelf. There were some students doing water color painting by looking at the actual objects on a large table. I told my mother that I was interested in fine art rather than piano. The instructor told me to start sketching a piece for him in front of the still life table. So I did. He asked if I took lessons somewhere else. I said I never took any lessons before. He said I did really well.

Missing Yarns and Needles

When I was in middle school my teacher, Mrs. Kang,

misunderstood something and treated me as a thief. I wanted to erase that awful experience from my memory but I have never been able to.

One late afternoon all the students were gone after class but I was standing outside of the classroom in order to finish reading my book—*Rage of Angels* (1980) written by my favorite American author Sidney Sheldon. I only had a few pages left and I wanted to know how the story ended so I stayed outside of the classroom after the last class and finished reading the book.

The next day Mrs. Kang called my name before the class started and took me to the teachers' office room. She looked at me as if she despised me for some reason. I was scared and did not know why she was staring at me like that.

I said nervously, "Yes?"

She looked at me out of the corner of her eyes and demanded out of the blue, "RETURN IT!"

"Return what?"

"You know exactly what I am talking about! Return it now when I am telling you nicely."

I had no idea what she was talking about. She said I stole her knitting yarn and needles. I just became speechless and stood there perplexed. I had to defend myself but didn't know where to start. God knew that I had nothing to do with her knitting tools. She said that *someone told her* that I was the last person who stayed late after school. I said I stayed late to finish reading my book. She said go back to my desk and return before the school was over that day. I was scared and did not know what to do. I was afraid of telling my mother about what happened at school. I had to face accusation to some petty crime that I had not committed. I did not know where to go and who I should talk to. I felt miserable. There was my mother at home and the teacher at school. I was afraid of them both and hated them both.

When I went home that day I decided to write a letter to Mrs. Kang as if it was my mother who wrote the letter but I copied my father's handwriting because his handwriting was very distinctive as an adult's handwriting.

I wrote, "Dear Mrs. Kang, My daughter came home today and told me what happened at school regarding your knitting items. She came home a little bit late yesterday and told me that she was reading her book and wanted to finish it. I did not see her carrying any yarn or needles. I wanted to visit you on this matter but since it is not something pleasant to discuss I am kindly sending you this letter via my daughter. Thank you for your understanding and I am very sorry about your missing items. Sincerely,"

In the letter, I tried to sound like a grown up person. I gave the letter to Mrs. Kang the next morning before the class started. I was very nervous if she could find out that it was me who wrote the letter. But after reading the letter, she did not look at me like she did the day before. She seemed to be content. Maybe she found her kitting items, I was not sure. It was the most terrible experience to me during my three years of that middle school period. Most of the teachers at school knew that I was a good student and they treated me fairly well but I could not believe that my own teacher treated me as a thief!

We used to wear school uniform but the school decided that students could wear casual clothes from now on. I was still in Mrs. Kang's class. My mother bought me expensive brand name clothes and shoes to make me look nice despite her tight budget. She wanted me to have things that she could not have when she was growing up. Mrs. Kang had a survey one day to see how much money students spent on their clothes since we stopped wearing school uniform. She asked students to raise their hands if the price range she called was describing the price of the students' outfits that they were wearing that day. I raised my hand at the very end which was the highest range. Other students said, "Wow!"

I was very glad that Mrs. Kang had the survey. I felt as if I proved myself that I was not a cheap thief that she thought I was. When we were wearing school uniforms we all looked pretty much the same. But with my brand name clothes, *NIKE* leather shoes, and the fine art lessons after school my classmates were curious about me and asked what my father's occupation was. I said my father owned his own construction business. At least I looked nice to the outside world. Indeed I always acted as a cheerful happy girl to disguise my miserable abusive life at home. They had no idea what I was hiding underneath the expensive outfits that I was wearing—the terrible bruises and fear of the horrible abuse from my mother.

Sometimes I skipped going to the art school. I didn't want to go home early either so I started following a bunch of trouble making girls after school for a couple of months. Those girls did not treat me as one of their real friends and indeed they did not care whether I followed them or not. They usually hung out at a video game room where a bunch of boys from other schools hung out too. One day I heard one of the girls whom I was following whisper something to another girl sitting next to her playing a video game.

The girl stopped playing the video game and asked, "What? Who?"

"The guy standing over there but don't look at him now."

"So what did you say??"

"I said NO!"

I learned later that they were talking about having sex. We were only 14 or 15 years old. I was afraid of listening to that kind of conversation and felt that I should stop following them. I saw them tearing a text book, stamping on it and spitting on it. I was shocked by their troubling behavior. They talked about each teacher who treated them badly at school and cursed on them with all kinds of dirty words.

We had to take a high school entrance exam. When we passed with a certain score we were eligible to apply for one of the high schools in the city, but if we failed our options were going to schools outside of the city. I did not take it seriously. My time spent with the troublemakers caught up with me. I thought I would pass the test. But I failed. My father was disappointed and said he was shocked. He never doubted that I would pass the test. He thought the test would be a piece of cake for me and I would pass it easily. I was very sorry to him and regretted that I followed the troubled girls.

My mother and I visited one of the schools in the suburbs. The school was very small and everything at the school seemed to be old and outdated. Rice fields were all around the school. After visiting the school my parents told me to try the exam again next year, so I registered at a private preparation school called Hak-One. All the students at the Hak-One were the ones who failed the high school entrance exam. I had to focus on the subjects that I did poorly on in the exam. One of them was English. I was always confused by the confusing grammar then lost interest in learning English and I almost gave up by the end of my school year. The Hak-One turned out to be a great opportunity for me to build basic English grammar again. I stopped going to the art school and focused on studying to prepare for the test. I did not have any contact with the troubled girls either. I just went to Hak-One and home.

My mother did not beat me as much as she used to since my father came back from Saudi Arabia but still complained about an endless number of little things. On one occasion I had a very difficult exam. Most students at Hak-One performed poorly including myself. We all complained that the tests were really difficult. My overall test score turned out really bad. I was afraid of bringing the report card to my mother. As I expected she scolded me harshly and said that I was not doing anything but wasting money. I asked one of the girls in my class whom I often studied with if her parents said anything about her recent report card. She said her parents said they understood and she could do better next time. She asked me what my parents said. I said that my parents said the same thing. I wondered why my mother couldn't be like other parents—gentle and understanding. I finally passed the high school entrance exam. The best part of the whole preparation was that I was able to learn English grammar again from the basics and definitely gained confidence in English.

I don't have God

High School was a little bit awkward at first to be with younger classmates, but one year old difference was not too bad. I did not have to tell anyone that I had to retake the high school entrance exam. Students were from several different middle schools and they did not know each other. Everything was new and I liked the new beginning. I wanted to do well especially in

English. I was no longer afraid of English.

My mother's physical abuse was not as much as it used to be but she never stopped complaining or verbally abusing me. Some of the expressions were ones that I never heard of in my life. They were immoral and humiliating. I wished I would be stupid and not remember all of that. Isn't a mother supposed to protect her own precious daughter? How could she say such awful things to me? I truly believed that she could not be my birth mother. She did not deserve to be my mother. I hated her with all my heart and soul. I did not have any close friends or relatives to talk about my life. I was lonely. So I started writing in several notebooks which I used as journals.

I asked God, "Lord, are You really there for me? I am miserable here. Where are You? I need You NOW! I feel like dying. Please do something for me. Please… I beg You."

Nothing seemed to be happening at all. Sometimes I doubted if there was God. If there was, why was my life so miserable and He did not do anything for me? Why does God not answer my prayers? How long should I live a miserable life like this? I felt that I was neglected and abandoned by everyone including God. I never heard anyone saying "I love you" to me. I concluded that if there was God, He was for other people but not for me.

I said to myself, "I don't need God who does not care about me. From now on, I am on my own. I don't have God."

I was sad and depressed. When I woke up one morning after feeling so miserable, the first thing I remembered was that I denied God the night before and it was just me alone from now on. All of sudden I felt some kind of huge emptiness inside. I felt so lonely. In the past I used to talk to God all the time in my mind whether He answered my prayers or not.

"My Lord, please protect me today. Help me not to be beat again."

But I could not talk to Him anymore because I decided to be independent without Him. I started having all kinds of weird negative thoughts. I felt something was not right. I was getting nervous to think that I was absolutely alone in this world without

God. I had no place to be comforted. It was not hard to find myself distracted very often. I could not focus on my studies.

I often looked outside of the window in my classroom. It was raining one day. I saw two girls running after each other in the pouring rain on the school track field. They were having fun. This only made me feel worse. I felt like having a long walk in the rain. No particular destination in mind. I just wanted to get out of my miserable life and do something for myself freely. I wanted to go somewhere and never come back. I wiped my tears and decided that I was going to run away if the crazy woman cursed on me three more times. I knew she was going to but hoped not. *I am going to run away for real! I will give her the final three chances.* She had made me feel little, like a nobody. She had humiliated me. She had no idea what I was going to do and finally used up her last three chances.

"THAT'S IT!"

I decided to call my mother "Ku-Yeo-Ja" from now on—"The woman." I knew my father gave Ku-Yeo-Ja some money for Choo-Suk (Korean Thanksgiving) a few days before. I stole her money, about 300,000 Won (which was about $300) from her purse. I packed a few clothes and secretly left the house through the back door. I started walking fast as if I was almost running. My heart was pounding hard and racing fast. It was raining outside. The misty rain gradually soaked my hair and clothes. I wiped my eyes. I thought *MAYBE* there was God and *MAYBE* He was sad for me now. That was why it was raining. Thinking that way was actually comforting for me a little bit.

"God, please help me. I need You," I prayed.

Runaway Girl

I was sixteen years old. When I was running away in that rainy late afternoon, I did not care about the shock my mother may experience after I was gone but I was worried about my two helpless younger brothers. I could not protect them anymore. I could not do anything for them before, now, and forever. I was hopeless and powerless before her. Now it didn't matter anyway. I was running away from the woman. Everything was over. I felt my eyes were getting warm and blurred. I swallowed the deep sadness from my throat. The rain was getting heavier now. I wiped my eyes again. I had to get to the express bus terminal as soon as possible before the crazy woman found out that I ran away and was coming after me.

I bought a bus ticket with the money that I stole from the woman's purse. 300,000 Won was big money for our family. I did not know how long the money was going to last and what kind of future was waiting for me. I just thought that I would survive and somehow would be successful for sure. Then I would go back to rescue my brothers. That was my plan. But for the crazy woman, I wouldn't even say "Hi" to her. I would completely ignore her and not even look at her. I would treat her like dirt.

While sitting in the bus I lowered my body and looked around carefully to see if there was anyone who could recognize me. There was a teacher from my school standing at the bus terminal as if he was looking for someone. I was not sure if he was there to catch any troubled student running away like me or waiting for someone. I started preparing my story in case he would board the bus and ask me where I was going. I would say that I was going to my uncle's house in Seoul, though this would not have made sense because this was not a weekend. "Well", I thought, "then I just need to be careful to avoid eye contact with him." What about other people? If someone comes up and asks me where I am going, what am I going to say?

I would say that my father's business got bankrupt and I could not continue my school. That's why I am going to Seoul to get a job and I am going to stay with my uncle.

That was my story to tell people. Although my uncle did not live in Seoul anymore, I felt like that I should start my new life from there because the area was the only place that I was somewhat familiar with and knew how to get there. So my uncle's old house became my starting point.

The large red numbers on the digital clock mounted on the bus dashboard were turning 4:58, 4:59, 5:00 PM. Then the bus started moving slowly. I liked the bus driver because he kept the timing so precisely without any delay. I saw the rain drops flowing diagonal on the large bus windows. I thought about my brothers but there was no turning back. The bus was speeding up now and it was running on the highway gradually reaching its full speed.

Good bye! I will come back when I am successful. I will show up in front of the woman with my pride held high and I will ignore her. You were not meant to be my mother. It was God's total mistake from the beginning. I am on my own now. Watch me when I come back. I will make you feel embarrassed, shameful and miserable for what you have done to me. It has been more than enough but it's over now. You are not my mom and I am not your daughter!

The bus stopped at two rest areas for ten minutes for a bathroom break each time. People got out of the bus. Some went to stores and brought something to eat in the bus. I just went and used the restroom and came right back to the bus. I did not talk to anyone and did not have any eye contact with anybody. We finally arrived at Gang Nam Express Bus Terminal in Seoul after a little over five hours of driving. I got out of the bus following other passengers and walked toward a bus stop. I heard from the news that abductions were happening in Seoul those days. Bad people kidnapped innocent young girls who came to Seoul to make money and they sold them for prostitution. I had to act like a smart girl. I forced myself to erase any sign of sadness on my face and put on a game face instead; as natural as possible and confident. I wanted to show I blended into Seoul like other students of my age. I did not want to give any impression that I just arrived in Seoul from a small city. But the problem was that I had such a strong southern accent which was not easy to cover up all of a sudden. However, when I had to survive in the big city it was not fun at all but I had to force myself to speak like others.

I knew one of my aunts, my mother's youngest sister, lived somewhere in Seoul but I did not want to go to her. If I did, she would definitely send me back to my mother right away. It was a dumb plan, so I decided to start my new life from my uncle's old house as my starting point. He was my mother's first younger brother. When a bus came that had a sign of Kimpo International Airport, I was onboard. My uncle used to live close to the airport because he worked as an airline dispatcher for one of the major

Korean airline companies. They moved to Anchorage, Alaska a few years back and I didn't know who was living in his old house, but somehow, going to his old house felt right.

I remembered exactly where my uncle's old house was although I visited there only once when I was in the sixth grade. My watercolor painting was selected as second place at a junior art competition held by UNESCO (United Nations Educational, Scientific and Cultural Organization). So, my parents and I went to Seoul to receive the prize and we stayed at my uncle's house for a couple of days. We visited Chang-Kyung Zoo and Kyung-Bok Palace after I received my prize. That was probably the only one good memory with my parents that I could recall. When we were taking pictures at the palace, my mother put her arms around me behind my back and put a big cheerful smile on her face. Whenever I saw the photo, I asked myself if my mother's happy smile at that moment was for real. I heard from my uncles and aunts that I cried a lot when I was baby. It had to be my mother who always held me to stop my crying. I believe she loved me and cared for me when I was a baby. When I was about five and my younger brother was three, my mother took us to a park and we had a photo taken by a photographer at the park. In that old black and white photo my brother and I were nicely dressed up holding a half split apple each. I saw my mother standing right behind us and gently put her hands on our shoulders and smiled. She was a beautiful and loving mother in that photo. I wondered what happened to her. What caused her to change her personality drastically to be such a mean and evil person all of sudden? I could not understand it at all.

After about 30 minutes of the bus ride, I got off the bus at the bus stop nearby by my uncle's old house. There was an isle about thirty feet long to the entrance door. I walked to the house and looked into the house through the gap between the doors. It was quiet. No one seemed to be in the house. I turned around and walked. I imagined myself as if I was coming out of the house to go somewhere.

It was almost 11 o'clock at night. I needed a place to spend the evening. I found a Dok-Seo-Sil where students paid money to study and stay overnight. Some students preferred Dok-Seo-Sil to studying at home because they didn't want to be distracted by watching television or something else. Libraries closed at certain hours but Dok-Seo-Sil was open all night. I had been to Dok-Seo-Sil before but never spent all night at one. When I entered the Dok-Seo-Sil it was warm and I felt comfortable. The anxiety of being followed by someone or abducted had disappeared and I felt safe there. I paid money and entered the study room. Girls went to the girls' room and boys went to the boys' room. There were probably about 20 small desks but there was only one girl sitting in the corner. I liked that it was quiet and not many students were there. Although I once decided to do everything alone without God for He seemed to be not caring for me at all, this time I couldn't help but asking Him to help me. I thanked God that I could spend the night at the warm safe place and asked Him, "My Lord, please help me. I cannot do anything without You. I was wrong before that I denied You. Please forgive me. I need You. In the name of Jesus, Amen."

It was almost midnight. The girl in the corner and I were the only ones in the girls' study room that night. She came to me first and greeted me. We exchanged our names and ages. She was a couple years older than me. So I called her "Un-Ni" which means "Older Sister" in respect. In Korea, if a person is older or we meet someone for the first time regardless of their ages, we use "Jon-Ching" which is a way of speaking with respect and we do not call their names directly.

Unni said she was working for a German bakery shop in Young Dung Po, which was the biggest bakery shop in the area. I remember she told me that she was living with her sister but when she went home late, the door was locked and the lights were off. Instead of disturbing her sister to get up, she came to the study room to spend the evening. I asked Unni if I could get a job at the bakery shop where she worked. She said it was not easy to get a job there because a lot of girls wanted to get in. She told me that I should try a manpower company. They had many job options such as Ka-Jung-Bu (maiden service for cooking and cleaning), Da-Bang (serving at coffee shop) or just a simple cleaning job. I did not know how to cook. So I couldn't apply for Ka-Jung-Bu. Da-Bang was a coffee shop but back then coffee shops were not like these days. I heard Da-Bang was a dangerous place for a young girl to work. Some old men went to Da-Bang and sit all day long to play with young girls working there. Sometimes young girls worked as prostitutes secretly. That's what I heard. So I never gave a second to think of working at Da-Bang. A cleaning job sounded easy enough for me to handle. So I decided to get a cleaning job. I was so glad that Unni was there at the study room that night.

As Unni told me, I went to a manpower company the next day. The guy at the manpower company asked me how old I was and why I wanted to get a job. I told him the story that I prepared in the bus before I left my hometown—my father got bankrupt with his business and I had to get a job to support my family. He said there was a family who was looking for a cleaning woman. He made a phone call to someone and said Mr. Park was on his way to meet me.

While waiting, I prayed to God, "My Lord, please let me meet nice people. In the name of Jesus, Amen."

Mr. Park arrived. He was the driver for a wealthy restaurant owner. He was wearing thick black frame glasses, a thick black down jacket, black pants and black shoes. He seemed to be just black from head to toe. But he had a soft Seoul accent when he greeted the manpower guy which made me feel less scared. He asked me the same question that the manpower guy had asked me. I told him the same story. He also asked if I had a cleaning job experience before. I said, "No."

"When can you start working?" he asked.

"Today."

So I got the job.

While driving, Mr. Park told me that the place where we were going was a Naeng-Myun (cold noodle) restaurant. The owner was originally from North Korea but fled during the Korean War (1950) as a refugee so he still had a little bit of a North Korean accent. The owner and his wife had three children; two boys and one daughter. Although we were going to the restaurant, I was not going to work at the restaurant but upstairs for the family. We arrived at a three story modern building. The first floor was the noodle restaurant, the second one was used for storage space and the third one was the residential area where the owner and his family lived and also the place where I was going to stay and work for them.

When Mr. Park introduced me to the owner, he demanded me to show my hands.

"Let me see your hands."

He examined my hands and said to Mr. Park that he found the right person for the cleaning job. He said cleaning people should have hands like mine that showed knuckles. Too soft or long skinny fingers were not suitable for a cleaning job but my hands looked fine for the work. I felt like he was examining me as if I was a healthy slave. The owner said to his wife loudly that a new cleaning girl came. His wife did not come out of the room but responded loudly.

"Tell Ms. Jang to show her what to do."

Ms. Jang came out of the kitchen. She was under five feet tall, a petite lady, wearing an apron. She was in charge of cooking for the family. I greeted her and she showed me the room where I would stay. There was no bed. Five girls who worked for the family and the restaurant downstairs used the one room all together. Ms. Jang gave me two blankets that were used by the previous cleaning woman. There was one tall dresser in the corner which had several drawers and a closet for putting coats and other garments. The bottom drawer was mine. After I put my stuff in my drawer I followed Ms. Jang. She showed me where I could find brooms and rags. Then she showed me bedrooms and bathrooms where I should clean. When we entered the owner's room, his wife was reading a magazine and I greeted her there for the first time.

I started cleaning the house right away. I cleaned the owner's three bedrooms, an office room, two bathrooms and a living room. I swept the floor first then knelt down to wipe the floor by hand. After that I cleaned all the windows. Mrs. Lee, the owner's wife, told me to wipe her closet surface with wood polisher then dust several dozen of her tiny perfume bottles. When I finished all of that, Ms. Jang showed me how to do the family's laundry. It was surprising that this rich family did not own a washer or a drier. It was the cleaning woman's job. I was shocked to see how Ms. Jang did the laundry. It was not doing laundry at all. She just dipped the clothes in water, rubbed a laundry bar front and back once or twice, then put it back in the water, shook it roughly, then squeezed. That was it! It took less than one minute to wash a pair of pants. To me it was not doing laundry but just pretending to do laundry. I did not do it how she did. I thoroughly washed the clothes like I used to do at my house.

The owner or his wife sometimes told me to bring noodles for them from the restaurant downstairs. When I went to the kitchen I chatted with the guys working there while they were preparing noodles. They were nice and kind to me. I heard from one of the servers that the restaurant was famous for Pyong-Yang style cold noodle. The noodle dish was made of noodle, beef broth which was cooked for several long hours with beef and bones, then chilled in a refrigerator to make it ice cold. They garnished the noodles with thinly sliced beef, cucumbers, pickled sweet radish and a half cut boiled egg on top with wasabi on the side. When famous entertainers came to eat the cashier or Mr. Park gave Mrs. Lee a phone call. She would come down and prepare the noodle dishes herself.

I did not have to go outside unless Ms. Jang told me to get something for her. If I had to go out during my work hour, then I had to let Ms. Jang know where I was going. It was getting cold outside so I preferred to stay indoors anyway. I was afraid of being noticed by someone and caught, especially my aunt who lived somewhere in Seoul. I cleaned the house and did laundry every day. I worked from 9 A.M. to 6 P.M. I was tired but I was able to handle it. I don't remember how much exactly I made a month but the owner gave me half and he kept the other half as a deposit. Mr. Park said when I was coming from the manpower company that the owner would give me the other half when I quit my job. I heard from other people that the owner kept the money so that people would not run away.

While I was cleaning, I noticed one day that there was a full set of 19th century literature books in the office room. They were translated books in Korean. The books seemed to be a little bit old but in practically new condition. They were just luxurious decorations for the office. I breathed in the smell of the old books. I was so excited as if I found a treasure box. I thought maybe God put them there for me. I decided to read all the books. I thought that I could educate myself by reading those well-known works of literature instead of going to school like other students. Then I wouldn't completely waste my life as a cleaning girl.

Some of the books were Jane Eyre (1847) by Charlotte Bronte, Wuthering Heights (1847) by Emily Bronte, Tess of the d'Urbervilles (1891) by Thomas Hardy and Great Expectations (1861) by Charles Dickens. I secretly brought each book to our room and started reading when I was not working. After I read them, I returned the books to their original place. I didn't tell anyone that I was reading the owner's books. Among the books I read, the one that most impressed me was Thaïs (1890) by a French novelist Anatole France (1844-1924). Thaïs was well known as an opera or as violin music "Meditation De Thaïs" but I did not know about it back then.

The novel was based on a beautiful courtesan, Thaïs of Alexandria who became Christian by Paphnuce, who was a monk. He led Thaïs to repent her sins and live a humble life. She left everything she had and lived a pure life after her repentance for the rest of her life. When she was dying, she saw the heavens opening before her eyes, but the monk was obsessed by her beauty and became lustful. He told her that he loved her so much and the heaven she saw was an illusion. Then he became a devil himself after she died.

After I finished reading the book I was so sad and felt a heavy burden in my heart. I thought about my own life. Why did God let me read the book? What does He want me to do? What kind of life should I live from now on? I could not think of anything else for a while. I must not become like Paphnuce. That's for sure. What about Thaïs who repented and lived a pure life for the rest of her life? I believed God put the books in the office for me for sure. I was truly sorry to God that I denied Him once before in my miserable days. I apologized to Him and asked for His help so that I could live a good life.

One of the guys at the kitchen downstairs was called "A-Ra-E." He had his own name but everyone called him "A-Ra-E."

I asked a server at the restaurant what that meant. She said it meant "a dish boy" as North Korean slang. He washed dishes in the kitchen. One day the A-Ra-E called me quietly behind the kitchen door and asked if he could borrow some money from me. He sounded very desperate. He said he would pay me back as soon as he got his next pay check with a whole month of interest although there was only a week left until the next pay day. I wanted to help him so I lent him 100,000 Won (about U$100). The next morning I noticed some guys were gathered in the kitchen and chatting. I asked what happened. Someone told me that the dish boy ran away the night before. I felt as though someone hit the back of my head. I was so ashamed that I trusted him and lent him my precious money. Obviously he thought I was naive to trust his lies. All of sudden I felt a strong fear of men and thought I should never trust anyone from now on. I had to protect myself.

Every night when I was about to fall asleep I heard a church bell nearby. I did not know where the church was but it sounded really peaceful.

I felt God was telling me, "I am here for you. I am watching over you."

I cried and prayed.

"God, please protect my little brothers and help me do well. In the name of Jesus, Amen..."

I decided to visit the church someday. A woman who worked at the restaurant often cried when she came to our room after work. She was from a small town in the countryside and came to Seoul to support her family. She said her daughter's name was the same as the owner's daughter. She cried every night missing her two-year old baby daughter left in her hometown. I was sad for her but there was nothing I could do except listen to her. The woman could not stay any longer and quit her job before Christmas. A new woman was hired. She was in her fifties and I found out that she was a Christian. We promised to visit the church together where the church bell sound came from on Christmas Eve.

We went to the Christmas Eve night service. There were lots of people at the church that night. The pastor gave his Christmas message but somehow I was dreaming of my old Christmas Eve when I was in elementary school. I got my mother's permission to stay overnight at one of the church Elder's house along with other students in my Sunday school on a Christmas Eve. We played a Korean traditional game called Yoot and ate Duk-Guk which was rice cake soup the elder's wife made for us. At dawn, all of us headed out to visit other church members' houses. In front of their entrance doors we held candles and sang Christmas carols. My favorite carol was "O Holy Night!"

O Holy Night, the stars are brightly shining; it is the night of the dear Savior's birth! Long lay the world in sin and error pining. Fall of your knees! Oh, hear the angel voices! O night divine, the night when Christ was born; O night, O Holy Night, O Night Divine!

I loved the carol so much and never was tired of singing the same song again and again. I had tears springing up when I sang that carol. When we were singing the Christmas carols I was happy and felt that I was special in the group. It was sad though that we couldn't go to my parents' house to sing.

While I was dreaming of my old days, the pastor's Christmas sermon was almost over. I looked around to see other people. I saw many students who seemed to be of a similar age as mine. I wondered what the differences were between them and me. All of sudden I became so embarrassed by a thought that people might recognize me as a runaway girl. A huge feeling of insecurity covered me. My cheeks were getting warm and red. The woman whom I went to church with started sobbing when she was praying. She started having short breaths. People around us stared at us. I did not want to get too much attention and wanted to get out of the church as soon as possible. We hurried out and came home.

The next morning Ms. Jang asked me, "Where did you go last night in that late hour?"

"I went to church."

She was so upset and said, "How dare you? Do you think you can do whatever you want now? I am not complaining that you went to church, but what I am saying is that you left the door wide open all night! Are you going to be responsible if any guy downstairs ran away?"

It was so unfair for her to say that. Anyone could come in and out. Why should I be responsible for the guys? She did not question the other lady who went to church with me if she was going to be responsible for the guys. I knew she wanted to control me. Although I didn't tell her where I went in advance, it was after my work hour, so technically I didn't have to tell her anything. Since then I did not talk to her much unless I had to. She hardly spoke to me either but when the owner's first son came to the kitchen and talked to her about his latest blind date, she laughed and flattered him as if she was the most kind, generous and happiest person in the world.

When I began to clean the house the next day it seemed like someone already had. Several dirty rags were scattered right in front of the owner's room. I asked Ms. Jang if she cleaned the house.

"Yes, I did. The house was so dirty and the window frames were so dusty. If you are not going to do your job right why don't you just quit and go somewhere else?" she said.

She wiped the narrow corners of the windows and doors where it was high up and hard to reach and put the rags in front of the owner's door on purpose. If the owner asked her what the dirty rags were about then she was going to tell him that I was not doing my job and wanted to see me fired.

Once in a while the owner called me in his room and asked me to give him a shoulder massage. His wife was sitting in the same room reading her magazines. They casually chatted while I was giving him a massage. He would lie down on his stomach on the bed and ask me to rub his shoulders then his legs. One day when his wife was not there he laid down on his back and pointed toward his crotch and motioned me to rub it. I looked at him in shock and was speechless. He said, "It's okay."

Suddenly I felt my head was spinning. I stood up right away and got out of the room immediately. I went to our room, closed the door and sat in the corner. My whole body was trembling. I could feel that my heart was beating so hard and I could almost hear it. Ms. Jang walked in the room and saw me sitting in the corner with my head down in my crossed arms. She asked me if something was wrong. I told her what the owner had asked of me and I did not do it and came out of the room just now.

Her eyes got bigger and said, "Oh, Really? The girl who worked here before you also said the same thing. She was a little bit retarded, so I did not believe what she said. I guess she was telling the truth then."

That night Ms. Jang was kind to me for the first time in a while and asked me if I wanted to eat something special. I asked for two sausages.

The next day, early in the morning, the owner came out of his room and was looking for me with so much rage. He shouted and yelled at me. I thought he became crazy overnight. He shouted with all his guts that I was not doing my job properly and the house was so dusty. How could the house be so dusty when I wiped the floor every day? He said if I would not clean the house thoroughly that day I would be kicked out of the house immediately. He was so furious. Ms. Jang and I knew why he was acting like a crazy man all of sudden. Obviously he was embarrassed when he remembered what happened the previous day and I was disobedient to him. He wanted to threaten me that I would be fired. I cleaned the same spots again and again all day long. Nothing happened.

Washing the clothes by hand with a toxic laundry bar was a real bad thing. I did laundry with my bare hands every day. The skin of my fingertips started to peel off like onion skins and blood was even smearing. It was painful to put my hands in the soapy water. I showed my fingers to Ms. Jang.

She said, "You should have done laundry like the way I showed you before. If you listened to my advice your fingers wouldn't have to be like that."

I remembered how she did laundry. I thought maybe I should have done it like that, but then it wouldn't be honest work. Even though I did not agree with how she did it, I started doing the laundry as she showed me before. Just dip the clothes in water and rub the laundry bar a couple times here and there, then rinse it roughly and it is done. I didn't feel good about it but could not do more with my blood smearing fingers.

Once the owner told me to touch his body I did not want to stay at the house any more. I also didn't feel comfortable to work with Ms. Jang. I wanted to go somewhere else. Now I had experience at a cleaning job. It was about nine o'clock at night. I went to the owner and told him that I wanted to quit because my fingers were bleeding and hurting from doing the laundry.

"Let me see your hands."

I showed him my fingers.

"Your fingers are just fine! How dare you come to me and lie that your fingers are bleeding!! Get out of my sight NOW!!!" he yelled at me.

I couldn't understand him. A couple days ago he yelled at me because he was going to kick me out of the house if I didn't clean the house thoroughly. Now he yelled at me as if he did not want me to leave.

I came back to our room quietly with my head down. Ms. Jang asked me how it went although she heard everything outside. I said he could not see how bad my hand condition was because of the dimmed light. My fingertips were red but they looked fine and smooth to him under the dimmed light. The next day he called me.

"Let me see your hands again."

Maybe he wanted to fire me this time if my hands were fine. We were standing in the living room next to the window. So he could clearly see my hands under the natural light. He was disgusted and furrowed his eye brows. He said to his wife, "Hmm. Her finger tips are not like what I saw last night. They are really bad."

They told me to ask Ms. Jang to get rubber gloves and use them from now on until they buy a washing machine. I felt better that I was proven to be innocent but lost the chance to leave the house. I was not sure how long I should stay at the house as a cleaning girl. I wanted to study and take a GED test so that I could go to college.

I wondered what my mother was doing. Perhaps she was

shocked at first when she found out that I ran away with her money then fought with my father. She probably struggled with her tight budget because I stole her money. Instead of remembering her as a crazy woman, I had pity on her. I thought *"Mom, I am really sorry that I stole your money. I will pay you back."* I felt like sending her some money to help her so I went to post office. The woman at the post office told me to fill out a form. I stood by the table to fill out the form but struggled with what address to use; a real one or a fake one. I wasn't sure what to do. I was afraid of losing my money in case I used a fake address. I didn't want to lose money again like I did to the A-Ra-E guy who ran away with my money. So I sent the money with my real address of the noodle restaurant. I was a little bit nervous but it was out of my hands.

On a Saturday morning Mrs. Lee told me that she was going to pay for me so take her daughter to a public bath house. She used to go with Ms. Jang but this time I was told to go with her. Since we had to take off our clothes in the bath house she refused to go with me. Mrs. Lee almost forced her to go with me. She cried and refused the first time but we finally went there together and I helped her by rubbing her back where she could not reach. Ever since then, she and I became good friends. She came to me and talked to me more often. One day she came home after school and showed me a flyer.

She said, "Unni, I saw this on the news board at the police station on my way back home. Isn't this person you?"

"Let me see. Let me see."

IT WAS ME! My heart was pumping so hard. My family was looking for me! They had called the police. They printed the flyers to search for me. Thank God that she saw this and let me know first before anyone else at the house, especially Ms. Jang. I kindly asked her not to tell anyone, then I would do anything she ask me to do and help her with her homework every day. I folded the flyer and put it deep in my pocket. I did not want to throw it in the garbage can in case the witch lady Ms. Jang saw it and picked it up.

The second son was getting ready to take his high school entrance exam. When he was about to leave the house I gave him a couple of useful tips. I told him not to spend too much time struggling with difficult questions but move on to the easier ones. Take care of those easy ones first then go back and deal with the difficult ones. Otherwise he was not going to finish the entire exam. Also make sure to complete both sides front and back of the test sheets not to miss anything. The owner seemed to be impressed and said that I gave his son really good advice.

I heard that Ms. Yoo, one of the servers at the noodle restaurant was going to quit after almost ten years and she was going home to get married. She showed her loyalty to the owner and was leaving the job for a good reason. She seemed to be very excited and happy. The owner ordered Mr. Park to give her a ride to the train station. I saw her getting in the back seat of the yellow Mercedes. Ms. Jang told me once that yellow was Mrs. Lee's favorite color. Ms. Yoo was treated as a VIP that day. I envied her not because she was riding in the fancy car but she was leaving the noodle house. I wondered how many employees had that kind of special treatment from the owner. I bet that the crazy owner never asked her to touch his crotch or even give a normal massage. If he had, how could anyone work there for such a long time?

I had to find a way to study and take a GED exam. I was flipping through newspapers to search for a night school to prepare for the GED. Then the cashier at the restaurant downstairs called me to come down for a moment. I thought she had something for me to bring to the owner. I went downstairs. There stood a policeman with my youngest aunt, Sook. As soon as I saw them, I started walking far away from them. Mr. Park shouted "Stop her!" The policeman came after me and caught me. My aunt Sook cried and asked me what I was doing there and wanted me to go home. She told me that everyone in the family had been worried and was looking for me. Mr. Park told me to go upstairs right away, pack immediately and come back downstairs. I did not have much to pack. I took out my back pack and walked out of the room.

I said good bye to the owner who was standing in the middle of the living room. His wife was in the room but did not even bother to come out. He said he wondered how I could give such smart advice to his son for his high school entrance exam and now he understood that I was a clever runaway girl. I said I was sorry and thanked him for the opportunity to work at his house. The owner phoned the cashier at the restaurant to give me my half salary that he had kept.

I avoided eye contact with Ms. Jang. I had no idea how I would handle my current situation but I was happy that I did not have to listen to her crap any more. She used to brag about her educational background. She said she attended a prestigious girls' high school in Seoul. I wondered why she ended up as a cook at someone's house instead of having a professional job. Ever since I went to the church without telling her she had been so mean to me but now the game was over! I ditched her and was happy to leave the house, finally. I had somewhere else to go now but she was still stuck at the house as a cook for the family.

The cashier at the restaurant gave me my salary that the owner had kept. I stayed at the noodle house a little over four months. I didn't have to go to the police station.

The officer asked my aunt, "Is she your niece?"

My aunt verified, "Yes, she is. Thank you very much."

Then we were on our way. My aunt took me to a breakfast restaurant. We ordered hot beef bone soup which was a common menu for Koreans who usually had a hangover in the morning. The soup tasted really good and I felt comfortable eating my own food in a long time. I never felt comfortable eating the food at the noodle house. I always ate the leftovers after Ms. Jang prepared for the owner's family. I used to go to a nearby convenient store or street food vendor to buy snacks. My aunt said I gained some weight and it was hard to recognize me at first. I asked how she could find me. She said they traced my address after I sent the money to my mother. I was not sure if it was a good thing that I wrote the real address or not, but that's how I came back home.

When my mother saw me, she wiped her tears but I did not feel anything. I did not apologize to her. I felt that I became brave for the past four months. I made up my mind if she ever beat me again then I was going to run away again. I did once so why not again? *Bring it on, Woman!* That's how I felt. My father wiped tears from his eyes. I felt profoundly sorry to him that I made him shed his tears. I felt guilty. I don't remember what my mother asked me but my father asked me how hard it was while

I was away from home. My brothers welcomed me and said that they were worried about me. My mother tried to be gentle and kind to me which made me feel awkward. I was not sure how long her temporary kindness would last but she seemed to be a little bit different now. I thought she was afraid that I might run away again.

Bullied

At my first day of school after I returned home, my previous teacher, Mr. Kang, took me to the teachers' office and he introduced me to my new teacher, Mr. K.S.

He said, "She is a returning student. I would appreciate your kind attention."

It was very kind of him to say that but I knew right away that my new teacher Mr. K.S. was not welcoming me as one of his students very much. He slightly smiled to Mr. Kang as a nice gesture and said, "Sure. No problem. I will."

But when he looked at me he did so with a distrusting glance out of the corner of his eye. Mr. K.S. taught English and I heard that he only wore black golf shirts and black pants 365 days of the year. He liked good students only and didn't even bother to talk to students who caused trouble. I bowed to both of them and got out of the office. When I was walking back to my classroom, I decided firmly that I was going to change the way Mr. K.S. looked at me by studying English really hard and prove that I was a good student.

During the first week at the school some of my old classmates visited me in my classroom during the lunch break. When they asked me what I did while I was gone, I told them that I was on a medical leave. Freshman's name tags were green, sophomore's blue and senior's were red. When my old friends were wearing a different color of name tags as they visited me it was obvious that I was older than my new classmates. Some students called me Un-Ni right away but some others never even said "Hello" to me. The class was divided in two groups. One group called me Un-Ni with respect. The other group called my name although they knew that I was two or three years older than them. Younger people calling older people's names intentionally was considered being disrespectful.

The small group who called me Un-Ni liked me. We studied together and I helped them with their studies especially English and Algebra. Two students were paired to sit together for each week. We called it JJAK-JI, which means a pair. Each week all the students wrote their student numbers and mixed them to pick our next JJAK-JI. Some of the girls who called me Un-Ni wanted to sit with me continuously. So I had to change my number with others several times. One of them I sat with for three weeks. We got along really well. The other group was different. One of the girls from the other group was either confident or arrogant. She said one day in front of other students, "My mom and dad said that even though you are two years older than us, we did not have to call you Un-Ni since you are in the same class with us."

It sounded logical but it was not like Korean culture. I wondered what kind of other things they talked about behind my back. Usually the girl and her group had strong opinions and gossiped behind my back. I saw them gathering during lunch break or while we were cleaning the classroom. They put their heads together glancing at me once in a while, chatting and laughing out loud. Those girls ganged up on me and bullied me. No matter what I did or what I said, they gossiped as a group, talked back to me sarcastically and laughed all together at me. I was afraid of being close them. I wished that I would not pick a number of those mean girls to sit as a pair. When I had to sit with one of them we hardly spoke to each other. I just studied hard and focused on English especially. I wanted to make the mean girl sitting next to me feel insecure by my English language ability.

In three months after returning to school I lost my weight significantly and became slim like I used to be. My test scores were high. My English score was better than Korean. The way my teacher Mr. K.S. looked at me was different from the first day we met. I gave myself one year but it took only three months to change the way he looked at me. Now I was one of his top students whom he liked.

My favorite classes were geosciences, fine art, and English. I was fascinated by the mysteries of earth and the universe in general; the stars, the invisible magnetic forces, ocean tides controlled by the moon and fish fossils discovered on top of dried mountains. It was really interesting to understand how scientists could analyze layers of the earth and tell what happened thousands of years ago. I imagined Noah's ark drifting in the Grand Canyon and he was sending a dove out to see if there was any dry land after 40 days and nights of the flood. I tried to understand how big the universe was. I put a dot on paper and drew a circle around it and another circle around and another circle after that. It was just thousands of endless circles. I thought I would go crazy if I had to figure out how big the universe was. Wow… Who created it? God? The God who comforted me with the church bell sound when I was a cleaning girl at the noodle house? He created THE endless Universe AND He knows me?!

"Who am I?"

The Holy Spirit said, "A child of God."

"Really? Am I that important of a person?"

"Yes!"

"Yet to all who received him, to those who believed in his name, he gave the right to become children of God—children born not of natural descent, nor of human decision or a husband's will, but born of God."

— John 1:12-13

Fine art class was a piece of cake to me as I took fine art lessons in the past. My art teacher asked me to help him to sort hundreds of paintings that his students submitted for grading. There were about 50 to 60 students in each classroom and total of 10 classes. So about 500 to 600 students submitted their paintings and one art teacher had to sort and grade them. For other subjects such as Korean, English or mathematics, there were two teachers for each grade, but for fine art and music, only one teacher for each grade. That's why my teacher asked me to help him sort the paintings. I really enjoyed doing so.

When I was in middle school I didn't like English much

because I was confused by its grammar. To make a sentence in Korean we place the subject, object then verb, like "I apple eat." But English is subject and verb then object, like "I eat the apple." It was so confusing to rearrange the words like a puzzle each time I wanted to speak. One of my English teachers said, "When you study English turn off the Korean knob and turn on the English knob. And try to think everything in English. Eat with English and sleep with English."

I couldn't find the knobs to turn it on and off. It was too dark for me. But at the Hak-One, when I was preparing for the high school entrance exam, I learned English grammar and vocabulary from the beginning. I couldn't believe that English became one of my favorite subjects at school.

I purchased a set of English learning cassette tapes with the money that I earned from the cleaning job. It was "English Alive" made by British people. I enjoyed listening to the tapes a lot. One of my uncles, from my mother's side, was a college student majoring in teaching English. Even though he was not a Christian, he sometimes brought Mormon missionaries to my grandparents' house and I saw them communicating in English. I found that to be quite interesting. I wished I could talk to them but my English was not nearly well enough to communicate with any native speakers yet.

Sometimes I went to a national park nearby our house over the weekend. It was usually quiet early in the morning without many people visiting. I practiced my English that I learned from the cassette tapes. I acted for two people. I questioned and answered. I imagined that a foreigner was with me and asked, "Would you like to have a cup of tea?"

Then I answered, "Yes, please."

During the week I awoke early in the morning to listen to my favorite radio program called *Good Morning Pops with Oh, Sung-Sik.* Mr. Oh played pop songs, translated, and explained the lyrics. He taught English grammar and vocabulary with the pop songs he played. I tried to write down the songs in English but it was not easy. I recorded some of the songs, wrote the sound in Korean, then listened to the songs again and again to memorize them. I did not quite understand what some of the songs meant because I wrote down the pronunciation in Korean. One of the songs I wrote down was F.R. Davis' *Words*. When I hear that song nowadays the lyrics are very simple but back then I understood only partially what was sung. But I still thought that it was cool to mumble the song as if I sang in English.

The importance of sports, music and arts was minimal at school at that time. It was not like these days. There were no pro sports teams. Studying hard and entering universities was the most important thing to students. If someone said he or she was a student attending a university in Seoul, people looked at them with envy. I heard a rumor that a boys' school motto was,

"The Better Universities the Better Wives."

When I moved up to the second year of high school my teacher was Mr. Kang again, who had been my very first teacher before I ran away. Some of my classmates were the same but most of them were new.

One incident that I remember is that the student captain was not nice to me. We had to bring our tuition to her then she collected and brought the money to our teacher. One time I was not able to bring my tuition on time. I informed my father that I had to pay the tuition but he did not have money. It was 100,000 Won, about $100. The captain went to the blackboard and wrote *"Students overdue with tuition"* with three students' names underneath. I couldn't ask my father again and again. I just waited but when I went to school the captain asked me in front of all other classmates why I did not bring my tuition. Everyone looked at me. I said my parents were out of town. I couldn't wait for my father any longer. Other students paid but I passed through a whole week so I kindly reminded him that my tuition date was overdue. He said, "I am sorry. Let me give it to you tomorrow."

I had to wait one more day. The captain girl had no idea what was going on at our house and she did not like me. Anything she said was usually cynical and sarcastic. She wrote my name every morning until I paid my tuition, though when my teacher came in the classroom he saw my name written on the board and erased it.

I recall a test day which lasted all morning. I don't

remember exactly how it started but the captain said something sarcastically about me. It was not the first time she had done that. My opinion was not respected at any time. If I spoke, she always stood up and said in front of the class, "I heard *someone* said so and so and I don't agree with that. What do you guys think?"

Then the girls who usually hung out with the captain girl agreed with her and made me feel isolated and embarrassed. I could not take it anymore. She aggravated me for months. So I pushed my desk and left the class room this particular morning. I went to the third floor and hid myself in a dark corner close to the roof top. I sat there and buried my head in my crossed arms. I was tired of the mean, sarcastic attitude from those girls. I was miserable at home and I was miserable at school. I wondered why my life had to be that way. I had no place to go. Home and school both mistreated me.

Everyone was taking the test but me. While they were taking the test I wondered how my life would end up. Then I heard a dragging sound, which turned out to be my teacher's slippers. I could also hear my name being called. I knew he was looking for me. I did not make a sound. After the test I went back to the classroom. The students all stared at me but no one said a word. Before my teacher dismissed the class he told me to come to his office. I followed him. He asked me why I did not take the test. I told him what happened before the test. I said the captain and some other girls were always mean to me and I couldn't take it anymore. He asked where I had been. I said I was hiding on the third floor and heard him calling my name when looking for me. He did not punish me but just let me go. I didn't know if Mr. Kang said anything to the captain girl or not, but at least she stopped addressing me as "someone" anymore and we hardly spoke for the rest of the year.

Jesus my Savior

Students usually stayed at school until nine o'clock at night although all the classes were over. No teachers came in the class room to teach but a designated teacher each day walked in the hallway and monitored students to make sure they were quiet and studying. If students were chatting and did not study, then the teacher walked in and supervised the students. The after class study time was called "Free Study Hour" although it was mandatory. I would hardly have called it "free".

All private schools competed against other schools for a higher rate of college entrance. They wanted to maintain their school reputation for how many students entered universities. So the students of second year (junior) and third year (seniors) had to stay until nine o'clock at night to study. After nine, all of them rushed out of the school and went to the bus station to catch buses to go home. No parents came to pick up their children. There was a boys' high school nearby our school. Then several hundreds of students came out all together to catch the buses. Although it was after nine o'clock at night, because of the bright street lights and jam packed buses with the students, it was like bright daylight. We went home, washed then went to sleep, got up early in the morning and then began the same routine all over again.

I saw an interesting poster one day. It was advertising something called Spiritual Revival Crusade. An American pastor was coming to our town. It was somewhat unusual to see a foreign pastor coming to our city to preach because there were not many foreigners ever seen in our town. When there were foreigners people used to stare at them. When I was in middle school I and a friend of mine, who attended the fine art school with me, followed a foreigner in downtown just to say "Hi." When I asked the foreigner, "Where are you from?" he kindly responded that he was from The Netherlands. After that I could not continue my conversation in English because I did not know what to ask or how to speak in English, though it was fun and exciting to see a foreigner. I don't remember who the American pastor was but the Korean pastor who was going to interpret for the crusade was Pastor Jang Hwan Kim (Dr. Billy Kim). I wanted to go to the crusade.

On the day of the crusade, I skipped the Free Study Hour and secretly got out of the classroom along with a few other girls who called me Un-Ni. I had a good relationship with them, especially one whom I told about my dream one day. In my dream, I was standing in front of the Egyptian Pyramids. I saw one big camel in front of me and I heard someone asking me a question in the dream.

"How could the camel go through a needle's ear (which is a Korean expression)?"

"It is impossible by human's ability but with God's help, it is possible." I responded to the voice.

My friend asked me if I read it from somewhere.

"No. It was just my dream."

"It is really strange that you had such kind of a dream because the story is in the Bible."

I probably heard of the story at a church but I did not remember it. The next day after I told my friend about the dream, she brought her Bible to school and showed me the scripture. I did not know she was a Christian until then but we became good friends and decided to go to the crusade together.

> "Again I tell you, it is easier for a camel to go through the eye of a needle than for someone who is rich to enter the kingdom of God."
>
> —Matthew 19:24

A lot of people came to the city sports arena where the crusade was held. We took off our shoes and carried them when we walked on the polished wood floor in the sports arena. We put our school bags and shoes in front of us and sat on the wood floor. I had never been to any worship service that large before. The American pastor preached and the Korean pastor interpreted right after. It just felt so right to be there. I repented all of my sins. At the end of the worship service, the pastors asked if there was anyone who wanted to accept Jesus Christ as a Savior then please quietly stand up where they were. I knew it was the right moment to confirm that Jesus Christ was my Savior and dedicate myself officially. That was the whole purpose why I went to the crusade, even skipping the Free Study Hour at school.

It was a little bit awkward to stand up at first because I didn't want to get attention from other people but I stood up quietly not to lose this opportunity to confirm Jesus as my Savior then I saw other people were standing up too. I remembered that I denied God once when I was in my misery but this time I promised God that, no matter what, I would never deny Him ever again for the rest of my life. I said to Him that I was truly sorry and I was wrong. "God, please forgive me. I accept You as my Savior. Please come into my heart." After the unforgettably special crusade I walked out of the arena feeling that all my heavy burdens were lifted and even my heavy school bag felt so light somehow.

> "Whoever acknowledges me before men, I will also acknowledge him before my Father in heaven."
>
> — Matthew 10:32

The next morning Mr. Kang said, "Whoever skipped the Free Study Hour last night, come on out right now."

The other girls who went to the crusade and I stood up and walked to the teacher in front of the class. There were about five of us. I was the oldest. Mr. Kang never showed his emotion much. He was calm and quiet. When he walked he always dragged his slippers as if they were heavy. He slowly walked toward me and asked, "Where did you go last night?"

"We went to a Christian Crusade."

He paused for a moment then asked, "You are the oldest one here. So, let me ask YOU. Tell me, WHAT is God?"

I did not know what to say when he gave me such a broad question abruptly. I looked down for a moment and said, "God is a BEING whom we cannot see with our eyes but we can FEEL in our hearts."

I had no clue how I could say that. I felt someone else just said that through my mouth. I thought I was not smart enough to say such a thing right away. With my own limited understanding I would have probably mumbled something to the affect of "God is a spirit" or "I don't know how to describe God exactly." He looked over at the window then looked at us, "You can go back to your seats now."

When the class was over the other girls came to me right

away and said, "Wow! Because of you we are alive! You saved us today!"

The girls said that they were so nervous when they were called out in front of the class. So was I but I felt really good that day.

"On my account you will be brought before governors and kings as witnesses to them and to the Gentiles. But when they arrest you, do not worry about what to say or how to say it. At that time you will be given what to say, for it will not be you speaking, but the Spirit of your Father speaking through you."

— Matthew 10:18-20

I kept my diary in several plain notebooks. All the contents were pretty much about how badly I was treated by my mother. In the notebook, I called her not my mom but *the woman*. She said awful things to me. Physical abuse had been replaced by more aggressive verbal abuse. Some of the things she would say were truly detestable. For instance, she would infer that I was somehow sexually related to an animal. I was humiliated when she said such awful things to me. I thought about running away again but I wanted to finish high school this time. When I couldn't say anything against her I felt like killing her. A few times I imagined myself smacking her head and killing her with the laundry bat that she had used to beat me. I would use all my energy and power to smack her head. She would probably beg me for mercy when she was dying. It was a poisonous imagination that Satan put in my mind. I even thought about what I was going to do with her dead body. If people find out that I killed my own mother no one would forgive me. They would never see me as a victim who had been tortured and abused by my crazy mother for years. They would probably say no matter what I shouldn't have killed my own mother. The world would hate me and condemn me. So killing my mother wasn't a healthy way to think and I still feel uncomfortable knowing that I felt that way at one time.

I was afraid someone could read the notebooks that were full of painful memories. I kept the notebooks in a secret place but I was often nervous in case my mother was to find them. So I stapled the notebooks all around. I did not want to read them again and I did not want anyone else to read either. However, one day I unstapled all of them and decided to burn them. At school I waited until the lunch hour was almost over so that most of the students would head back to their classrooms. When there were not many students around I went to a place called "So-Gak-Jang" which was about a 12 by 12 foot small concrete building where all the garbage at the school was collected and incinerated. I brought a match box and the notebooks. I was going to burn the notebooks in the corner of the burning lot where I saw some empty spaces. The notebooks were set on fire in the corner and gradually burned. I wished all my pain would be burned away with them. I did not want to remember any bit of the content. I wondered if there was any easy way to erase my memories. It was getting too hot to hold the edge of the notebooks and I could not hold it any longer. I had to drop the burning notebooks into the lot and now the fire was spreading to other scattered papers one by one. I tried to extinguish the fire desperately, but the fire was rapidly spreading to another pile of the paper and finally the entire garbage pile was burning. The gray smoke and burnt black debris were coming out of the So-Gak-Jang. It was out of my control. I was so scared but didn't know what to do. I had to go back to the classroom but I could not leave the place like that. I stayed there until most of the garbage was burned down. Luckily no one came and asked me if I knew about the fire. It was my lucky day that I was not caught by anyone. Since then I stopped writing about my miserable life because I did not want to remind myself of my painful memories.

When students moved up to the third year (seniors), they were all busy to prepare for college entrance exams. I wanted to go to an art school to major in fine art but my father told me not to because it was too expensive for him to support me financially. To be accepted at an art school, students had to take lessons for years and take art evaluation tests for acceptance. Monthly lesson fees to prepare for art school were an extra burden to my father. So I had to give up on that idea. It was very disappointing but I understood. My next option was majoring in English so that I could get a job after college. I did well in English but my overall score was not high enough to apply for the university that I liked. My second choice was Chung-Ang University that had two campuses; one in Seoul, one in An-Sung. The city, An-Sung, was about one hour of driving distance from Seoul. I liked the fact that Chung-Ang University was a Christian school. I submitted my application to the College of Foreign Languages, Chung-Ang University, An-Sung Campus. I was glad that I would be able to graduate, finally, from high school and move on to college. I wanted to be away from everyone and everything that was attached with my past.

While I was preparing for my college application, a group of girls sarcastically said loud enough to let me hear, "I heard someone is planning to apply for a college out of town! It is not easy to get in a college even in this city. What a waste of time!"

The other girl said, "I agree. I think it's hilarious!"

And they all laughed together. No matter what grade I was in, there were always some mean girls around and they ganged up on me with their cold attitudes. I was upset and wanted to go slap her face right away but I stayed in my place and pretended that I did not hear anything although I heard clearly every word that they said and laughed about. With my boiling anger I wanted to do something to those mean girls, but I asked God, "My Lord, please help me."

My sad days at the high school were almost over.

"Do not repay anyone evil for evil. Be careful to do what is right in the eyes of everybody."

— Romans 12:17

2

Ugly Name for Blind Date

If I couldn't go to college, my next option was joining the military but I became a college student in the spring of 1989. I moved into a women's dormitory on the campus. Two students shared one room. We could get up anytime in the morning but we had to line up in front of our room at 10 o'clock at night. All the names of the students who lived in the dorm were called and checked. After that, the main entrance door of the dorm was locked and nobody could get in or out. I liked the military style rules. Male students were not allowed to get in the dorm except Open House day once a year. Students had to maintain a minimum GPA to be qualified to stay in the dorm. If they did not meet the minimum GPA they had to apply for the next semester.

College was a lot different from high school. Students were from all of the different parts of the country. No more uniforms and matching book bags. Girls without make-up on the campus were hardly seen. I attended girls' middle school and high school but now men and women were mixed. It felt a little bit awkward to sit with men in the same class.

Most of the girls in my class were two or three years younger than me but there were some older guys who returned to school after serving their military service for two and a half years. I did not hang out much with the girls and was not close to them. Not just because of the age gaps, but I just did not find any interest in listening to stories about their blind dates. Sometimes a group of girls met a group of guys from other classes or schools. I never joined any blind date meet ups during the entire four years of my college. I was very insecure and hated introducing myself in front of other people. Girls who went out on blind dates were younger than me and they spoke with a soft Seoul accent while mine was still a strong southern accent.

I hated my original name, Bong Nam, that was made by a name maker and I used to be teased when I was little by other kids because the name sounded similar to one in a funny children's song. My mother didn't like the name at all. She never called me Bong Nam once in my life. She called me Nami. She argued with my father that he went to a name maker and paid for the ugly name without discussing it with her. Even my birthday was registered wrong by the clerk's mistake at the town government office according to what my mother said to me. On my birth certificate, it says May 5th, 1968 which is Children's Day in Korea, but my mother told me that my real birthday was September 26, 1968 by the lunar calendar. I was actually born on Saturday November 16th, 1968 by the solar calendar. I just hated introducing myself in front of other people with my ugly name and my old complicating age. I never thought that I was pretty at all in my life. When I was growing up I heard from older people sometimes that I looked smart but never heard that I was pretty. So going out on a blind date with those young classmates was not in my interest at all.

The Club C.E.L.A.

There was a study club called C.E.L.A. which stood for Chung-Ang English Learning Association. The main difference of this club from other clubs was that it was financially supported by the university, so we had a foreign professor who came to the club to help students with English before the regular classes started. Students had to take a written exam and an oral test to be accepted as a member. I took the test and passed it easily. The way of learning English at the club was a lot different. Senior members lead the club by turn. The classes were composed of dictation, debating, reading and translation. For dictation, they usually played the recorded *A.F.K.N.* (Armed Forces Korea Network News), *ABC News* with Peter Jennings, *NBC news* with Tom Brokaw, and pop songs. For debating, the student leader gave a certain subject each time and members were divided into two groups to discuss, then would debate against each other. For reading and translation *TIME* magazine or *Newsweek* magazine was used.

I had never heard that kind of fast speaking English news before. Debating was absolutely nerve racking. Before jumping on debate, I had to know how to speak English first. Reading and translation were completely different from high school text books. In order to read one paragraph in those *TIME* or *Newsweek* magazines, I had to use an English-Korean dictionary at least a dozen times and write down the individual translated meanings in Korean under each English word. Besides, without general informative knowledge on what's going on in the world, it was not easy to understand any story in the magazines at all.

I thought I was very good at English when I was in high school. But at the club, I felt that my English was like a preschool level. A senior leader would play a recorded news cast several times then the members wrote down what they listened to. I could not catch what the news anchor just said right before he even started the news for the evening. I told the leader that I had no clue. The leader played the same part at least ten more times for me and asked.

"Can you hear that now?"

"No… I am sorry."

"It was *Good evening everyone*."

I was embarrassed and felt so stupid that I couldn't even listen to such a simple greeting. He played it a few more times and now I could hear a little bit that it was "*Good evening everyone*" indeed. I just sat there and realized that my English was so far behind compared to other members. So I got up early in the morning and studied English. I played the fast speaking news thousands of times and tried to write it down.

For the spoken English I usually had to write down on a piece of paper what I was going to say then memorize it. Some of the members spoke English really well. I was surprised they sounded like native speakers. Then I learned that they used to live in English speaking countries when they were young so English was their first language. But they had hard time with Korean language instead. It was not easy for them to study in Korean.

Any subject that required a lot of memorization, such as Korean history, was definitely challenging for them.

One day I saw an English speech contest poster that was held by Kyung-Hee University in Suwon. It seemed to be an interesting challenge to try so I decided to attend. For the contest I wrote down an essay and brought it to my professor, Mr. Bomhart who was American. He reviewed and corrected my English grammar. Then I memorized the two pages of the entire essay on Korean culture. Mr. Bomhart helped me correct my pronunciation. My English was not perfect but I did my best. I won second prize. The first prize went to the student from the hosting university. The auditorium was filled with students from the university and they cheered for the candidates from their school but I went there all alone. No one from my school went there with me but I was not discouraged or sad. I just wanted a challenge of something different and wanted to accomplish something. It was my goal. That's all. It didn't matter whether our school knew about it or anyone supported me or not. I truly did not care. Honestly it was better that way. I wanted to be different from other students in my class. Chatting about blind dates or what kinds of new outfits or cosmetics my fellow students bought over the weekends was absolutely meaningless to me.

My parents sent me $100 each month for food and spending money. My father told me that if I needed more money he would send me more but I never asked him for more money. I wanted to get a part time job where I could practice my English. I did not want to work at restaurants or coffee shops though. It was wasting my time. The minimum wage as a server was about $1 per hour nearby the campus.

I went to the Job-Help office at the school and applied for part time jobs at the International Trade Exhibitions in Seoul. I also worked as an assistant for American Adoption Families, who provided a service to Americans visiting Korea with their adoptive children to show them their native country. Most of the parents had their own biological children. One family particularly caught my attention. The parents introduced themselves as pastors. They also had their own biological children but they adopted a handicapped child. The boy had down syndrome and definitely needed assistance for everything. It was impossible to imagine a Korean family who had their own children to adopt a handicapped child. I wondered what motivated them to adopt children from another country. The whole process of assisting the adoptive families made me think of serving other people and also planted a dream of adopting a child someday too.

One of the International Trade Shows in Seoul that I worked for was a British silverware company. I worked with another girl from a different school. She was very tall and beautiful, like a model. However she hardly spoke English and did not understand what the British guy was talking about when he spoke of his products. They both struggled to communicate all morning and she kept asking me, "What did he just say?"

Finally he told her to leave but I stayed and worked until the end of the trade show. After the exhibition, the business man complimented me that I did a wonderful job and really appreciated my help. I made $5 an hour at the trade show, five times more than a restaurant server. I felt real good that day. Sitting in the bus coming back to my dorm, I looked through the bus window. Some people were standing in line at a bus stop. I thought about the mean girls at my high school who sarcastically talked about my decision of going to a college outside the city. I was wondering what they were doing now while I was enjoying the very opportunities that I could get in Seoul instead of the small city where they chose to remain.

Another part time job that I had was as an assistant at a tailor shop. One of the English club C.E.L.A. members, Bok, introduced the job to me. His sister and brother-in-law owned the tailor shop. Bok's major was government administration and he spoke English quite well. The tailor shop was located near one of the U.S. Army bases in Pyong-Taek. Bok used to help his brother-in-law when he had spare time but he was often too busy with his studies so he introduced me to take over his job as an assistant during summer vacation. I was excited to practice my English with G.I.s at the tailor shop. They came to the shop and looked through magazines to pick which style of suit they wanted then they chose fabrics. Bok's brother-in-law measured their sizes and I wrote them down. G.I.s really liked custom tailored outfits.

Sometimes they brought pictures cut out from popular magazines and asked if the tailor could make their suits like that. Then the tailor said okay and made them look very similar. They came back for a fitting once, then their suits were ready in a few weeks. They were really excited with their custom made suits and shirts. They usually ordered these kinds of special suits right before they moved back to the U.S.A., or they ordered for their loved ones in the country and mailed them.

It was a real easy job to do but sometimes I got bored and did nothing. I would just sit there and flip through magazines or chatted with G.I.s once in a while. One of the G.I.s who came to the shop was Rich. I asked him what he was doing in the military. He said he fixed helicopters. He joined the army to get scholarships for his college. He suggested going to Nam-Dae-Moon market and Itaewon for shopping together. Those two places were very famous for foreigners in Seoul. I thought it would be a fun trip to practice my English with a native speaker and also shop at the open markets. So I agreed, "OK, let's go."

I met him at a bus stop nearby the tailor shop after work. The bus we were onboard was not for Korean civilians but for G.I.s and their families only. I thought it was cool to be in the bus as if I was related to the U.S. Army.

We arrived at Nam-Dae-Moon market and walked through the crowds of people. Rich wanted to buy some clothes there. People usually tried to bargain at Nam-Dae-Moon market. If a merchant said $35, then we asked how about $20 then the price usually met in the middle. So, I tried to negotiate the price for him.

I said to the salesman, "Would you give us some discount please?"

He looked into my eyes and said, "You and I both make U.S. dollars. Why are you trying to bargain for him?"

At first I could not understand what he meant but soon I realized that the man thought of me as a prostitute. I found myself so embarrassed all of sudden and my cheeks were getting so hot. I never imagined that people would look at me like that. So I told Rich that I wanted to return to my dorm right away. We did not buy anything there and I started walking as fast as I could as if I was escaping from there. I did not want to walk close to him. Because of him I was treated as a prostitute. How embarrassing it was! Of course he could not understand why I was acting so strangely all of sudden. He followed me and kept asking me what the problem was and what the guy over there just said to me. I just cried and could not speak anything in English.

I started being afraid of people. I could not hold my face up. I felt that all the people were looking at me as a prostitute. I was not even wearing anything provocative. I was just a student who was excited to practice English with a native speaker, but it was my own thoughts. Rich was getting so upset because of my unexpected weird behavior. He said he was going to go back to the guy at the market and ask him what he said to me unless I explained to him. I said no need to and I tried to explain but I could not stop crying. He said he was sorry and understood. He came to my school campus and said he was very sorry again. I told him it was not his fault and finally returned to my dorm. Since then I did not want to meet any foreigners.

School Celebrity

Whenever I went home during my vacation, I visited my grandmother in the country. One time there was a gentleman who was about to leave after visiting my grandmother. My aunt, my father's oldest brother's wife who lived with my grandmother, introduced me to the gentleman.

She said, "Nami. Why don't you come here and greet your grandfather? He is one of our relatives. You can call him as grandfather."

She told me that he was the President of Chung-Ang University in Seoul. I was surprised that such kind of a high profile man was visiting my grandmother in the deep country. I politely introduced myself to him that I was a freshman at Chung-Ang University, An-Sung campus. He gave me his business card and told me to visit him as soon as school starts after the summer vacation.

I went back to school and checked in the dorm again. I

remembered that the grandpa president told me to visit him but I thought he would be probably very busy and did not have time to see me. One day when I came back to my dorm room after a class, the teaching assistant who was in charge of our dorm phoned me and let me know that the President of the University stopped by our dorm to see me with a group of his staff. I became an instant celebrity at the dorm. It was quite surprising news among the students and the cleaning ladies who worked in the building. All of sudden they started recognizing me as the President's granddaughter.

Although Chung-Ang University had two campuses; one in Seoul and the other in An-Sung, he usually stayed at the Seoul campus and came down to An-Sung once in a while. When he came to our campus he visited me. I felt really special to be remembered by someone like him and very much appreciated his kindness. When I visited him in his office, he asked me how my school life was. I said that I was doing great and told him about the English Speaking Contest that I competed in at Kyung-Hee University and won second prize. He asked if our school knew about it. I said, "No. I just went there alone."

He congratulated me then said that he was going to recommend me to the Korean American Scholarship Foundation so keep up the good work. He also recommended me to get an opportunity to travel on an academic trip to China that was sponsored by the Ministry of Education, Korea. I sincerely appreciated him for his kind encouragement. He was the very first person who gave me such kind of encouragement and generosity in my life.

I had to study hard in order to continuously stay at the dorm and get the scholarship from the Korean American Scholarship Foundation. My parents were extremely happy and thankful for the unexpected scholarship news. I did my best and received the full scholarship each semester until I graduated from the college. One of the reasons why I decided to go to Chung-Ang University was because it was a Christian school. I had no idea that I was going to meet the University President at my grandmother's house and would take the scholarship. I was so lucky and thanked God.

I felt something wonderful was happening. With the President's recommendation, I was able to join the China trip. About a dozen students from the Seoul campus and a dozen from An-Sung gathered for the China trip. A couple of professors and an officer from the Ministry of Education joined us as well. It was my first trip to a foreign country. Not many people traveled to foreign countries back then, especially a communist country like China in 1990. Since we were going to a communist country, we had to take a mandatory orientation on how to react or what to say when we encountered North Koreans. We went to the Kyung-Hee University in Suwon where I participated for the English Speaking Contest before. There were a few civilians as well in the orientation class. They were not going to China but to Japan. After the orientation we received our passports that were valid for six months only.

China Trip

The students for the China trip gathered at the Inchon Harbor which was well known for General Douglas MacArthur's (1880-1964) successful landing during the Korean War (1950). The West Coast of Korea, where the harbor was located, was shallow compared to the East Coast of the Korean peninsula, so North Korea did not suspect that Inchon would cause them to retreat. North Koreans already marched down to Pusan which was the second capital city of Korea. General MacArthur and his marines landed in the Inchon Harbor secretly and reclaimed the capital city Seoul from North Korea. General MacArthur has become a legend and a hero to Koreans since then.

I saw an enormous ship next to the dock. I had never seen anything like that in my life. The ship was huge and looked like a ten story apartment complex. We were onboard and assigned to our bunk beds. I was too excited to fall asleep that night. I went out to walk around in the ship with a couple of other students. We walked like drunken people in the narrow, tilting isles. We were so excited and had so much fun. We did not know where we were going and ended up at a dead end. We opened the door and all of sudden there were hundreds of people sitting on the floor. Some were lying on the floor. They did not have their own rooms or beds so they sat on the floor in the large room together to go back home. We closed the door gently and went up to the upper deck. It was late at night. We were in the middle of nowhere. I could not see anything on the black ocean. Only the stars in the sky were ever so bright.

I slept only a few hours then woke up early in the morning. So did the other students. When we were getting close to China, someone shouted.

"I can see China now!!!"

We went up to the deck and saw some watermelon skins and other debris that were drifting from the land. Everything seemed to be different: the colors of the buildings, the people, the atmosphere, the air and everything.

After we checked in our hotel, we visited a university and met with a group of Chinese students. They gave us a lecture on Chinese culture and history. After the morning class we went back to our hotel and had to gather at the lobby to go to a restaurant for lunch. I was standing with our professors waiting for the elevator to go down. When the elevator door was open, I saw several North Koreans in the elevator! They were all nicely dressed in suits and had their great leader, Kim Il Sung badges on. I was a little bit nervous to see North Koreans for the first time in my life. I only read about them in text books. I remembered from the orientation class that the North Koreans traveling outside the country were usually high profile government officials. Our professor greeted them first.

"Hello, are you from North Korea?"

"Yes, we are from Pyong-Yang. Are you from Seoul?"

"Yes. We are from Seoul. We are going to Baek-Du Mountain (Changbaishan in China)."

Then one of the North Koreans politely replied with a smile on his face.

"So are we. Baek-Du Mountain is the one where our ancestors' spirits reside. Someday, we should all go there via Pyong-Yang when North and South Korea reunite in the near future!"

I thought it was so cool that a North Korean talked about

reunification like that. Our professor also kindly replied, "Yes, of course. It was very nice meeting you. Have a wonderful trip!"

"Thank you. You too."

When all the students gathered at the lobby, we talked about the special greetings with the North Koreans in the elevator. The other students were wowed that we actually met some real North Korean people face to face.

We arrived at a huge Chinese restaurant. An interesting thing at the restaurant was that there was a glass case at the entrance where snakes were kept. I could not walk by the snake tank so I ran into the restaurant. Like Indiana Jones, I have been frightened to death of snakes since as long as I can remember. We ordered lots of Chinese food from the menu and the large round table was full of all kinds of delicious looking food but the flavor was very strong and unfamiliar. After the dinner we came out of the restaurant and some of us complained that we should have ordered Coke instead of Jasmine tea. The oily foods were not settling in our stomachs. Soon a student came out of the restaurant with a can of Coke. We were delighted to see the red can. It was not chilled at all, though everyone was eager to sip the warm Coke as if we found water in the desert. Although it was warm Coke, it really tasted good especially after the greasy, strong flavored Chinese foods.

We were laughing and having fun while waiting for others to come out. Then one of us mentioned that there was a tour bus nearby and some North Koreans were getting off of the bus. I looked at the bus. I could tell all the people sitting in the bus were looking at us with curiosity. We were curious about them too. A group of the North Koreans from the bus walked toward us and said "Hi." We greeted them and introduced ourselves as students from Seoul. They were all nicely dressed up in suits and dress shoes. Contrarily the students from South Korea were wearing sunglasses, sleeveless shirts, short pants and sandals. Women wearing short pants were probably not allowed in North Korea. I had never seen any North Korean women wearing short pants on television. We asked them where they were from. They were professors from Kim Il Sung University. Then one of us asked them if they could exchange the Kim Il Sung badges as a souvenir.

One of the professors advised us that it was not just a simple badge but the symbol of their Great Leader and we were not supposed to consider it as a souvenir. The girl immediately apologized to him. He then gave us his name cards. He was very kind and so were the other North Koreans.

We were supposed to go to bed early that night to catch an early flight the next morning. But many of us gathered in the senior guys' room. They started drinking Chinese vodka called Ko-Ryang-Joo. I was there too. The Chinese vodka seemed to be really strong. One of the seniors lit a lighter on the vodka and it was really burning with a flame! All the students in the room had a drink. Although I was not good at drinking alcohol, I joined the gang and had a few shots with them. We talked about what we experienced that day especially meeting with the North Koreans at the parking lot. Being in the group without being bullied made me feel accepted and comfortable.

The next morning I was exhausted from drinking the Chinese vodka and had to force myself to get up. We gathered at the lobby and waited for the others to come down. Our main schedule for the day was flying to Beijing and visiting the Forbidden City and the Great Wall, but because of the students who couldn't get up from the drinking the night before we missed our flight and the professors discussed how we were going to go to Beijing. They decided to hire a bus driver. After several hours of bus driving, we finally arrived in Beijing and were able to visit Tiananmen Square, Forbidden City and the Great Wall. Seeing all three landmarks in a day was a bit much. I felt like we were rushed. It was not a real tour but instead, stopping by each place just for the record. We were still behind schedule. We were supposed to take a flight going to Baek-Du Mountain in the afternoon but after we visited the three places, we were too late to catch the flight. There was no flight available in the evening. Baek-Du Mountain was a historically important and symbolic mountain to Koreans and visiting the mountain was considered as a once in a life time opportunity. The mountain was right between the border of China and North Korea. Since we couldn't visit the mountain via North Korea, we had to go to the other side of the mountain via China. So our professors decided to give up all other tour schedules and focus on visiting Baek-Du Mountain only. They hired two bus drivers and we ended up riding in a bus from Beijing to Baek-Du Mountain for almost 30 hours. Except short bathroom breaks and meal time, we stayed in the bus and stared at the endless corn fields until we dozed off. When we finally arrived at a city close to the mountain, we felt we had enough of China and wanted to go home. But the lunch we had was a lot like Korean style, probably because we were close to North Korea. We were served rice, Kim-Chi and hot green peppers with bean paste. We really enjoyed the meal and missed our home food.

Baek-Du Mountain was famous for a lake on top of it, called Heaven Lake. The lake was formed by volcanic eruptions and the size was about 8 miles around and 820 feet deep. Legend said there was a dragon living in the lake. I wondered how we were going to climb up 9,000 feet of the mountain. We climbed the mountain by bus on paved asphalt then walked to the final peak. Far from the grandeur and spectacular scenery as we heard numerous times about the mountain, when we got there, the lake was completely obscured by thick fog and 30 mph strong winds carrying sand and dust. It was almost impossible to open our eyes. At the bottom of the mountain it was humid hot summer with no wind at all, but at the top of the mountain it was so cold, windy and rainy. One of the professors shouted at us not to open the umbrellas we brought because we might be blown into the lake. We just desperately wanted to take some pictures as evidence that we had been to Baek-Du Mountain. Since we had a hard time to open our eyes we did not know where the photographer was. A guy with a camera shouted.

"Here! Here! Look at me here!"

So we just posed toward the sound and took some photos. Even though the weather was terrible and we could not see the beautiful lake at all, all of us laughed, jumped up and down with excitement and cheered out loud.

On the way back to Korea the students who received the name cards from the North Korean professor threw them away in the ocean. We did not want to be questioned by Korean government officials why we possessed the North Korean professor's name cards.

The twelve-day China trip was over. The group gave me a

sense of camaraderie and a meaning of friendship that I had not experienced in my school life from elementary school to middle and high school through college. There were no bullies or any sarcastic talk against me. I thought the trip might be the first and the last overseas trip in my life. I felt emptiness but I also felt so lucky to know Grandpa President who helped me get the unforgettable opportunity.

Summer vacation was over. When the new fall semester started I heard from a few classmates who went to Australia during the summer vacation for their English language training. I was very interested in listening to their experiences. I thought about going to the U.S.A. for language training but I had just come back from the China trip so I decided to take some time to think about it then ask my parents if they would help me. The more I thought about the language school the more I became excited. As soon as the fall semester was over I moved out of the dorm and went home. When my father came home after work, I kindly told him that I wanted to go to America to take a language course for eight weeks. The tuition was $1,050 and the approximate total costs for eight weeks including housing, meals, books and insurance were $2,620 in total. He was concerned about money. So he told me to ask my mother. Despite my mother having financial hardships, she still managed saving money as much as she could. So I asked my mother if it would be fine with her. She said it was fine and that I should go ahead.

I deserve to go to hell

The relationship between my mother and I was no longer what it used to be. Ever since I left for college I heard her complaining about her financial difficulties on occasion, but she was no longer a mean person like in the past. I thought the long distance helped.

One day she said to me, "What I did to you and your brothers is impossible for anyone to forgive. I deserve to go to hell." I was shocked when she said that and felt a deep sympathy for her. As soon as she said that, I told her, "Mom, I forgive you. You only did that to us so that we could do better and live better lives. Don't feel so bad, please. We all forgive you." I knew I had to forgive her because of my faith in God. However, I forgave her from my mind, but not from my heart at that time. My mother was regretting profoundly for what she had done to us. It was like her awakening from a terrible dream. She had been in her own imaginary world and suffered from her dangerously serious depression. She should have been treated by a psychiatrist on regular basis, but we just thought that we were the victims only and we were the ones who needed help, but not her. As mistreated children for so long, we had no room to understand her. Forgiving her was nothing but a nice gesture. I am unsure of my sincerity.

Now that I had my mother's permission to go to the U.S., I had to decide which school I would attend, then get a new passport, a student visa, and purchase airplane tickets. Since I was going to the U.S. during winter, I decided to go to a school somewhere in the South. So, I submitted three applications to three different Universities in the South in order to get an acceptance for my student visa. The next step was applying for my passport. The passport that I got for my China trip was for one time use only.

I called Suji whom I met during the China trip and asked her if I could stay at her house when I would go to Seoul for my passport. She lived with her parents and they welcomed me to stay with them. Suji's parents owned their own kitchen furniture business in Gang-Nam, Seoul. Suji's parents asked me why I needed a new passport. So I told them about my plan of going to America to attend an English language school for eight weeks during the winter vacation. They said it was a wonderful idea and suggested that their daughter, Suji, should also take that kind of language training.

Suji's parents listened to my plan and complimented me for being independent and passionate. Suji's father told me that he used to travel all over the world for his business and he was very excited about my trip to the U.S. He then offered that he wanted to take me to the Ministry of Foreign Affairs and Trade building and help me with the application. I could have gone by myself but I accepted his generosity. Suji's father said that I might get a one-year passport since I was a college student but we were surprised when I received a five-year passport a week later. I really appreciated Suji's parents who helped me and encouraged me as if I were their own daughter. Later Suji went to Japan for a year for her language training and I heard several years later that she translated some children's books from Japanese to Korean after she graduated college. She also married one of the guys whom she met at the China trip. Her younger brother went to Russia for his language training and majored in European economics.

No agent needed. I have God.

My passport was all set and I had to get my student visa next. When I visited the office of the Ministry of Foreign Affairs and Trade to get my passport, I noticed that there were many travel agencies and notary offices in the area. There were so many agencies and I had no idea which one was better than the other. Instead of staying at Suji's parents' again, I decided to commute by bus from my hometown to Seoul in a day. It was about a five-hour bus ride each way. My plan was to take a first bus leaving my hometown at five A.M., visit the office, then take a bus coming home in the afternoon. Then I would arrive home by 10 o'clock at night. Although it was a tiresome plan, I was more than willing to go through with it for my exciting trip to America.

In the bus going to Seoul, I remembered the time when I was running away from my mother several years ago. My destination was the same but the purpose of the trip was much different. I was running away from my mother back then but now I was going to apply for a visa to go to the U.S.A. America was just a country that I heard of, but now I was actually planning on going there! Wow! I thought I could handle more than ten hours of a bus trip in a day.

I stepped into a travel agency in Jong-Ro, Seoul. Since there were too many travel agencies in the area, I just chose one with a big sign that said "VISA." I told a guy at the travel agency that I needed a student visa to go to the U.S.A. He said I would need several required documents to submit and asked about my father's occupation and how much money we had in our bank account. I told him that my father was a carpenter and ran his own small construction business. He said my father's occupation was not nearly good enough to impress the U.S. Embassy to get my student visa. However he could make some fake documents that would show that my father was an executive officer at a well-known corporate company and show fake income statements. In order to do that, he requested me to pay him an extra 1,000,000 Korean Won (about US$1,000) on top of the application fee and the visa service charge. I said I understood and would get back to him after I discussed it with my parents first. When I was walking down the stairs from the travel agency on the second floor, my legs were shaky and my eyes were blurring with tears.

I went to the express bus terminal directly from the travel agency. I sat in the bus going home and buried my head in my hands. I was so upset about what the agency said regarding my father's occupation. I was humiliated. My father did his best to raise his children but the travel agent said that my father's occupation was not nearly good enough to "impress" the U.S. Embassy. I was so sorry to my father. I was not going to say a word to my father what I heard from the travel agent. The more I thought about it the more I became depressed. I wanted to reach something in the sky but I felt that someone was dragging me from the bottom. I faced a dead end. There was no way to go further. That was it. Going to America was not meant for me. I told myself that the China trip was good enough and an eight-week language school in America would not give me a happy successful life.

It is too short anyway. I tried to convince myself. Let's give up on going to America. I could still study English in Korea and get a decent job. It was not the end of the world. Thinking that way was comforting to me a little bit. I did not have to feel so miserable after all.

I came home. My mother asked me how it went. I told her that I decided not to go to America. She asked, "Why not?" I did not say anything to my father, but I told my mother what I heard from the travel agency. She said she would try to come up with the extra money so I should continue my plan. I thanked her but I said I was no longer interested in going to America.

In my dream that night, I saw myself walking on the path in a rice field in the middle of nowhere. 10,000 Korean Won (about US$10) that was in my pocket fell out behind me, but I saw myself keep walking without knowing it then I saw myself realizing that I lost the money. I was looking around but the money was nowhere to be found. I felt really bad. If it was just a quarter or a dollar I wouldn't care much, but 10,000 Won was not small change to me. I said to myself in the dream, "Nami. Why don't you go back? There is your money not that far from where you are. Just turn around and go back. You will find it."

Then I woke up from the dream and still remembered the dream vividly. I thought about what the dream meant. What was God trying to tell me?

> "In all your ways acknowledge Him and He will make your paths straight."
>
> — Proverbs 3:6

What was the 10,000 Won for? Was it just money and a meaningless dream? Why did I not turn around and go back to find it? I wanted to close my eyes and go back to pick up the money but it was too late. I was not sleepy any more. I tried to understand the dream. Was the money something important to me? What is the important thing to me now? Going to America? But I didn't want to go back to the travel agency and pay the extra money for the fake documents. I wondered what God was trying to tell me. Should I continue my plan of going to America? But how?

I decided to prepare the visa application and the supporting documents without using the travel agency. So I went to school to get a copy of a certificate that I was a student of Chung-Ang University and my transcripts. Since the winter vacation had just begun there were not many students on the campus. After I took care of the errands I walked on the campus deep in my thoughts. I was going to take a bus going to the express bus terminal but I saw a school bus waiting at the bus stop on the campus. I didn't know school buses were running during the vacation. School buses connected between the Seoul campus and the An-Sung campus. Instead of riding in an express bus going to Seoul, I felt like riding in the school bus for the first time. Since I used to live in the dorm on the campus, I never had a chance to ride a school bus before. I thought it would be fun to try something different.

There were only a few students sitting in the school bus. Among them, I noticed one of the seniors. Her name was Jen. One of my classmates told me that she used to live in the U.S. for several years. She was a senior student and had already been hired as an in-flight interpreter for one of the major airline companies in the U.S. She was tall, beautiful and spoke English really well. We were not close friends but easily recognized each other. We exchanged greetings and sat next to each other. She asked me what brought me to school during the winter break. I told her about my language school plan in the U.S. and came to school to get some supporting documents for a student visa. She listened to me and said it was a great idea and asked if I received an acceptance letter from the school I wanted to attend. I didn't have it. When I called the University of Alabama, I was told that they mailed the acceptance letter and it was on its way. Then Jen told me that I did not have to get a student visa if it took so long to get the acceptance letter. Instead, I should get a visitor's visa. So I told her what the travel agency told me about the extra fee.

She said, "You don't need to pay the extra fee to the agency. A friend of mine works for the U.S. Embassy Visa Department. Let me ask her if she could help you out. Nothing to worry about. Everything will be fine. Do you have your documents translated in English?"

"Yes, and they are notarized."

All of a sudden I felt my heart was pumping so fast. I thanked God a million times. *Oh, Lord, Thank You, Thank You, Thank You!!!* Besides the application and the supporting documents, I also had an affidavit from my cousin who was a high school mathematics teacher to guarantee my return to Korea after visiting the U.S.A. Jen asked me if I purchased airplane tickets. I said I almost gave up on going to America after what I heard from the travel agency, so I did not even think about purchasing airplane tickets yet. She said, "Airline companies usually require a minimum of two weeks prior notice for tickets but let me call my company and see if they have any tickets available for you." I felt that I was so lucky to be onboard the school bus that day and sit next to her.

While waiting for the visa I was able to stay at a teaching assistant's house in Seoul, whom I met at the church on the campus. He was a graduate school student and was married. Unfortunately, I forgot his and his wife's names. While I was staying at the couple's house, he suggested reading a Christian devotional book called *The Imitation of Christ* (1418) by a German Christian monk Thomas à Kempis (1380-1471). He said the book was widely read among Christians. So I got a Korean version of the book and started reading it. When they both were gone to school early in the morning I decided to do a 24-hour fasting.

I took a shower first. Then I got my Bible, a hymn book and the devotional book of *the Imitation of Christ*. I sat down on the floor and started singing some of my favorite hymns and gospel songs. Then I started praying and repenting all my sins as far as I could remember, even the tiniest of things. Whether it was small or big I repented everything. I kept praying and praying. I sang more of the songs in the hymn book. I meditated on the lyrics while singing. They were so comforting, humbling and honoring to God. I thanked God that He had protected me no matter where I had been and guided me so far. I thanked Him that He sent me Jen for the visa and the flight tickets. I thanked Him for the T.A. and his wife who kindly allowed me to stay at their place. Among everything, I thanked Him for forgiving my sins and accepting me as who I was.

In my quiet time with God, I could picture everything that had happened to me. God showed me the strange dream of losing the money. He let me feel that I had to go back and start over instead of giving up. He stirred my heart to get onboard the school bus that day at the exact time and let me meet Jen who happened to have her best friend working at the U.S. Embassy Visa Department and happened to be an interpreter for an airline company to get me the last minute airplane tickets going to America. Everything seemed to be fitting into its own place precisely at the exact moment. I felt someone who knew everything in advance orchestrated the whole thing in such a short period of time. It was certainly not me. I could not do it on my own. I almost gave up, but I believed that IT WAS GOD who worked everything on behalf of me without losing any minute. Wow… this must be a miracle and THE miracle was happening to me…

"Do I deserve this?? No… definitely not. Wow… Who am I?"

"A child of God…." He said to me in my heart.

I felt His Being surrounding me. The more I prayed the more I was closer to Him. After repenting all my sins, I kept thanking Him and honoring Him. I started realizing that my fasting and my prayers were not just limited to get the visa so desperately. I really enjoyed the time with God. I cried and cried. I just could not stop crying. I did not know how long I cried and prayed like that. My legs were sleepy. I tried to move and get up to go to the bathroom but I felt the lower part of my body was someone else's. I once heard rubbing the tip of your nose with saliva would help when people had sleepy hands or feet. I tried but it did not help. I was glad no one was home. I barely stood up. I felt that I was standing up on hundreds of tiny needle points. I made it to the bathroom and saw myself in the mirror. My eyes were popped out so badly. I looked like someone else. I washed my face with cold water several times to calm my eyes.

I realized that fasting for 24 hours without even drinking water was really challenging. I could skip one meal for my diet easily. Skipping two meals would be uncomfortable but I thought I would be able to handle it. However not taking anything for 24 hours was not something that I expected. My hands and legs were shaky. I had never studied how to fast properly before. But I liked the way of my own fasting. Nothing but the help from the Holy Spirit! That was exactly what I needed.

> "For the kingdom of God is not a matter of eating and drinking, but of righteousness, peace and joy in the Holy Spirit."
>
> — Romans 14:17

I prepared rice soup that I was going to eat later when the fasting was over. It was just one part rice to ten parts water boiled together. No salt. Nothing. It was just plain rice gruel. When the fasting was almost over, I was so excited and overwhelmed by a full sense of joy and accomplishment. At last I did it! I repented all my sins and just had my 24 hours of a spiritual bath. I felt so great! I thanked God that He helped me to complete it! Wow!!! What can I do without YOU, my LORD!!! Thank you, Thank you,

Thank you so much!!! My rice gruel soup was ready to eat—my first meal after taking the spiritual bath. But I waited for another ten more minutes as a nice gesture because I did not want to show God how starved I was! I thought that God would laugh at me when He read my mind though.

The next day I went to the school library and collected all the books related to a U.S. visa interview. I read every single part of the U.S. visa interview. I wanted to prepare myself for the interview. I practiced so many times with different answers about what to say when a visa officer asks me questions about my trip to the U.S. Some of the basic questions were "Why do you want to go to the U.S.? How long will you stay? When will you come back? Basic stuff. If I had to speak English really well, this was the time. I did not want to disappoint my parents and other people who had helped me so far. I wanted to do my part to be the best!

How many average people in the world would get their U.S. visa in one week? Not many. Probably high profile government officials only. How many average college students would get their U.S. visa in three days without a visa interview? Only one in the world and it was ME—A child of God. God gave me my very first U.S. visa in three days without an interview. I just said Thank you God, Thank you, Thank you, Thank you!!! I really appreciated Jen and her friend at the U.S. Embassy. That was over twenty years ago. I hope that Jen's friend at the embassy wouldn't be in trouble because of my sharing this old story today.

Jen came out with her boyfriend. She handed me my visa and the airplane tickets. They congratulated me. When I looked at the flight tickets, I was a little bit nervous that I had to transfer airplanes several times; Seoul to Memphis, TN; Atlanta, GA; Birmingham, AL then finally on to Tuscaloosa, AL. Jen's boyfriend told me that one thing to remember in America was not running in public no matter how much I was in a hurry. In Korea, it was common to see people running to catch buses. They said Americans don't run in public and if I did, they would stare at me. I thought that was an easy thing to keep in mind.

"I promise I won't run in public. Hahaha!"

I thanked Jen sincerely from the bottom of my heart.

I went back to my parents' house to pack and leave for America. Riding in a bus for five hours felt like just a regular commute after the numerous bus trips back and forth between Seoul and Jinju, my hometown. When I went home, there was an acceptance letter from the University of Alabama English Language Institute. The school knew that I was coming and a teacher from the E.L.I. would come to the airport to pick me up and take me to the dormitory. It did not matter whether I had the acceptance letter or not since I had my B1/B2 visa now. I thought about the man at the travel agency who tried to coax a bribe out of me to forge documents. I wondered how many students he lied to like he did to me. Without God I could have been deceived by him too. I couldn't thank God enough for everything He had done for me.

Before I left I visited my grandmother (my father's side) and other relatives to let them know that I was going to America. It was only for eight weeks but it meant a lot to me. My grandmother wished me well and I promised that I was going to write a letter to her. I also visited my other grandparents (my mother's side) and said good bye to them. They all wished me well. I thanked my parents for helping me financially and allowing me to go to the U.S. Then I left home.

There were a lot of U.S. soldiers in their uniforms aboard the airplane. I almost felt like I was sitting in a military plane with the soldiers. They were stationed in Korea and going back home. I thought about Rich, my friend whom I went with to Nam-Dae-Moon market. I remembered the day when I was treated as a prostitute by the merchant at the market. It was one of the terrible memories of my life. It took quite some time to get healed from the emotional trauma and get rid of the fear of people. I used to walk looking down on the ground for a while in order to avoid eye contact with anyone. When Rich went back to the U.S.A. after finishing his military service, he sent me a letter that he started his school and was going to become a pilot as he always wanted to be. He wanted to finish his school as soon as possible. So he took many classes during the weekdays and did not have much time for anything else. I was glad that he was doing really well.

The long airplane trip was tiresome but it was not like

the endless bus trip in the corn fields in China. I was not bored but excited. First I arrived at the Memphis International Airport in Tennessee after probably about 18 hours of flying. I followed the other passengers who got off the same airplane I flew in. At the immigration inspection the officer asked me if it was my first time visiting the U.S. and how long I was going to stay. I said it was my first time and I was going to stay for about two months. The officer asked me how much money I brought in. I told him, "US$3,000." He asked me to show him the money. I showed him the exact amount. He said great and stamped six months on my passport.

I walked to the next gate to transfer to my next flight. When I was walking by, I noticed photos of a man everywhere. I wondered who he was. His face was printed on walls, postcards, books, calendars. On my next flight I asked a person sitting next to me who the famous guy was at the Memphis Airport. I learned that it was Elvis Presley, the King, and Memphis was his hometown. Oh, I heard of his name before but didn't know he was from Memphis. I learned something new. I flew to my next stop, Atlanta, Georgia. I did not see any recurring photos of a celebrity icon there but noticed peaches were very popular. I thought Georgia produced peaches a lot, but someone told me that the peach was the official state fruit of Georgia. I finally arrived in Birmingham, AL and still had one more flight going to my final destination in Tuscaloosa. I don't remember exactly how long it took for the entire flight but at least 24 hours. I found my luggage at the baggage claim then met a teacher waiting for me from the school. She welcomed me and took me to the school dorm—the Rose Towers.

Never used perfume

I checked in my room. Four students shared two bedrooms. My roommate's name was Jaclynn. Two others were Acura and Nykee. The three of them knew each other already. They welcomed me and said that I was their first international roommate. Jaclynn showed me where the kitchen and the bathroom were and she also told me that I could share the kitchenware with them. I never thought about cooking until then and realized that I had to cook now. At my school I just went to the school cafeteria and paid for the meals but now I had to cook even though I had no idea what to cook. I was thankful that I didn't have to buy any cooking ware at least.

I went to the English Language School the very next day to take a level test. I met some new friends from other countries after the test. There were several Korean students too but I wanted to practice my English with students from other countries. The test result came out the next day and my level was intermediate. Some Korean students had been there for over six months and even a year, but they were still in the intermediate level. I thought that I saved at least six months of time and money since I already started at the intermediate level. In my class I met a Taiwanese friend. Her name was Mao. Mao and I became good friends. We sat next to each other and took our classes together.

Mao and I went out to see a basketball game one night with other E.L.I. students. The University of Alabama played against a college from Illinois. I had never been to a basketball game before, so I became so excited to be at the game. We all cheered out loud, "B.A.M.A. BAMA!!!" We had a real fun time that night. There was another girl whom we liked to talk to. I forgot her name but she was from the Middle East. She always wore her black traditional dress Hijab when she came to school. We only saw her beautiful big eyes. She spoke English really well compared to us. She said she was an English teacher in her country and came to the U.S.A. for her husband who was a graduate school student. One day she invited Mao and me to her place. When we went to her apartment, she was not wearing the Hijab but a pretty red sweater and a long black skirt. We could see her long beautiful dark hair. We could not recognize her right away. We had to cover her face with our hands except her eyes to see if it was really her. We all laughed and giggled. She said her tradition was wearing Hijab outside but when they were home they could wear anything they liked.

Mao and I never had Arab food before. We all sat on the carpet floor and ate the homemade Arab food. She put the food plates on a large vinyl sheet instead of on a table. Everything looked interesting and delicious. They said they usually ate food with their hands but if we wanted to have forks and spoons we could use them as well. She and her husband were very kind to us.

Mao and I said we did not expect they were going to prepare that much food for us. We really appreciated their warm hospitality. Her husband said that being kind to others was written in the Quran and they told us about the prophet Muhammad. I thought the story about Muhammad and the Quran was pretty interesting. I remembered that there was an Islam temple in Seoul. I thought I was going to visit the temple when I went back to Korea. Mao and I had a real good time at their house.

When the class was over in the morning, I usually went to my dorm to have lunch then went back to the afternoon class. After school I usually spent time with Mao at the library to do our homework. A few times I met with Korean students and had dinner with them. When we went to the mall one day, I decided to have my ears pierced as a memento of my trip to America.

When I went to the dorm to have lunch one day, I saw Nykee was lying on the couch. I walked toward her and said, "Hi, Nykee!" I saw her eyes closed and her long eyelashes were rapidly blinking but she did not respond to me. I thought it was odd because she usually wanted to spend time with me.

She liked taking me out to her friends' dorm and introduced me to them, "Hey Guys! Meet my new roommate Nami. She is from Korea."

Nykee also took me to a library to show me around. But that day she did not answer to me. I thought maybe she was trying to take a nap so I did not bother her.

I usually ate Ramyon noodle or an unknown dish that I created. I stirred a little bit of ground beef, drained the fat, then added cheese, salt and pepper and mixed them all. I ate it with a couple of slices of bread. It was unhealthy food and not my typical eating habit but it was easy to make. Honestly, I did not know how to cook. I ate the foods that my mother cooked until I graduated from high school then I ate at the school cafeteria all the time at the college. I never learned how to cook. As soon as I finished eating, I took my books and went back to my class.

When I came back to the dorm after school the three roommates were all standing together in the living room. I said Hi to them and walked into my room.

Jaclynn came after me and asked, "Nami. Do you have a minute?"

"Yes."

I went out to the living room and looked at them. They all stared at me as if I did something wrong. I did not know what was going on.

Jaclynn asked, "Did you go into their room and touch anything today?"

"No. Why?"

They showed me broken glass fragments gathered on the coffee table. It was a broken perfume bottle. Jaclynn asked if I broke the perfume bottle.

I said, "No! I did NOT!"

I had never used any perfume in my life. Why would I go in someone else's room and break the perfume bottle? I was absolutely innocent. All of a sudden I felt a huge fear covering me and became speechless. I struggled how to prove my innocence to them in English.

I just said, "No, I did not do it! Believe me! I did not do it!"

I was learning English at the language school but it didn't mean that I was fluent in English. I was so nervous and afraid of all three of them. When they were in the dorm, usually they played music so loud and I could not concentrate on my study at all. It happened pretty often. I asked them to be quiet a little bit but they just laughed at me and went back to their partying. Now they were accusing me for the broken perfume bottle that I had never seen before. I told them that I stopped during my lunch break to eat my lunch and get my books but I did not go into their room at all.

"Nykee was at the dorm when I came."

"But she said she was sleeping."

The three of them ganged up on me and looked at me as if I was a criminal.

"Call the police," I said.

Then they all screamed at me, "WHAT??? ARE YOU

OUT OF YOUR MIND? WE ARE NOT GOING TO CALL THE POLICE!!! If you didn't do it, you didn't do it. We just want to hear from you!"

I believed that it was Nykee who touched the bottle and broke it. Then she pretended that she was sleeping on the couch when I got home. I should have called the police and have the finger prints on the broken glasses checked. I should have told them to smell my hands if they could smell any perfume. But I could not speak to any of them in clear English because I was so flustered.

I just cried and said, "I did not do it. Please believe me."

Acura said it was okay, but it was not okay with me. My old memory of being treated as a thief by my teacher when I was in middle school had always followed me like a shadow. It had been torturing me for years. Now those three girls ganged up on me and accused me for something I did not do. And I couldn't defend myself in their language despite that I could think lots of things in Korean. I couldn't understand why those awful things were happening to me. I felt so small and helpless. I wondered why I wanted to come to America so badly. To meet these mean girls and be bullied?

The next day I went to my teacher and told her everything that had happened at the dorm. She told me to move to a new dorm room right away after I was done with school that day. I said there was only three weeks left and I would endure until I move out. She said, "It might be Korean culture to endure but in America people would change their roommates right away in this kind of situation."

I felt good when my teacher seemed to understand me and tried to help. She called the teaching assistant who was in charge of the building and said to me to meet him right away. So I did.

The T.A. gave me a chair to sit down and asked me why I wanted to change my room. I told him what happened as much as I could. I could not help but showing my tears when I was telling him how mean the three girls had been to me. I felt they discriminated against me. When I finished talking to him he said he understood everything I had explained to him. He also said,

"People who experienced discrimination in the past discriminate against others on purpose because they know how it feels."

Surprisingly he said that he already talked to the girls and heard their story before I went to see him. I did not know that he already talked to them. He wanted to hear my story to compare to theirs. I did not know what they said but I knew that I did not do it and God knew that I was innocent.

The T.A. said that the three of them had been friends long before I became their roommate. So they were together all the time. They would discriminate no matter who becomes their new roommate. He gave me a new room and I moved all my belongings right after I got out of the T.A.'s office. The three were not at the dorm at that time so I did not get a chance to say good bye to them.

When I met two new roommates, Andrea and Shannon, I remembered the day when Nykee took me to the library. Nykee asked a white female student, "Is this seat taken?"

The girl screened us from head to toe and said, "NO!"

I told Nykee to go somewhere else because I didn't want to sit next to the mean girl. I felt really bad and insulted by the way she looked at us. When I met the new white roommates, I remembered the mean girl at the library and wished that they were not like her. I prayed it would go well this time.

Early the next morning I was walking from the Rose Tower dorm to my class. Suddenly, a car stopped next to me. It was Jaclynn and the other two girls. I said Hi. Jaclynn asked me kindly why I left without saying good bye to them. I told them that I talked to the T.A. and he told me to move that day. Jaclynn and Acura looked at me while they were talking but Nykee was sitting in the driver's seat. She just sat there and stared at the wind shield. It was her who used to take me to her friends' dorm and the library, but that morning she didn't even look at me. I could tell why. Jaclynn said to visit them sometime then we departed.

My new roommate was Andrea. She was a basketball player and I heard that she was very popular among the guys at school. She was usually out and I hadn't had much time to talk with her. Shannon did not have a roommate so she used her room by herself.

After the perfume bottle incident I was afraid of people again. I did not feel comfortable looking at people just like the experience that I had from Nam-Dae-Moon market in Korea. I wanted to be alone. I decided to have a long walk. A couple of guys honked at me when they drove by me but I didn't care and just kept walking. I thought about lots of different things that had happened to my life. I felt so lonely and sad. I just could not understand why God allowed those awful things to happen to me. It was unfair and the more I kept thinking about them the more I became depressed.

I was going to a Korean grocery store. My legs were getting tired. I thought about going back but I walked too far to go back, so I kept walking. After about five miles of walking, I finally arrived at the grocery store. I wanted to sit down somewhere. The woman at the grocery store welcomed me and asked me where I was from originally. I said I was from Jinju and she could not believe that I was from the same city where she was from. We both shouted out at the same time, "What a small world!" She asked me how I came to the grocery store. I said I walked. She was surprised with her eyes big and asked a guy shopping at the store if he could give me a ride back to my dorm. He said, "Gladly!"

He was a graduate school student at the University of Alabama. He drove a fancy red sports car. Coming back to the dorm from the grocery store took only about ten minutes. I thanked him for the quick ride. As he dropped me off, he gave me his phone number to go out sometime, but I never called him. I am very sorry to say this but I did not feel comfortable to go out with him because he had lazy eyes.

The February weather was still warm in Alabama compared to Korea but people in Alabama seemed to be afraid of having cold winter. When it snowed one day, they said it was the first snow in the last ten years and the whole campus was shut down. Most of the stores were also closed that day. Only wild crazy young students came out on the campus and they screamed out loud. They tried to have snowball fights although there was not much snow that fell on the ground. A few cars on the campus honked constantly and the students shouted at each other with excitement.

Toward the end of the spring session the E.L.I. offered several different trip options for students to choose from. I chose going to New Orleans. We left very early in the morning. A teacher and a teaching assistant drove two separate cars. I was in the car with the T.A. We drove from Tuscaloosa through Mississippi to New Orleans, Louisiana. In the car, the T.A. played lots of pop songs that he recorded on tapes and I heard the song *Forever Young* by Alphaville for the first time and the song instantly became my new favorite song, although I did not quite understand what the lyrics were about because of my lack of English language ability. I just really liked the singer's voice and the melody.

Before I went to New Orleans I had no idea why people were so excited about the city, but when we went there I realized that the city was a lot different from where I was from. My hometown was just a plain, peaceful city where people got up and went to work or school in the morning. The atmosphere of the city of New Orleans was that people got up and were ready to have a party every day and night. Tourists were everywhere walking around with colorful beads around their necks. I walked into a couple of bars out of curiosity and came right out. I was uncomfortable to look at those half naked women serving the customers. We stayed one night at a Holiday Inn then went to a café the next morning to have the famous French Quarter Beignets and cappuccino for breakfast. Korean people never considered donuts as breakfast. Donuts were a snack to us. Just a couple of puffy donuts and a small cup of cappuccino were not enough to fill my stomach as a breakfast. I could have eaten a dozen more of the white powdery sugared donuts but I thought I would have been embarrassed if I ordered that many donuts for myself.

Time at the E.L.I. went by quick. But I kept my promise to write my grandmother a letter as soon as I started my school. I did not expect her to write me back but I wrote her a letter as early as possible just in case if she ever replied me, then I would get her letter when I was still in the U.S. I told her that I was doing really well in America. Although I did not expect her reply, she kindly replied to me. We wrote letters from left to right but her letter was written from top to bottom right to left and some of the characters were old characters that were no longer used in modern Korean language. The letter was the only one that I had from her and made me feel very proud of her. It was written in blue pen and sounded like a poem that had rhythm when I read it. I could tell from the characters that her hands were weak and shaky.

It started as "Baby, my dear baby. How far are you at? I am sitting here in a deep deep country and my memories are getting faded day by day."

She said she was very proud of me. She wrote the letter and my uncle who was my father's oldest brother living with my grandmother wrote the addresses on the envelope then mailed it to me. She also enclosed a photo of her, modestly standing with her two hands put together in front of her next to a bunch of white lilies at her garden. The letter and photo became my priceless treasures.

It was time to leave the E.L.I. after eight weeks at the University of Alabama. Except the perfume incident and being bullied by those three roommates at the dorm, overall I had a great time with Mao and other students at the school and I gained some confidence to speak English. Mao stayed and continued to the advanced level at the E.L.I. and was accepted at the university for her Master's degree. In January 1992 at the University of Alabama, I learned how to exchange e-mail for the first time. A teacher showed us how American students exchanged their e-mail for academic purposes. Mao and I did not have internet access or e-mail accounts. She and I had exchanged hundreds of letters by mail for many years when we returned to our countries after the E.L.I. I visited Mao in Taiwan and she and her friend visited me in Korea.

I was onboard an airplane flying from Birmingham, Alabama to Atlanta, Georgia. An old man sitting next to me started a conversation with me. I told him that I just finished my eight weeks of English language training at the University of Alabama and was going to visit my uncle and his family in California on the way back to Korea. He asked me if I had a good time and what was the most memorable experience in the U.S. I told him that among the experiences that I had, visiting the Arab friend's house for dinner was one of the fun experiences and I was also interested in learning about the Islam religion, especially after I heard about the prophet Mohammad. I said that I would visit the Islam temple in Seoul when I go back to Korea. The old man smiled and kindly said to me, "It might have sounded interesting to you but Islam is not about love but revenge. They teach eye for an eye and tooth for a tooth, but our Christian God is the loving God. He says when anyone slaps you on the right cheek turn to them the other cheek too. I am sure you are a smart person and you can choose what is right and what is wrong."

After I talked with the old man in the airplane I thought maybe visiting the Islam temple was not for me and I should stay with Jesus. Every time I think of the language school at the University of Alabama, I think of the old man as an angel from God who guided me to the right direction.

I flew from Atlanta to Los Angeles to meet my uncle and his family. I did not plan on visiting him when I was in Korea, but when I called him, he suggested that I change the flight tickets and visit him on my way back to Korea. My uncle's house in Seoul was the one that I used as my starting point when I ran away from my mother when I was sixteen. My uncle was stationed in Anchorage, Alaska for several years when he first moved to the U.S. for his job. He eventually quit his job and immigrated to the U.S. permanently, then moved to California. I met my uncle and aunt and my two cousins. We all went to Disneyland together and after the Disneyland trip, my aunt and uncle bought me a ticket traveling to Grand Canyon and Las Vegas.

I traveled along with a group of Korean tourists in a bus. I had an opportunity to visit Grand Canyon, Bryce Canyon, Giant Canyon and Las Vegas. In the bus, some people asked me how old I was. They were at least my parents' age or older and said that they had such an opportunity to see the magnificent Grand Canyon at their middle age but I was still very young compared to them. So they said how much more wonderful experiences lay ahead of me when I become their age so they blessed me to do good things in my future.

After spending about nine weeks in the U.S., I finally came back to Korea. I felt confident compared to the time before I went to the U.S. I learned something new and I saw something new in the country. I told my parents about my general school experiences and my visit to my uncle's house in America but I did not tell them about the broken perfume bottle and the three mean roommates. I did not want my parents to feel bad or upset for something they could not do anything about. Every time I thought about the perfume bottle and the girls, the hurt and anger came back. The more my English skill was advancing the more I came up with things I could have said to defend myself at the time. It was no use. Only God knows that I did not break the perfume bottle.

International Trading

I moved out of the dorm in An-Sung Campus for the last semester of my senior year in 1992 and moved into an accommodation house nearby the Seoul campus to get a job in Seoul. I paid 130,000 Won (about $130) a month to the accommodation house for two meals a day and a small room to share with a roommate. There were about a dozen students living in the house.

I started searching for a job where I could use my major in English as soon as I graduated. My previous part time job experiences at the International Trading Exhibitions, the English Speech Contest, the E.L.I. in the U.S.A. and even the China trip gave me some confidence that I could put something on my resume and something to say about myself for job interviews. I was scheduled to have two job interviews in Yoido, Seoul in one day. I went to one of the two companies and took a written test which was translating several sentences of a business letter from Korean into English. After the written test, I was asked to come into a different office. There was the human resource manager and the company president, Mr. Chang Kim.

The president looked at my written test sheet and read one of the questions in Korean then asked me to answer in English. I told him that my answer would be exactly the same as I wrote on the test sheet. He said it was okay even though it would be exactly the same. He wanted to see if I could speak English. So I told him the exact same answer as I wrote on the written test. Then he asked me what I was going to do in the afternoon after the interview. I said I had another job interview scheduled at a different company. He said that I didn't need to go there but should start working for him from next Monday. That's how I got my first job. The salary was $500 a month. It was an average salary for an entry level position. My parents were glad to hear that I had a job right away before my graduation. They didn't have to send me my monthly spending money anymore which was about $200 a month.

The company that hired me was an international trading company. They mostly imported chemicals from Italy for the semi-conductor industry, shock absorbers from the U.S.A. for the aviation industry and industrial robots from Japan for assembly lines. My title was Coordinator and the main duties were translating the salesmen's business letters from Korean to English and interpreting for international clients and salesmen. Men wore suits and ties, but all the nine female employees wore uniforms that the company paid for; white blouse, deep green vest, jacket, and skirt. A tailor was called into the company and measured our sizes. It was very common in Korea that female employees wore uniforms rather than casual attire.

There were three sales departments. My Department was in charge of the chemical and industrial robots. Mr. Tae was our manager. At the beginning I noticed Mr. Tae talking comfortably with Ms. Lee, an admin assistant in our team. But he didn't say much to me except exchanging greetings in the morning. Female employees did not have to serve men with coffee unless they were meeting with clients. However, I heard Mr. Tae comfortably asking Ms. Lee for his coffee once in a while or Ms. Lee brought him coffee voluntarily. They seemed to be getting along well. Ms. Lee graduated from a technical high school so she was good at the computer and had been working there for years. But I was not good at using a computer at all and I never used a program called *Lotus 123* until I started working there. I had to learn the basics from Ms. Lee. She was a high school graduate and I was a college graduate but she trained me with the computer basics. I never took any computer classes. In 1992 personal computers were not commonly used at home, only schools and offices. People used to use 5.25 inch floppy disks. There was no USB or CD drive in the computers at this time. I only used computers at school a few times to type my school papers. Most students wrote their resumes by hand, not by computer. So did I. I thought the manager did not like me because I was not good with the computer and I did not meet his expectations.

One day our main client whom Mr. Tae talked on the phone with very often called from Italy, but the manager was out of the office. The receptionist asked me if I wanted to take the call instead. I said I would. The Italian client called to let us know that the items we ordered were on shortage in their headquarters so they were going to send the products from their branch office which was in a different city. Therefore the shipping schedule would be delayed, inevitably. The Italian client's English accent was hard to understand but I wrote down what he said and gave the memo to Mr. Tae when he came back. He read the memo and asked me who took the phone call. I said I did. Surprisingly, I saw a smile on his face. He told me to give the memo directly to the manager at the accounting department to inform them of the new shipping schedule. I wondered why he smiled and emphasized on giving the memo directly to the accounting manager. Did I do right? Did I catch all the Italian city names and changed shipping dates correctly? It must be right. Otherwise why would he smile?

Once a month all the employees gathered and Mr. Chang Kim, the company president, gave his speech in front of the employees. Usually it was to announce recent company news, promotions or sales reports, but sometimes the president told us about his personal stories how he started his business and became one of the top middle and small business companies in Korea.

He originally came from North Korea as a refugee and was an orphan during the Korean War (1950). He had no family or relatives in South Korea. He started his business from selling chewing gum. He earned small profits each day but did not have much to spend. After he finished his work, he went to a food vendor on a street where sweet buns with brown sugar, called Ho-Duk, were sold. He wanted to eat it so badly but he had to save his money to grow his business. So he stood next to the food vendor and smelled the Ho-Duk from the vendor for a while then went to his place wiping tears.

I didn't know how other employees reacted to the story

but it really touched my heart. He was a Christian and an elder at his church. When he got a fax from his church for a donation, I heard him ordering the accounting department to send a donation to the church immediately. I admired him very much. He was a modest, humble, and hard working man. He started from selling chewing gum after the Korean War and now he owned his own multi-million dollar business and helped others.

There were nine female employees and one of them was Ms. Hwang. She had been working for the company over ten years. I noticed that she showed me such a cold attitude anytime I saw her. I did not know what I did wrong to her. One day I wrote a small note and put it in her coat pocket hanging in the closet. I said I wanted to have coffee sometime with her if she didn't mind. So we went to a coffee shop after work one day. I told her that I noticed her avoiding me a few times and I would like to know why. Besides, if there was anything that I had done to offend her, I did not mean it and wanted to apologize. She paused for a moment and smiled. Then she said that I did not do anything wrong to her. She was just not happy about the company president showing favor to me who just joined the company not long ago. She said she had been working for the company over ten years and she never got that kind of favor from the president. She was insecure that she never went to college and couldn't speak English. So she was jealous of me and did not like me. When all the female employees were going out for lunch together, she asked other girls if I was going too. When they said yes, then she told them she was not going with. She apologized to me for being mean to me. I thought I was the one who might need to apologize to her if I did anything wrong but I was surprised that it was her who apologized to me instead. I thanked her for being honest with me and said that I was a likeable person once she knew me better. We laughed together. I thanked God for the good conversation that we shared that day.

The company used to be located in Yoido Island in Seoul. They used to rent a whole floor in one of the buildings in Yoido. But the company was prosperous and built a brand new building in Gang Nam which was a modernized business district in Seoul and recognized by luxury residential areas. When they moved to the new building, they also hired some new employees as well.

Among them, there was a female employee who was supposed to do the same kind of job that I did; translating business letters. Her name was Ms. Kyung. She majored in French at one of the well-known women's universities in Seoul. Although her major was French, she seemed to be doing fine with translating letters in English. She had a great pride about her college background and hated the fact that she was working with me, who graduated from Chung-Ang University, An-Sung Campus, not Seoul Campus. Her desk was right next to my desk. The girl sighed heavily and said loudly to let me hear her, "I'd better quit this job soon and find a new one. I did not go to a prestigious college to end up with someone who graduated from a second rate campus! I don't understand what I am doing here. What a waste of my time!"

Then the salesmen returned to the office after visiting their clients in the afternoon. She got up and ran to them. All of a sudden she was smiling and flirting with them. I remember the day when I went back to work after taking a day off because I had the flu. I asked her if she was busy while I was gone. She kept typing, looking at her computer screen, and said sarcastically, "Because I had to do your work all day long yesterday, I had no time to do mine."

She never looked at me or asked me if I was feeling better. As much as she disrespected me and hated working with me at the same company, I also hated going to work every day to put up with her crap. She was always happy with all other guys at the office but there was no single kind word to me. As far as I remember, she was mean, cold, rude and disrespectful.

The receptionist at the company was a Christian. Her name was Ms. Chung. She suggested to me to go to her church one day. I felt comfortable being at the church. Since then I started going to the church and it became my home church. It was called Sa-Rang Church. When I was sad and depressed by the mean girl, Ms. Kyung, I went to the church during my lunch break and prayed to God with tears. I could not simply forgive her. She was a little devil to me each day. I wondered why God put me in the situation. Maybe it was time for me to leave the company.

I heard some of the girls who were in my class at the college got their jobs at foreign companies. Their pay was good and they did not have to work overtime. I wanted to get a job at a foreign company too. But most of the girls who got their jobs at well-known companies had some connections with influential people. They were recommended to get the jobs. I didn't know any influential people except my President Grandpa who recommended me to receive a scholarship and get the opportunity of the trip to China, but I could not ask him to help me get a better job.

I remembered vividly what one of the managers, Mr. Park, at the company told me at a company dinner party. We were drinking beers and I happened to be sitting next to him at the same table. He asked, "Ms. Ha. Do you know any high profile people?"

"No. Why?"

"I think you are brilliant and talented but if you don't know any powerful men who could help you, it would be really difficult for you to be successful in your future."

I liked his compliment but at the same time I did not appreciate that he predicted negatively on my future.

I wanted to quit my job so badly and get a job at a foreign company. So I submitted my resignation paper after I got a job at a small Hong Kong liaison office dealing with textile business between Hong Kong and Korea. When I submitted my resignation, the company president called me in his office and said, "For my own sake, I do not want to let you go and keep you here. However I do know that you are a very bright and ambitious young woman, so I will let you go but there is one thing that I want you to remember for the rest of your life. Please remember that you learned the basic knowledge in society at MY Company."

I smiled and kindly said, "I promise you that I will surely remember that. Thank you." Then I politely bowed to him and left his office and the company.

Acme

I began my job at the liaison office of Acme Textile in Seoul. The owner, Mr. Choi was from Hong Kong. He used to have frequent visits to Korea for his business and now he moved to Seoul and was looking for a Korean assistant who could help him with interpretation. He used to work at his apartment alone, but after he hired me we found a small office in Gang Nam. There was no need to decorate the office. A few of his long time Korean business friends in Seoul sent some plants and flowers to the new office.

When he visited other textile companies I went along with him and interpreted between him and Korean salesmen. That was my main job. I wrote some business letters and sent faxes to his clients. Mr. Choi knew how to count in Korean and understood basic Korean quite a bit, but before we would enter a meeting, he told me not to mention to Korean guys that he understood Korean. I remember two Korean salesmen who were talking their offer prices in Korean. They thought Mr. Choi wouldn't be able to understand what they were saying, so they discussed their price freely in front of him. I was embarrassed and really wanted to give them a sign not to speak any more. I glanced at Mr. Choi. He showed no emotion on his face but was concentrating on their discussion. Mr. Choi and I visited many different textile companies to get the most current market prices in Korea and he tried to sell cheap textiles from China at much lower prices than his competitors in Korea.

Mr. Choi hired a salesman to help him. Most of the time the two of them went out together, so I did not have to go with him as his assistant any more. Ever since I started working for Acme Textile, I attended a language school and started learning Chinese from a native speaker from Beijing. I thought Mr. Choi would like that I was learning Chinese to help his business but he seemed not liking it at all. He did not like me taking the fax messages from the Hong Kong office which was his brother's company. Soon after he was off the phone with his brother the fax machine rang to receive a message. He came out of his office and took it right away. If there was any message he had to send to Hong Kong he sent it himself. I only learned basic conversational Chinese but he seemed to be suspecting that I might be able to catch their communications in Chinese.

Mr. Lee, the new salesman, was a nice guy and spoke English fairly well. When he was hired, Mr. Choi gave him a file case to become familiar with his textile business. Mr. Lee asked me who wrote all the business letters.

"I did. Why?" I said.

"I think the English was very well written. It's very simple and easy to understand."

Mr. Choi did not like us chatting in Korean whatsoever and told us to speak only in English in the office. He did not like Mr. Lee and, for a reason unknown to me, fired him after a couple of months. Right after Mr. Lee packed and left the office, Mr. Choi came out of his office and said to me, "Watch out if he comes back to the office and takes anything."

I told Mr. Choi that Mr. Lee was not that kind of person and he would never do such a thing. Mr. Choi never trusted any Koreans, including me. Soon after Mr. Lee was let go, Mr. Choi also told me that he was moving back to Hong Kong. I believe he came to Korea to analyze the Korean textile industry and find some new customers for several months then he went back.

Print Project

I went to see Ms. Jennifer, a headhunter, to seek a job at a foreign company. She was the one who introduced me to the previous job at the Hong Kong liaison office. She said that there was a publishing company in San Francisco looking for a new employee but there was a condition. The employee must work at their Headquarters in Korea at least a couple of years before moving to the San Francisco office in order to get used to the printing and publishing business in general. It sounded like a promising job to me. So I said that I was interested in meeting with Dr. Song, who was the owner of the publishing company in San Francisco.

I met Dr. Song at the Hyatt hotel coffee shop in Itaewon, Seoul. Having a job interview at a hotel coffee shop sounded very American style. Dr. Song explained that the printing and publishing business was considered as one of the professional occupations in the U.S. but most Korean people did not see it that way. Koreans considered printing as a lower class labor job dealing with small business cards and office stationery. Dr.

Song seemed to be a confident and successful business man. After talking with him for about an hour, I agreed to work at the Korean Headquarters for a couple of years before I moved to San Francisco. The Headquarters was at Gunpo City in Gyeonggi Province which was about an hour distance from Seoul. I was still living at the accommodation house in Seoul so I decided to take the subway to commute.

I started working at the printing company right away. It was a huge printing factory. One of the managers in the overseas department gave me a tour. I saw huge German printing machines on one entire floor, bindery machines on another floor, pallets with finished products waiting to be shipped out, and forty foot containers standing outside in the shipping yard. The press machine was quite loud and the operators had to wear ear plugs to protect their hearing, but I liked the constantly moving fast noise which made me so excited to work there. I remembered what Dr. Song said to me, "You probably speak English well now but I am sure that there will be a lot of new terms and expressions in English to learn at the printing company. Without understanding the printing process, it is not easy to work on the publishing side. That's why we also send our interns from the U.S. to the print factory."

I learned the overall printing process. I wrote job tickets and translated clients' job instructions from English to Korean, ordered cartons, pallets, and 40 foot containers to ship out the finished products to our international clients.

When clients visited the factory for their press checks I introduced them to the press operators and interpreted for them. Sometimes I stayed overnight at the factory. We printed everything from business cards, calendars, brochures to soft and hard cover books. We printed a lot of children's books and once in a while handled limited editions for world famous entertainers. The security guard at the main entrance checked bindery people's bags when they would leave work to make sure none of the finished books were smuggled out and sold in public. Most of the clients were American and European. The printed products were sold at famous National Parks and also distributed through major book stores and calendar distributors in the United States.

Printing was an interesting business indeed. From a computer disc to final product, when a project was completed it looked beautiful and gave such a sense of accomplishment, especially when I sealed the containers after the last pallet was loaded. When the long forty foot container trucks were slowly moving out of the shipping yard, I quietly prayed for the truck drivers in my heart that they would drive safely on the road and the containers would travel safely over the Pacific Ocean. I thought about the pitch black ocean that I saw when I was going to China. Now my containers would travel on the Pacific Ocean for at least fifteen days. We had to make sure that there was no hole in the containers for rain or that nobody was sleeping inside. I heard a man who worked at the shipping yard took a nap in one of the containers and other people did not know. They locked the container and the guy napping inside died because of lack of oxygen and no food.

The printing business required very detailed attention on every stage, otherwise thousands of printed materials turned out as useless garbage. One of the project managers, his name was J.K., handled multiple book projects. One of his projects was getting closer to send out to the client. He went downstairs to get some sample books for his client but he found out that the book cloth under the dust jacket was brown instead of black that his client had ordered. If people did not pay attention closely, it might look black because it was dark brown. The book spine was stitched with thread and the book cloth was already trimmed and glued to the hard board cover. All the books were completely bound and the dust jackets were placed. He was so upset that he mistakenly ordered the wrong color of the book cloth. His face turned red and looked like he was drunk. He went outside to chain smoke. When he came back to the office, reeking of cigarette smoke, he and his team manager were speechless and did not know what to do. J.K. blamed himself that he was color blind when he ordered the brown book cloth and kept saying that he could not believe that he made such a stupid mistake. He reported to his client about the book cloth. Very luckily his client replied to him that the dark brown might look better than plain black. When the client agreed to accept the books as they were, J.K. was so thrilled that he almost wanted to jump up and dance. He put a huge smile on his face and told everyone how lucky he was this time and went out to chain smoke some more to celebrate.

Postcard projects seemed to be simple and easy to handle but they were not. Some of the postcards looked very similar and were difficult to keep sorted. When I took over the postcard projects I double checked shipping lists and reported to my clients in detail. They were happy and complimented my work. They also sent me boxes of chocolates, sweaters and other complimentary gifts.

The department manager was a conservative man and was not fair. He discriminated against employees. There were international book fairs each year and he sent men only. One of the men was hired after me but he had an opportunity to go to the book fair and I was left out. I was told later that they talked about sending me but the manager voted against it because I was female. I was loyal to the company. Dr. Song, who hired me, promised that I may have the opportunity to move to the San Francisco office after a couple of years of working at the print factory. But the manager said that females usually quit their jobs once they were married and became pregnant. Then it would not be beneficial for the company.

There were two other female project managers in the department. I asked them what they thought of the manager's decision on sending men only to the book fairs. Surprisingly, they just smiled and did not say much. One of them said, "Those guys are from four-year universities and so are you but we are just from two year technical colleges. Besides, you speak English well. So, you might feel that you should have the same opportunities like those guys but we are okay."

I was shocked and disappointed by what she said to me. They just accepted the unfair reality. Her comment sounded like she did not even deserve to get an opportunity to attend the book fairs.

There was a female intern from the San Francisco office who Dr. Song sent. I still remember what she said to me. "All the girls work equally hard but I see that there is sexual discrimination going on here and I don't understand why. I am from the U.S. but if I were from here, I could have been treated the same way."

When I heard her saying this I was ashamed of our system. I felt that there was a big thick glass wall in front of me and there was no way to get through it.

I got along with most of the people at the printing factory but J.K., the one who made the mistake with the book cloth, was always mean to me for some reason. I did not know why. When I asked one of the girls if she knew any reason why he was so mean to me, she said to me she heard him saying that he wanted to see me making a huge mistake some time. I was shocked to hear such an immature comment from him and wondered why. When the team went out to drink one night I asked him about the comment he made and asked if he really said that. He was drunk and said,

"Ah, it was just a joke. I saw you doing really well and honestly I was impressed how you handled your projects. I just jokingly said that I wanted to see how you would react when you make a huge mistake. It was a joke. I am really sorry."

Then he filled my beer mug and said, "Cheers~." Since that night he was no longer mean to me.

We have two different dreams

I met Dion at the club C.E.L.A. when I was Senior at the university right after I came from my English Language Institute at the University of Alabama. He was a returning student from his military service. He lived in the men's dorm but went home in Seoul every weekend. When he came back to school on Sunday afternoon, we met and had dinner at the school cafeteria and hung out until we departed to each dorm.

One night I had a phone call at the dorm. I wondered who it could have been because my parents did not call usually. I answered the phone. The person on the other side said that she was Dion's mother and she wanted to come down to our campus and meet me as soon as possible. I became so nervous what the whole thing was about.

Dion's mother seemed to be quite young to have a college age son who finished military service. She came down to the campus on a Friday afternoon with a young woman. We went to a coffee shop nearby the campus. Dion's mother thanked me for coming out to meet them on such short notice. She said that Dion and the young woman had been dating since high school and they were engaged. She came down to tell me not to meet her son any more. She said that Dion had been avoiding his fiancé lately and she found out that he had been meeting me. Dion never said to me that he was engaged. I was really shocked. Dion's mother told me that his fiancé had joined all of their family events and was considered as one of their family members for years. Dion's fiancé had been sitting quietly and wiped her tears without saying anything. I told them that Dion never told me about his engagement and I was shocked.

After they left, Dion called me right away to meet me. I told him that I promised his mother that I was not going to meet him anymore. So, he came down to our dorm and waited until I came down to the meeting area. He explained to me that he met the girl when they were in high school but they did not get along for the past couple of years. His parents liked her and treated her as their daughter. I told Dion that I had no reason to step in someone's engagement and had no desire to date someone whose mother was against me. Dion said that his fiancé never went to college and started working right after high school. So she did not like when he talked about his college stuff and they argued a lot lately. However, when he met me, he said I seemed to be very cheerful and confident and he liked talking to me. He said he wanted to be with me and was not going to marry the girl. I said, "What about your parents?"

He said it was about his life so he would choose. Although I liked the fact that someone liked me that much, I was worried about breaking the promise that I made with his mother and his fiancé.

Although we met each other during the week days I started being insecure and jealous of his fiancé. When he went to his home on weekends he usually called me before leaving. We did not have cell phones back then. When I didn't know he was engaged, I used to call him at home and his mother answered the phone calls. That's how she found out about me. But after his mother's visit, I was afraid of calling him in case his mother answered.

He usually called me as soon as he arrived in Seoul. When I got the calls from him, I was excited because I thought he was thinking of me. But when he did not call me for several hours after he was gone to his house, I started thinking that he might be with his fiancé and they probably got back together. When he called me late at night, I was so upset and did not want to have a proper conversation at all. I did not use her name.

"What have you been doing so far? Did you meet *the Woman*? Did she ask you to come back and marry her?"

He explained what he had been doing and where he had been. Usually he had to help his father with their family business. Sometimes he said the girl was already at his parents' house and could not avoid seeing her and talking to her. The relationship between Dion and I was not based on true love. I was always worried that he would go back to his fiancé. I became very insecure and selfish. I did not want to lose him over another woman. Each time we met I started questioning him first about what he did, whom he met, what his mom said about me. Ridiculous questions.

A few months later, Dion told me that his fiancé married someone else as revenge toward him. She wanted to show him that she could move on with her life without him. He seemed to be down and sad. I was also shocked how she could find and marry someone in such a short period of time.

On my college graduation day I met Dion's parents. I knew they loved Dion's ex-finance but there was no reason to stop him from dating me anymore since his ex-fiancé married someone else. They met my parents for the first time that day. We did not go any place to sit down but just exchanged greetings on the campus and took a photo together. I did not tell my parents that Dion's mother visited me once to tell me not to meet Dion. If I ever did, my mother would be furious that I must not meet that kind of guy whose mother was not in favor of me.

Dion and I got married in 1994. We usually visited his parents on weekends. Dion's parents were hard working people but I was afraid of his mother. She told me that she was disappointed to see Dion's ex-fiancé married someone else. Dion's mother ran a clothing shop and she worked as a videographer for weddings on weekends. She drove her car everywhere for her job.

Back then not many females at her age drove a car and had that kind of video job which was usually for men. She had Dion when she was very young so she was still fairly young to have a married son. She kept saying to us that she was too young to be called as a grandmother. The first couple of times that I heard it I understood but she continuously repeated this and I did not know what to say to her. It was annoying to hear her saying constantly that she was not ready to be a grandmother.

Visiting Dion's parents over the weekends was fine but I told him that I did not want to go to his parents every weekend. I had to do our laundry, clean our house, go grocery shopping and take care of our own chores over the weekend. So I suggested to him that we visit his parents once a month instead. It was comfortable for him to visit his parents every weekend but not for me. Each time I visited his parents I felt it was another extended work day on the weekend.

One day after we came home from his parents I realized that my wedding ring was missing. I knew I took it off right before I started washing the dishes. I remembered that I put it in my pocket. I checked the pockets and searched my purse several times but could not find it. It drove me crazy all night. I could not sleep. I was getting nervous and searched the entire house a thousand times. I searched every single pocket of my jackets, pants, and bags. After searching for days, I concluded that I lost the wedding ring. I told Dion about it but he said he would prefer losing the ring over losing me. It was very sweet of him to say that. I was very sorry and also afraid of going to his parents' house even more. Though, this may have been a sign that this marriage was not meant to be.

One night we got a call from his mother and heard that Dion's grandmother, who had been ill for many years from Parkinson's disease, passed away. We all rushed to the hospital where the funeral was getting ready. All the relatives came and we wore traditional white funeral dresses for the funeral. It was cold snowy winter outside and the thin funeral dress was not nearly enough to keep us warm. I did not eat much all day because I was helping the visitors. Late at night I finally had a chance to sit down and have dinner. But there was a woman who kept staring at me. I had never met her before and I did not know who she was. She was unkind to me for no reason. She kept giving me a dirty look. She went to Dion's mother and complained about me loudly as if she wanted me to hear what she said.

"Look at her, Sister. How dare she sits down and eats dinner while you are still standing here and working!"

Dion's mother said with a lower voice, "Don't say that. She doesn't know anything."

I did not know what I was doing wrong. I hardly sat down all day long since I arrived at the funeral house the night before. I asked Dion who the mean woman was. He said she was a distant relative and he met her only a few times before. I told him how mean she was to me but he said just to ignore her. I could not simply ignore her. I tried to be nice to her first so I said Hi but she mumbled something and I could not hear her. The woman's dirty look aggravated me and I could not stand her any more. I went out to a phone booth and called my mother. I told her how lucky she was that she did not have to deal with such kind of a mean person and I told her that I wanted to take off the funeral dress and run away. I cried and complained about my situation to my mother. She told me to be patient and stay. The funeral was over, finally, and I was glad that I did not have to see the distant relative woman any more.

Later, I had a chance to talk to my aunt, who had come to the noodle house to take me back home several years ago. She said her relationship with her in-laws was awful and unimaginable. Her husband was the only son in the family and his parents did not like my aunt from the beginning no matter what she said or did. They literally hated her and mistreated her. Right after their honeymoon, they visited her in-laws to greet them. Her father-in-law threw dirty rags to my aunt's face and told her to wipe the floors. He did not hesitate to say awful things to her. When my aunt became pregnant her father-in-law asked her, "How many abortions did you have before you married my only son?"

My aunt's husband was a couple years younger than her, so her in-laws accused her that she married him to take advantage of their son. If the in-laws did not like what she said then they said, "Did your uneducated parents teach you to say that?"

My aunt could endure whatever they blamed on her but when they insulted her innocent parents she felt her blood was boiling over and wanted to kill them. My aunt was not happy because of her in-laws and argued with her husband quite often. When I visited my aunt once I heard them fighting. Their two young children stayed in the next room quietly and heard everything. It was really sad to see the kids in that kind of terrible environment. My aunt and uncle did not divorce though but they moved to a different city far away from the in-laws. Although my case was not even comparable to my aunt's situation, I could understand her better how hard it would be when relatives mistreated her.

Dion and I did not have much in common except that we both were interested in learning English when we were students. We did not argue but we had hardly any memorable experiences together except one time that we visited my friend Mao in Taiwan, who had been my best friend at the E.L.I. in Alabama. Dion liked singing and playing guitar. He was also good at break dancing. He was not a Christian when we got married but I asked him to go to church with me. We went to the contemporary worship service at the Sa-Rang Church in Gang Nam, Seoul. When he saw the worship team singing gospel songs on the stage he wanted to join the worship team but he had to take an audition first. So I asked Sherry, one of the girls who worked with me at the printing company, to help Dion for his audition. She was a pianist at her church and played guitar as well. He had several song choices. I was glad that Sherry was willing to help him. The three of us went to Sherry's church and they both practiced together while I was waiting for him. He passed the audition and became a worship team singer. Later he was baptized and accepted Jesus as his Savior.

Dion and I lived like college roommates. We got up, went to work, came home, had dinner, watched TV or played computer games late at night then went to sleep. He used one room and I used the other room. We did that throughout the week and visited his parents on the weekends or took care of chores at home. I told him about moving to the San Francisco office that Dr. Song offered when I got the job at the printing company. We agreed that he would continue his education to get a master's degree while I supported him, financially. So we agreed not to have a baby until he may finish his degree in the U.S.A.

When my American client, Craig, came to the print factory for his press check I told him about my plan of moving to the U.S.A. with Dion. Craig said it was a great idea and he was willing to help. Instead of going to San Francisco, I accepted Craig's suggestion of moving to Minnesota with his recommendation. When I told Dion about my plan moving to Minnesota, he liked the idea and promised that he would go with me.

When Craig was returning to the U.S. after his press check, he took two sets of my resume. Soon he told me that two printing companies in Minneapolis would like to meet me for job interviews. So I flew to Minnesota for a week. When I arrived at the Minneapolis St. Paul International Airport, I somehow felt very comfortable and excited that I might get a job there and live there someday. Craig picked me up at the airport and showed me around the Minneapolis and St. Paul downtown areas first. I visited Craig's house and met his wife, Susan. With Craig's suggestion, I checked in at a motel called Econo Lodge which was nearby his house.

The next morning I went to an Embers restaurant to have breakfast, across from the Econo Lodge. My server, Ben, came to me to take my order and he asked me if I was a Korean. I said, "Yes." He said he traveled to Korea for two months and loved Korean food. He said he even made his own Kimchi. Kimchi was pickled cabbage with hot red peppers mixed with fish sauce and lots of vegetable ingredients. I did not know how to make it yet. I was very impressed. He asked me what brought me to Minnesota so I told him about the job interviews. He wished me good luck and gave me his phone number to contact if I could get a job and would be moving to Minnesota in the future.

Craig knew the owners of the two printing companies where he sent my resumes. Both companies said the same thing—that they were going to let me know when they had an open position. A few months had passed after my job interviews and Craig called me again and said, "Bethel wants to hire you and you can come over to the U.S. now."

I was very excited and told Dion about it, but he said, "I think you and I have two very different goals in our lives and I don't think I would be able to support you. Why don't you go get the job in the U.S. as you have planned? I just want to stay in Korea."

We talked it over and I tried to convince him to move to the U.S. with me but in the end we agreed that there was no future together for us and let's just bless each other. We didn't need to see any marriage counselor or a divorce lawyer. We walked to the court and signed on the divorce papers. I remembered what my friend Suji's mother told me before I got married. She advised me that I should marry someone only when the relationship was truly based on love. She asked me if I loved him. I said, "I think so." My problem was that I was not ready to marry anyone. I thought I should be married after a few years removed of graduating college, like most people. So I thought I had to. I did not give enough time to think about marriage seriously. Marriage for me was just one of the things to do. I was not wise and did not know any better.

After Dion and I got divorced he told me that he was interested in Sherry, who helped him for his church audition. It was a little bit too soon to have a girlfriend but I thought they might be a good fit for each other since they both loved music very much. I sincerely wished them the very best for each other. They married later and had two children soon after.

Itaewon

Hanna was the assistant to Mr. Guenter—the plant manager at the printing company. Hanna and I became very close friends. We wanted to go out and party often but did not want to hang out nearby the company or where we lived so we went to Itaewon in Seoul. Itaewon was a popular shopping district especially for foreigners. There were many custom tailor shops like the one I used to work at in Pyong-Taek. Gift shops, bars, and restaurants were everywhere. When Hanna and I were getting out of work, we shouted, "Let's get out of this freaking place and get crazy! Hahaha!"

We went to a bar called Seoul Pub. There were dart boards and pool tables. A lot of G.I.s came to the pub too. Hanna and

I enjoyed the non-traditional English speaking environment and no one recognized us. We became regulars there. Once in a while some guys bought us beers or shots to party with us. Maybe they thought we were prostitutes and wanted to take advantage of us. We had drinks and played darts together at the pub. We both were not that good at drinking alcohol but we didn't pass up the free drinks. I vomited sometimes and had a splitting headache from the binge drinking, but that did not stop me from going there again. As we went to the pub on a regular basis we started recognizing people and we met two other regulars. One was from Special Forces, his name was Nick and the other one was a Military Logistician, Greg. Nick was a big guy and not my type. He and Hanna were paired up and I was with Greg.

Greg was divorced and had two children in the U.S. He told me that he was a Christian and he wanted to be a preacher once but he slept with a girl whom he met at their church. The girl told her friends and the rumor was spread around the church. People knew that he wanted to be a preacher but he slept with a woman before they were married. So because of his guilty conscience he gave up on becoming a preacher and married her to be responsible. He was stationed in Korea but she did not like living in a foreign country at all. He said, "She thought all the girls nearby the camp base were prostitutes. She also had a jealousy problem."

They divorced and she moved back to the U.S. with their children. I told him that I was divorced too after two years of marriage and I was going to move to the U.S. for a new job.

As soon as I submitted my resignation Dr. Song called from the San Francisco office and offered me $30,000 a year to come to the branch office in the U.S.A. I was very excited until the plant manager, Mr. Guenter, told me that $30,000 would be not enough for me to pay the rent and live well in San Francisco. However, the printing company that I had an interview with in Minnesota offered me $32,000 a year. Only $2,000 difference but it would be manageable with the cost of living in Minnesota but definitely not in the San Francisco area. So I took Mr. Guenter's kind advice and decided to move to Minnesota in July 1997.

Mr. Guenter was a German but he held Thai citizenship

as well. He used to live in Thailand for many years before he moved to Korea so he still owned a house there and had many local friends. We got along really well. He understood that I was not fairly treated at the company. He was a great listener and whenever I had any difficult projects to handle he stepped in and helped me to ensure the best outcome. I respected him and was glad that I had him on my side.

Before I resigned from the company, Mr. Guenter gave me a special gift. He arranged a trip to Thailand for five days for me. All I had to do was buying my airplane tickets. He called his best friend in Koh Samui, Thailand and allowed me to stay at one of the deluxe bungalows there for free. He gave me detailed information on how to get to the Koh Samui Island and explained about the money value there and how much tip I should give to taxi drivers or servers at the resort. He also wrote a wonderful letter of recommendation in case I needed to get a new job in the future and wished me the best luck.

Pity Party

Koh Samui Island was absolutely beautiful. I loved the comfortably warm ocean water and tropical trees and plants. The deluxe bungalow was gorgeous with cool air and a queen size canopy bed. It was spacious and everything was neat and clean. It seemed to be a very expensive place to stay if I had to pay out of my own pocket. I really appreciated Mr. Guenter.

After checking in and unpacking my luggage I went out to walk around the town. Lots of Europeans were there especially French nationals. Although Thailand was one of the popular countries for Korean honeymoon couples I did not see many Asians there except the local Thai people. Koh Samui was not a well-known place to Koreans. I liked that. At least I did not have to worry about meeting someone I knew.

The sunshine was really hot and I had to put a long sleeve shirt on to block the achingly strong sunshine. However, I saw a lot of women on the beach who were topless. It was impossible to see that kind of topless beach in Korea. Thailand was certainly different from what I was used to. I walked into a small local restaurant and ordered a bowl of rice with grilled vegetables. The server asked me how spicy I wanted my food. I said five peppers out of five shown on the menu. He said it would be really spicy.

"It is okay. Koreans eat Kimchi all the time which is made of spicy pepper."

He asked again, "Are you sure?"

"Yes."

But the Thai food was beyond my expectation. I never had any food that spicy in my life. My tongue was getting numb and I could not eat it any more. I just finished a bottle of beer and left.

Although it was so hot to walk under the strong sunshine, all of sudden it became dark and warm rain poured down for a short period of time then it stopped. I went to a couple of different bars and drank beer. Everyone seemed to be enjoying themselves in groups but I was probably one of the few people wandering alone.

When I went to one of the bars they were getting ready to open and not many people were there. I wanted to go somewhere else. When I was getting out of the bar, there was a guy who came up to me to talk. He was a French guy and came to the Island alone like me. He had been there for several days already. He asked me where I was headed. I said the place was too quiet and I just wanted to go somewhere else. He asked me if he could join me. I said, "Sure." So we walked together. When it was getting dark, the street was getting brighter and louder. People from the beach moved to the town to eat and drink. It seemed to be that there were more Europeans than the local Thai people.

There was an open bar where a stage was set up under a tent roof. The stage looked small and narrow, but some pretty girls were standing next to the stage to go up and dance for the night show. Around the stage people were drinking and waiting for the show. I was glad that I got there earlier to sit close to the stage. The bar was crowed and packed. It was still warm and humid but the pretty girls had their thick makeup and did not seem to be sweating much somehow. When the show started the girls came out one by one on the stage and danced. They played popular 70's and 80's dance music and one of the songs was Abba's *Dancing*

Queen. The speaker was really loud and the sound was terrible. Girls who were not on the stage were serving the customers. I saw one girl who was sitting on the long counter table where people put their drinks. She whispered to a guy something and he shook his head. I just sat there drinking and watched all kinds of people. I was in a totally different place from where I was from.

It was getting late but I did not want to go to sleep yet. The French guy and I looked like a couple now after spending a few hours of drinking together. It was the last day of his vacation and my first on the Island. We watched the Thai ladies dancing and drank beer without much talking. My limit was usually three bottles of beer but I probably had five. I was feeling sick and wanted to go back to my place. I said good bye to him but he said he wanted to walk with me to my place.

We came to my bungalow and sat on the bed together. Out of the heavy drunkenness we hugged and kissed. I knew I should not act like that but the dizziness dominated my thoughts and covered my guilty feelings. When I lay down on the bed I was unbearably sleepy but he desperately wanted to have sex. I did not remember when I slept with my ex-husband Dion the last time. The French guy was breathing short almost like hyperventilating and his hands were trembling. We could not have sex. His body was not functioning. I asked him what the problem was. He said he had diabetes and was not able to have sex. He just wished it would work this time. He wanted to stay overnight but I told him to leave. As soon as he left I locked the door. I was relieved that I was prevented from making a terrible mistake in my drunkenness.

While I was staying on the Island I spent most of the time at the beach laying down and drinking beer alone. I hardly talked with anyone except the bartenders or servers at the restaurants. I regretted my drunken behavior the first night with the French guy and I was so ashamed of what I did and felt guilty deep inside. I was supposed to enjoy a happy relaxing time on the beautiful Island, but the trip to Thailand turned out as a guilt ridden pity party. When I came back to Korea I looked like an African woman with dark skin that tanned so quickly in only five days.

I got rid of all my wedding photos. I put all my belongings into a ten foot container and sent it to Craig in Minnesota. Before

I left Korea my father asked me a couple of times to ensure that I was not going to regret my decision on the divorce and moving to the U.S. My mother said that getting a job opportunity in the U.S. would not come to anyone easily and she said I should take the great opportunity. I promised them that I was not going to regret my decision but do really well in the U.S.A.

The airplane that I was on board took off from the runway and started climbing. I saw the people walking on the street, cars, and houses through the small window. They were getting smaller and smaller and I could not see them anymore. It made me really sad and I cried. I knew I would not come back home soon. I missed my parents and my two brothers already. I was a little bit nervous about my new life. I knew my life was totally depending on God from now on and I felt so sorry to Him for my behavior in Thailand.

3

33 Hours of Greyhound Bus

I arrived at the San Francisco International Airport. There were a couple of former clients living there whom I used to work with closely. They knew that I quit my job at the printing company and was coming to the U.S. One of them invited me to his house. His name was Jake. One of the funny things at his house was that he and his wife had a two-car garage and their cars were exactly identical in and outside; same model and same dark green color. The only difference was the license plate numbers. Jake asked his wife while she was getting ready to go out for dinner which car they should drive.

"Oh, Come on, Jake. They're the same."

"But yours or mine?"

I just laughed and looked at the cute couple. Jake also gave me a ride to the Golden Gate Bridge. He let me get out of the car at one end and waited for me at the other end. It was like a dream. I only saw the red Golden Gate Bridge through the books and the calendars that I handled at the factory but I was able to walk on the bridge and touch it. I thought of the people at the print factory whom I worked with and how many of them would get such kind of an opportunity that a client would invite them to their house and give a tour of San Francisco. Probably none. I was an exceptional case. I felt very fortunate. Now I moved to the U.S. with a job lined up solely by the recommendation of my client. I was not treated fairly by the people at the printing company in Korea but my clients recognized my hard working effort and showed me their favor.

After staying one night at Jake's house I met Stephanie. She used to work as Mr. Guenter's assistant before Hanna. Stephanie quit her job and moved to the U.S. to go to school. I spent a few days with Stephanie. She seemed to settle down and was enjoying her life in the U.S. I used to envy her while we were working at the printing company together. She clocked out on time every day while I was still running around at the factory from upstairs to downstairs to meet schedules and pulling samples. I worked late almost every night. I thought I was doing all the tiresome laboring work while she was doing easy secretarial work. Now she seemed to be living a comfortable life in the U.S. I wondered what the significant difference was between us. Stephanie sounded like she was from a happy wealthy family. I couldn't understand why God blessed her with an easy life while He let me struggle with everything since I was a little child.

I flew to the Minneapolis St. Paul International Airport in July 1997. Craig picked me up at the airport and drove me to Bethel Printing to meet Jeff who informed us that he had an open position for me. When I met him he asked if I had a work visa. I said "No." I entered the country with a tourist visa. Jeff said that I needed to get a work visa in order to work at his company and he would wait for me until I bring my work visa. I thanked him and said that I was going to come back as soon as I get a work visa. So Craig took me to the immigration office in Bloomington, MN.

We went to one of the officers and explained that I wanted to get a job in the U.S. and apply for a work visa. The officer gave me a lengthy application to fill out. I asked how long it would take in order to get the visa.

"Three months to six months." was his reply.

I almost wanted to sit down right there. I did not calculate the unexpected waiting period in my American Dream. Now where should I go and stay for several months in the U.S.? And how long would the company wait for me to come to work for them? They might not be interested in hiring me by the time I get the work visa. It would be too late! They needed someone NOW to work. That was why they told me to come to work for them. Why would a company wait several months for someone like me? I was nobody to them.

First of all, I had to decide where to stay while waiting for the work visa. Craig had a guest room but I could not stay there for several months without a job. I thought about Ben who was my server at the Embers restaurant when I came for the job interviews. Although he gave me his phone number and we met a couple times to get a drink I could not ask him to let me stay at his house for an indefinite length of time. We did not know each other well. I thought about asking Stephanie in California. Not a good idea. She lived in a tiny studio apartment. I also considered calling my uncle in California but I did not come to the U.S. to be a burden to him and his family.

I called Greg, the military logistician, whom I met at the Seoul Pub in Itaewon. We dated for a few months in Korea. When he was returning to the U.S. he told me to visit him someday but I never thought of asking him to help me. I explained to him about my situation that I needed a place to stay for several months and asked him if it would be okay to let me stay at his place. He said it would be fine but I had to move out when his children come to live with him. He was not sure when he was going to bring his children home but I promised that I was going to move out for sure when it happens. So I decided to go to Greg's house in Georgia while I was waiting for the work visa.

I didn't have enough money. I thought I was going to start working right away and make money so I did not have enough money with me. I couldn't afford airplane tickets. Craig suggested that taking a greyhound bus would not be a bad idea. I could enjoy the scenery in different states. So he took me to the greyhound bus station in downtown Minneapolis. I purchased a total of ten tickets from Minneapolis to Columbus, Georgia by transferring ten different buses. From Minneapolis to Chicago, it would usually take about six hours but because of the numerous bus stops and railroad crossings, it took about ten hours. In the bus, I thought about the promise that I gave to my parents that I would do well and wouldn't regret my decision of going to America. They would probably think that everything was going well with me and I would start working soon, but in reality I was riding in a greyhound bus with some Amish people sitting next to me.

The first few hours were fine. Although I had lots of different thoughts and worries I tried to think positively and comfort myself that it was just a matter of time. Once I get the work visa everything would be fine and I would get right back on track. When the buses stopped for bathroom breaks I went out to stretch and got back on the bus. My lower back was feeling uncomfortable while sitting in the buses over thirty hours even though I had bathroom breaks from time to time. I tried to sit in different positions but it did not help. I wanted to shower and lay down on a flat bed. I thought about the bus trip after we missed our flight in China when I was in college. Back then, I thought it would be the longest bus trip ever in my entire life but I was just sitting in different buses in a different country for over thirty hours. Without knowing anyone in the bus and without knowing what was going to happen in my life, I could not really enjoy the scenery outside. I just felt that I was facing something big and I was not sure how to handle it. So I prayed to God. *My Lord, please forgive me for what I have done and help me.*

Finally I arrived at the bus station in Columbus, Georgia after 33 hours of Greyhound bus riding. Greg was there to pick me up. I was so happy to see him again and also a little bit embarrassed that I had to see him like this. I did not look like the girl whom he used to hang out with at the pub. Back then I was a cheerful party girl with a beer mug in my hand and was full of confidence. I had a job waiting for me in America and I believed that I would live a fantastic American-Dream-Come-True life, but now I looked so tired with no makeup after the long bus ride and was jobless and homeless. My grandeur American Dream had slammed into a brick wall and I did not know where to go but to him. He was kind and understanding of my unexpected situation.

Greg was eight years older than me. I liked the fact that he was older. It seemed most people around me were younger than me throughout my life. I was bullied by the girls at school and mistreated by the mean girl when I was working for the trading company as a coordinator. They were all younger than me. Even Stephanie was two years younger and Hanna was a year younger. My best college friend, Jinju, was three years younger than me. I had zero friends of my own age. After being with younger people for so many years, when I met people who were my age, I felt that they were older and more mature so I should show my respect. Over the years a thought constantly came and bothered me. "I am older. That means I should do more than other people. I am far behind from my own age group. I have got to do two or three things at the same time in order to catch up to others of my age. Otherwise I would waste my life." So I tried to keep myself busy all the time and stressed over the need to achieve something and prove to myself that I was not a loser. But when I was with Greg I didn't have to constantly remind myself that I was old and did not have the insecure feeling of needing to prove myself.

Once in a while Greg and I drove his pickup truck around the town to see some nice houses for fun. Columbus, Georgia was a rapidly growing city so there were many new buildings and houses to look at. One day he pointed that there was a Korean church nearby his apartment. I was not sure if I could go to church after what I had done. I was divorced, pretty much drunk every night at the pub in Itaewon, almost made a regretful mistake with the French guy in Thailand, and was now living with a man without being married. My mind and body were no longer pure. Though I had no other place to go and that is why I came to Greg I knew that living with him as boyfriend and girlfriend was an obvious sin against God. I felt so dirty about myself and not worthy to go back to God. However, I was also so desperate to pray for my work visa and wanted to move on. So I went to the church on Sundays to pray for my work visa and asked God to forgive me and understand my situation. Greg did not go to any church but watched television sermons at home while drinking his coffee. I knew why. He felt the same way I felt; dirty and shameful before God. A man who once wanted to be a preacher became a lost soul. He was afraid of going back to God. He lived a lonely life for many years.

After Greg left for his work, I usually cleaned the apartment. I vacuumed, did laundry, and washed dishes. I could not pay the rent or buy any groceries, so I did the house work. When I was done with cleaning, I watched television, took a walk, or read books. On TV, I used to watch some day time shows where people on the stage were yelling at each other, throwing chairs, and fighting. Audiences cheered for them to fight while security personnel were trying to separate them on the stage. I knew these kinds of shows were not good to watch but I felt better to know that my life was better than theirs at least. I also imagined marrying Greg and giving up my job in Minnesota. Why bother with the work visa and go through all the troubles of the waiting period? Besides, it was not guaranteed that I would get the visa. The immigration department might reject my case and send me back home. Why don't I just live with Greg and live a simple, happy life? He is a nice guy and I get along with him well. I wished Greg would ask me to stay there and marry him.

After I sent all my belongings to Craig in Minnesota, I brought only a few pairs of clothes for traveling. I needed some comfortable clothes to wear but I did not have much money. I had a little over a thousand dollars in cash but that was for the airplane tickets to go back to Minnesota or back to Korea in case my visa application was rejected. At the Wal-Mart nearby I bought two pairs of sweat shirts and pants, one pair of navy blue and one black. I bought lotion and a few cheap cosmetics. No matter how I tried to make myself look good in the mirror, I was always wearing either the navy blue sweat shirt and pants or the black. My hair was getting long. I felt I looked so ugly and didn't like the way I looked at all. I was desperate to move on and do something but I couldn't do anything in the country without a work visa. I was stuck in one spot.

Greg came home after work and told me that he had something to tell me. He said a social worker would visit his apartment soon to make sure that he had a decent, safe place to bring his children to live with him so he asked me to find another place to stay. I said I understood. I decided to call Rich, the G.I. whom I met when working at the tailor, to see if he could help me. I heard that he had a temporary job in a small town called Hot Springs, Arkansas. He was working as an aviation mechanic. I remembered him talking about his goals for his career. He said that graduating from an aviation school as a pilot would not give him broad opportunities to become an airline pilot right away. He would probably have to go through some small regional airline companies first then it would take many more years to become a major airline pilot at last. So he joined the U.S. Army and became an aviation mechanic to help pad his resume in addition to his college degree. He also wanted to get a scholarship from the U.S.

Government for his school. Rich was a goal oriented guy. Driven and focused.

I called him and explained my situation. He wanted to talk with Greg, so I put him on the phone. They both agreed to meet at a greyhound bus station in Birmingham, Alabama. So, Greg had to drive to Birmingham and Rich drove over 400 miles all the way from Hot Springs. I felt so sorry for both of them to drive that long distance because of me. On the way to Birmingham, Greg and I both took turns driving.

While I was driving, I kept thinking of what had happened to me in the past and had no idea what was going to happen in the future. The more I was thinking about my life the more I became depressed. I was miserable. My desperate prayers seemed to be going nowhere. I felt like quitting everything and just go back to Korea and start all over again.

I remembered the day when Rich visited me one time. I was working for the international trading company in Seoul and was living at the accommodation house at that time. I asked my landlady if it would be okay that Rich would rent a room for a week. When he arrived at the house I introduced him to the landlady.

After Rich checked in his room she pulled me aside and quietly asked me, "Nami. Is he a black?"

"No, he is not. He is a Hispanic."

She seemed to be reluctant to rent him a room but I told her that he was a nice guy and would stay at the house only for a week. He could have gone to a hotel but since the accommodation house provided two meals a day, I suggested him to stay at the house for his convenience but when I realized that the landlady was not welcoming him because of his race, I regretted that I suggested him to stay at the house. During his stay in Seoul, he visited the places he used to go when he was in the army and shopped alone. I was very sorry to him that I didn't spend hardly any time with him. Honestly I was afraid of going out with him in public because of the painful memory that I was treated as a prostitute while we were shopping at the Nam-Dae-Moon market. And yet he called me as his friend and drove over seven hours to meet me and help me. We had no intimate relationship. I just needed a place to stay. I thought it was a miracle that I still knew him as a friend without being disconnected for such a long period of time.

We finally arrived at the greyhound bus terminal. Greg and Rich both greeted and shook hands. We didn't sit down to talk. I just grabbed my luggage and the two of them stood and chatted a little bit about their driving. Then they thanked each other for taking care of me. I met Rich at the tailor shop when I had the part time job in college and I met Greg at the Seoul Pub in Itaewon, Seoul while partying with my friend Hanna. Who could imagine that the two guys would be my helpers when I became homeless in the U.S.?

From Motel to Motel

Rich was living in a cheap motel. There were a couple of pots and plastic plates in a small kitchen area. The bed was just a mattress that could be pushed into a slot on the wall in the day time and was pulled out at night to sleep on. Although we used the same room together we did not sleep on the same bed. He told me to sleep on the bed and he slept on the couch. He woke up and went to work early in the morning. While he was gone, I just watched television most of the time.

I read the Bible and books sometimes but I didn't feel like praying to God any more. When Rich came home he usually made spaghetti and pancakes. After staying at the dirty, small motel for about a week Rich said he did not want to stay there anymore so we packed our belongings and moved to a different motel. When we were getting out of the parking lot from the dirty motel, he spit out of the car window and said,

"We are not leaving this place. We are escaping!"

We moved in a motel that had two single beds this time and it was much better than the old one.

On a weekend, Rich suggested traveling to Little Rock, Arkansas to cheer me up. He was always kind and tried to make me laugh but I couldn't hide my depression. I felt that I was a total failure. Sad childhood, bullies at school and work, unhappy marriage and divorce, insecurity. This was the summary of my life.

My American Dream didn't exist anymore. I became a homeless and a jobless loser. No matter how hard and desperately I prayed with tears, I did not hear anything from God. He was silent and I could not figure out what He wanted from me. I told Him that I was nobody and there was nothing good that He could get out of me so please leave me alone and allow me to live a simple plain life but He didn't say a word to me.

Two weeks had passed with Rich. He concluded that it was impossible to please me. He said, "Look how much you have already accomplished! When I met you the first time, you hardly spoke English like you do now. Don't you remember that you and I went to Nam-Dae-Moon market and the guy mistreated you? You could not explain to me what was going on in English. You just cried there, but look at you now. You speak English so well, you moved to a different country and have a job waiting for you in Minnesota. You have done more than what average American people would do. So, why do you have to be negative all the time? I don't understand!"

I knew he was trying to encourage me but I just could not be positive at all with all the negative thoughts filling my mind. I just cried and felt hopeless and helpless.

While he was gone to work, I stayed in the motel room all day long and was depressed. I prayed but it was always the same thing. I asked God to give me the work visa as soon as possible. Then I thanked Him for the place to stay and the food to eat. That's all. I had no room to pray for others. I called Greg one day and begged him to let me stay at his house again since his children didn't come to him yet. The Three of us met again at the same greyhound bus station in Birmingham.

Rich said, "Now I see you smiling finally! Damn!"

I thanked Rich and said good bye.

I told Greg what I did in Arkansas and showed him a copy of Rich's resume. Greg was very impressed by Rich's career and his educational background. He said Rich was more than he thought from the first impression. The resume was full of technical terms related to aviation mechanics, licenses, computer hardware and software and his military career.

There was an elderly woman on the second floor across from Greg's apartment. I saw her reading books all the time at her porch. She always had a pile of books next to her on the coffee table. When she saw me, she asked where I had been and invited me to her apartment. I asked her what kind of books she was reading. She showed me hundreds of books in two plastic laundry baskets. Most of them were romance novels. She said romance novels were easy to read and fun so she liked reading them a lot. I wondered if she was a Christian. I looked around but could not see a Bible. However, I found a pistol sitting on the coffee table next to her books. She told me not to be surprised by the gun and added that she got it when she was living in New York City for self-defense. I was not that surprised by the gun but more surprised by the uncertainty of her lonely life. She had hardly any visitors except her only son who visited her once in a while. I couldn't imagine myself reading romance books or having a gun next to me to protect myself in my old age. I always wished that I would die while reading my old Bible or in the midst of my prayer to God. That would be a true blessing. I even imagined myself lying in a coffin peacefully holding my Bible and I wanted to be cremated with the Bible in my folded hands. It was sad to see such a sweet old woman living a lonely life without knowing God and without even talking to anyone all day long but hold on to those romance books to kill time with a gun to protect herself.

Fasting to sort things out

Greg had to go to Dallas for his work. I gave him a ride to the Atlanta airport. When we left home it was late afternoon. Day light was getting shorter and it was getting dark already when I dropped him off at the airport. While driving back home I thought about the work visa again which had become a habit since I submitted the application to the immigration office. I wondered why God put me in such a situation that I was stuck in one place and had no idea what's going to happen in the future. It was like a bad dream that I couldn't move my feet to run. Was it a part of His plan for me?

I remembered other Korean people's immigration stories. A lot of them used to live pretty comfortable lives in Korea. Some of them had master's degrees or PhDs but they couldn't get a green card after their visitor's visa or student's visa expired and became illegal immigrants. They could not stay in the U.S. any longer but did not want to go back to Korea with empty hands after spending all the money they brought from home. Some individuals who had PhDs worked at a chicken farm or at construction sites. A woman told me that her friend's family who were Christian had lived in the U.S. illegally for many years. People said it was for their children's education but I was not sure if their illegal status would give their children any confidence or pride of who they were. Maybe God had different plans for them but they kept praying for their green cards and chose to stay illegally even after their cases were rejected. I was never interested in becoming an illegal immigrant whatsoever. I did not want to live my life hiding from the law.

While thinking of all kinds of different things I missed my exit and did not know where I was. There was no car ahead of me or behind me. I did not know why but I wanted to turn off the headlights momentarily to see if there was any light. It was pitch black. I was in the middle of nowhere. I imagined a crazy truck driver was coming after me like some horror movie. I turned the lights back on and turned around. I drove as fast as I could with high beam lights on and finally reached the highway again. Whew…! I survived! When I came home, it was almost midnight. I took a shower and lay down on the bed. It felt really comfortable. I thanked God that I had a place to stay. The 33 hours of greyhound bus trip from Minneapolis to Columbus made me appreciate any place where I could stretch my two legs and lay down on my back.

I remembered my 24 hours of fasting for my first U.S. visa to go to the E.L.I. at the University of Alabama several years ago. It was a miracle to get the visa in three days without a visa interview. I felt an urge to do another 24 hours of fasting while Greg was away from home. It was a great opportunity to do so while he was gone. I did not have to worry about anyone but could concentrate on my prayer.

I knew 24 hours of fasting would not be easy but I felt a strong desire to do it. I was eager to talk to God intimately again.

There was no one in the whole world but Him that I could go ask for help. I got up early in the morning and prepared for the fasting. I showered up first then brought my Bible, a hymn book and my favorite devotional book, *the Imitation of Christ* in English this time, and a towel to wipe tears.

I started with singing gospel songs then repented all my sins. Although God knew everything that I said and did, I confessed all my sins one by one through my mouth and asked for His forgiveness. I told God that I was truly sorry for what I did. I felt the heavy burden in my heart was lifted and getting lighter. While I was praying, I could understand why He had been silent so far. He wanted me to repent before I asked Him to do anything for me. It had to be a true repentance, not like simply saying "I am sorry God."

After sincerely repenting, I said, "My Lord, thank you, thank you, thank you….thank you so much for forgiving me. You are so good and faithful. Thank you so much for patiently waiting for me to come back to You."

I cried and cried.

"And when you and your children return to the Lord your God and obey him with all your heart and with all your soul according to everything I command you today, then the Lord your God will restore your fortunes and have compassion on you and gather you again from all the nations where He scattered you.

"Even if you have been banished to the most distant land under the heavens, from there the Lord your God will gather you and bring you back."

— Deuteronomy 30:2-4

I took out the Bible and read my favorite scriptures where I underlined before. Then I prayed again. This time I literally begged God for the visa with uncontrollable tears and a runny nose then I realized how much I feared my uncertain future. I feared of moving out of Greg's apartment. I didn't know where to go. I couldn't go back to Rich again. He probably left Arkansas already since the job he had was temporary. I had no idea whether I could get the visa or go back to Korea. Everything was out of my control.

Skipping one meal was easy enough but after missing two meals and crying so much, I became so tired and sad. If someone could tell me that I would get the visa on a certain day it would have been easier to deal with and I would not have to worry about it for several months. But the result was unknown whether I could stay or would have to leave the country.

I kept questioning God, "My Lord, why did You put me in this situation? What do You want from me? I am nobody. Look at me. How can I do anything that could help others while I cannot do anything for myself? I am stuck here."

To forget the hunger and the fatigue I took a nap for a couple of hours holding the Bible. I got up and washed my face. Then I sang more hymns and prayed again. I thanked God for listening to my prayers, even my endless whining and begging. I thanked Him for providing me with the place to stay so that I could repent. It was quiet... I closed my eyes. Warm tears ran on my cheeks again.

In the silent moment, I realized how arrogant I had been. My American Dream to be successful with a nice car and a nice house was not what He had in His mind for me. He wanted me to totally surrender and be obedient to Him then acknowledge that He was in charge of my life, not me. I wept and wailed. I humbled myself and promised Him.

"My Lord. I was wrong… I am really sorry. I will live a humble life. I surrender to you… I surrender… You are my God. You are in charge of my life… Please forgive me."

I closed my eyes and took a deep breath. When I had calmed down finally, I heard His voice gently saying, "Be patient…"

I cried and wept again not because I was sad but because I was thrilled. I thanked Him for talking to me finally!!!

With help from the Holy Spirit I completed the 24 hours of fasting again. I did not drink water or eat any food. My drink and food were the words of God and the comfort of the Holy Spirit.

Whether I was whining or praying I believed the Holy Spirit was with me and God listened to my every single word that I spoke to Him in the name of Jesus. I promised God that I would not live a materialistic arrogant life but humble myself.

Army Wives

Some Korean women, whom I met at the Korean church, invited me for dinner at a Chinese restaurant. There were some more Korean women whom I never met before. They attended an American church. I was surprised that there were a lot of Korean people in the town. They were all army wives. Since they moved to the U.S. with their husbands, they started going to Korean churches to meet with other Korean people and they seemed to be very devoted Christians to me.

Among them there was Jenna. She was the oldest among the women. Everyone called her *Jenna Unni*, respectfully. A lady from the Korean church introduced me to her and I greeted her politely. The lady told Jenna Unni that I was waiting for my work visa and would move to Minnesota when I get the visa later. She asked me if I had family or relatives in Columbus. I told her that I was living at my boyfriend's house. She said her house was very close to where I lived and invited me to her house.

I walked to Jenna's house. She was a devoted Christian. She said she bought a new Bible each time she finished reading an entire Bible. She was once married to a Korean man and had a son but she was forced to get divorced by her mother-in-law so she had to leave her husband and couldn't see her son ever since then. Later she met her current husband and moved to Georgia. Her husband retired from the U.S. Army and lived on the military retirement pension. They had two sons. I met their second son but saw the first son, Ron, in the pictures hanging on the wall. Jenna said he was in jail. She said Ron was very smart and talented but hung out with some bad kids and caused trouble. She didn't seem to be worried but faithfully said that God would use Ron as His good servant someday for sure and until then the Lord was molding him. She believed that God put him in jail on purpose to be away from the bad friends and let him think about how he was going to live his life.

I visited Jenna every day as if I was going to work. She took me to her church one Sunday. After the worship service she walked to the senior pastor and asked him for a letter of recommendation for Ron's college application and the senior pastor asked her in a friendly manner if he got out of jail. I was slightly embarrassed but she seemed to be not caring at all. She laughed out loud and responded that her son would need a recommendation letter as soon as he gets out of the jail. So she wanted to prepare it in advance. When she talked about Ron, she always said it was not just Ron who did something wrong but there was a spiritual battle going on between him and Satan.

Jenna told me that it was not right to live with a man without marriage especially as a Christian. So she suggested to me that I move into her house. Although I was living with Greg because I didn't have any other place to go, I wished people wouldn't ask me where I lived. I couldn't tell my parents where I was living so I lied to them that I was living with my friend Stephanie in California. I told Greg that I was going to move to Jenna's house the next day. He said he understood.

I used to dream of flying once in a while. I pushed the ground hard with my two feet to jump up high in the sky then I started flying with my arms spread out like wings of a bird. Sometimes I was lost where electric power lines were all over in the dark sky. I tried to jump up and fly but because of the web of power lines, I could not fly through. A few times I fell off from a high peak with an unbearable super speed and woke up scared and felt awful. Then I grabbed my Bible and read here and there quickly to get rid of the bad feelings. I thought I had such kind of bad dreams because I neglected reading the Bible so my mind was clouded with ungodly thoughts. However, when I read the Bible and stayed closer to God, I saw things that were impossible to exist in real life. I never imagined such things would exist but I saw them in my dreams. One time I saw gigantic mountains of rocks. The sizes of those rocks were indescribably huge. One huge rock, alone was the size of a mountain and there were many of them. The rock which I stood on had a beautiful pond. I thought it was really weird to see the pond on the top of the rock mountain. It was not shallow but I could see the deep bottom of the clear pond. When I had that kind of unusual dream, I tried to figure out what God was trying to tell me and couldn't wait to go back to sleep and see some more unusual things.

On the last night at Greg's, I had another dream. It was the best dream ever in my entire life. I was flying and found a beautiful garden. I could feel the warmth of spring and a cool breeze in my dream although it was actually January. I saw willow trees along the sparkling stream that was running through the garden. I did not have to push the ground hard to jump up high. I gently pushed the ground then bounced back to the sky and continued flying comfortably. I never felt such kind of peace before. I flew all over the beautiful garden with such a big smile on my face. I did not want to wake up but I felt that I was smiling while I was sleeping. I was awake. Oh, No... I wanted to fly more over the paradise...

I wondered what the dream meant. Is everything going to be all right? That's why God gave me such a beautiful dream? What a beautiful dream it was! I prayed to God to let me dream the same dream one more time.

I moved into Jenna's house. She told me that I could stay at her house but when her son Ron gets out of the jail, I had to move somewhere else. There was a woman whose name was Mai. She was from Vietnam and was Jenna's church friend. Jenna said she was going to give her a call and ask her if she could let me stay at her house later.

Jenna and her husband sold vitamins and she had her own clothing alteration business. Their vitamin business was doing really well. The vitamin company gave them a brand new sports car for their highest sales record. She drove the red sports car all over to deliver the vitamins to her customers. For her alteration business she fixed all kinds of dresses, pants, and blouses. She had sewing machines and a huge collection of several hundreds of colorful sewing threads on one side of the utility house in the back yard. Either her customers brought their clothes to her or she went to her customers' houses to pick up their clothes. She sold vitamins, altered clothes, and did Bible study in the utility house. Jenna was very talented with many things. She made her own dresses and cooked really well, especially traditional Korean foods. Jenna and her husband also had a lot of dogs. They raised

Chihuahuas and sold the puppies.

While I was staying at Jenna's I washed dishes after each meal time and followed her wherever she went whether it was for her business or church. One day she asked me to join her to hand out gospel newspapers. We knocked on each apartment door and handed out the newspapers and told them about Jesus. At one of the apartments a man answered. She asked him if he was a Christian.

He said, "No."

He was an Asian so we asked him if he was Korean.

"No. I am Chinese."

Then his wife walked to the door and asked him, "Who is it?"

The guy said to us, "But my wife is Korean."

Jenna and I both said, "An Nyung Ha Sae Yo?" which means "How are you?" in Korean.

The wife saw us holding the Bible and standing in front of their entrance door. She frowned as if she saw something disgusting and complained loudly.

"Totally unbelievable! Korean Christians are awfully stubborn. They bothered me when I was in Korea and now they followed me to America to talk about the church thing! Absolutely stubborn and unbelievable! Please go away and never come back. We are not interested!"

The guy seemed to be embarrassed by his wife's unexpected mean attitude so he mumbled, "Why do you say that, Honey?"

But she cried out, "Go away! We are not interested in becoming Christian."

Then she shut the door in front of our faces. I could still hear her complaining inside her apartment. Jenna and I stood there perplexed. I was speechless, but Jenna said, "The husband seemed to be a good man but I guess he will go to hell because of his wife."

Instead of being offended by her, we just laughed together then left the apartment building.

"And if any place will not welcome you or listen to you, shake the dust off your feet when you leave, as a testimony against them."

— Mark 6: 11

While I was staying at Jenna's, I missed Greg sometimes and wondered how he was doing but I never met him alone although it was just walking distance from Jenna's house. I only went out of the house when Jenna was going out. I didn't want to have her worry about where I was and what I was doing. One day when Jenna and I were coming back from visiting her client to pick up some clothes for alteration, we saw Greg on the road. We stopped the cars and greeted, briefly. That was all.

Jenna brought me to her Bible study group on Wednesdays and regular church service on Sundays. Jenna and I shared our personal stories and enjoyed talking about how wonderful God had been to us. I thanked God for letting me be with such a devoted Christian woman. After a few weeks Jenna told me that her son was coming home so it was time for me to move to Mai's house.

Mai was from Vietnam and came to the U.S.A. with her G.I. husband. But he cheated on her and left for another woman as soon as they moved to the U.S.A. So she had to raise their son as a single mother. She had all kinds of jobs to survive. She spoke English fairly well and spoke French too. She was old enough to receive Social Security benefits but she could not prove her original birth certificate in the U.S. and her passport showed that she was five years younger than her real age so she still worked at a carpet factory for 40 hours a week. Her son lived in California and called her once in a while to ask for money.

Mai's house had two bedrooms and one bathroom. In addition to the main house, there was an extra room extended from the back of the living room. It was a large green house. There were lots of tropical plants which reminded me of Koh Samui Island in Thailand. I enjoyed the bright natural sunshine in the warm green house. Mai owned a lot of neat collections of antique items. They were all nicely kept and displayed in the cabinets.

There were photos of her and her family hanging on the wall. I especially liked an old photo of her and her sisters wearing beautiful Vietnamese traditional dresses when they were young. Everything was neatly organized.

I said, "Mai, your house is so clean and beautiful!"

She said, "Thank you. I try to keep my house clean to honor God because He is everywhere."

I was impressed by her faithful comment and I thanked God that He guided me to another wonderful Christian woman.

Mai let me use her second bedroom and told me not to go outside if possible because of safety. I wanted to help her with cleaning the house or laundry. When I washed the towels in the bathroom, she said to me, "We wash hands or shower first then use the towels so they are still clean. You don't need to wash them every day." So there was not much for me to do. I only washed a couple of the dishes that I used and prepared dinner before she came home. Rice and Kimchi. That's all. One of the women whom I met at the Korean church heard that I was going to move to Mai's house so she brought me a bag of rice to help me.

"I tell you the truth, anyone who gives you a cup of water in my name because you belong to Christ will certainly not lose his reward.

— Mark 9: 41

When Jenna gave me a ride to Mai's house we stopped by a Korean grocery store and I bought a jar of Kimchi. Although it was not a fancy dinner at all Mai appreciated me for the dinner and we enjoyed our time being together.

I did not go anywhere. I stayed in the house most of the time. I read the Bible, a devotional book and watched the TBN Christian Channel sometimes. Mai's neighbor was quiet and peaceful. I did not understand why she said it was dangerous to go out. I did not walk around the neighborhood but just sat on the front porch to get some fresh air. Some little children rode bicycles, shouted with excitement, or ran after each other in the street. After sitting outside for a while, I came in the house and prayed again. Every time I prayed, God responded nothing but one thing—"Be patient."

I knew I had to be patient but most of the time my prayer ended up with the same question. "For how long?"

I wondered how Greg was doing. One day I took a taxi and went to his apartment. I still had his apartment key. I saw the old woman reading her romance book on the porch. I said, "Hi." She said she was wondering where I had been. I told her that I moved to a friend's house and we chatted a little bit. At Greg's apartment I fixed his bed, did laundry, cleaned the kitchen and vacuumed then I came back to Mai's by a taxi again. Greg called me later and said he thought an angel stopped by and cleaned his place. I felt really good to surprise him like that. If he asked me to marry him and stay in Georgia I could have said "Yes" but it was my own imagination to escape my reality.

Jenna visited Mai's one day and took me to a big Chinese restaurant. It was not like any other Chinese restaurants I had ever been to. The restaurant was huge and decorated with Chinese dragon statues and authentic Chinese red furniture. There was also a garden and a pond with lots of koi fish in it. Jenna took me there to see if I could get a part time job. The owner said I spoke English well and liked me but without a work visa I could not even get a part time job. In the car driving back home, Jenna said, "I wish you would marry Greg, get a job here and stay nearby me." It was very sweet of her saying that. She always treated me kindly as if I were her own daughter. She became my role model. I learned from her how to walk with God. No matter what difficult situations she faced whether it was big or small, she opened her hymn book, sang and praised the Lord. The utility house in her back yard was her own sanctuary. As she always prayed and hummed her hymns, she seemed to be happy all the time. I couldn't believe that she had a son locked in jail on and off.

Packing for an unknown future

Five months had passed since I submitted the application to the immigration department. Craig called me unexpectedly and said, "You might get your work visa sooner or later since it has been several months already. Why don't you come back to Minnesota now and get ready in case you need to start work as soon as you get the visa?" It sounded so positive and promising.

Craig was always a positive person. I had never seen him being negative. One time his calendar was misprinted at the print factory in Korea. Several hundreds of the printed sheets became garbage all of sudden. It was supposed to be a number *26* but there was a large space between the 2 and 6. No one caught it until it was printed. When the press operator brought the press sheet to Craig, he was in the middle of eating an ice cream cone. If it was me who had the unpleasant report, I would stop eating the ice cream right away and pay attention to the matter. But he was still licking the ice cream with a serious expression on his face.

I asked him, "Craig, is your ice cream still delicious?"

"Yes. Why?"

"Well, I thought you would be worried about your calendar. I don't think I could eat ice cream at this moment."

"I AM worried about my calendar but even though I quit eating the ice cream, it would not fix the problem. So, why should I stop eating my ice cream?"

It made sense. However, I couldn't help but laugh.

I hung up the phone with Craig and decided to go back to Minnesota. I had to find another place to stay. Besides Craig, there was only one person I knew to ask for help in the whole state of Minnesota. It was Ben whom I met at the Embers restaurant a year before when I came for the job interviews.

I remembered his parents had a big old house which was only two blocks away from the restaurant. I called Ben and explained that I was coming back to Minnesota finally and I needed a place to stay for a little while until I get my work visa. I asked him if he could ask his parents to let me stay at their house. He said it might be difficult because his younger sister got pregnant with her boyfriend who also fathered several other kids from multiple girlfriends. He said his parents were upset and it would be hard for them to have me in their house.

Ben's parents wrote a letter to their daughter's boyfriend to let him know that they would willingly help to start his family with their daughter and raise the baby, but they never heard a word from him. Ben's parents were very devoted Christians and raised their children with love. That's why it was so hard for them to accept the fact that their own daughter hung out with that kind of irresponsible guy and became pregnant.

Ben's parents did not believe in abortion. They decided to help their daughter raise her baby unconditionally. I still remember what Mr. Lee, Ben's father, said many years later. He said to me with a big happy smile on his face, "We thought the baby would be a problem, but now we realize that the baby is a blessing from God. We love him so much."

Ben also said that he and his brother decided to act as the baby's uncles and fathers. Meanwhile Ben suggested that I could stay at his place and he could move to his girlfriend's house until I find my own place. I really appreciated him.

I packed and was ready to leave Columbus, Georgia. Jenna came to give me a ride to the Atlanta International Airport. I said good bye and thanked Mai.

Mai said, "I am sure you will do well but always remember that God is with you everywhere."

Mai and Jenna were two angels God had sent to help me.

I did not see Greg but gave him a phone call before I left. In the car Jenna told me again, "It would have been really good if you could stay in Columbus, marry Greg and live nearby me. Then we can go to church together."

I just laughed out loud. I was not sure whether God would let me stay in the U.S. or He would send me back to Korea. I was not afraid of the immigration department but feared what God would say to me. I did not have the work visa but felt good inside somehow. I thought about the dream of flying over the garden. I felt something good would happen soon. Honestly, I was glad to leave Columbus, Georgia, finally. No more waiting!

At the airport, Jenna told me, "Do well when you get the job in Minnesota and don't forget about us here. Visit us sometimes when you have vacation. We won't go anywhere. We will always be here."

She gave me a big hug and said, "Find a good church when you get there and pray diligently. I will pray for you too."

I do believe that Jenna was my guardian angel from God.

As the airplane was taking off from the runway warm tears sprang up in my eyes. I swallowed once, "Good bye, Columbus, Georgia. Good bye, Atlanta. Thank you everyone for helping me for the past months. You were all my angels. I will come back someday. I promise! Thank you and good bye!"

The Band House

When the plane was flying closer to the Minneapolis St. Paul International Airport, I was excited to meet Ben again but also a little bit nervous about what would happen to me in this cold state covered with snow everywhere. I just flew from Georgia and I did not have any warm winter outfits.

Ben and his girlfriend, Heather, came to pick me up. Heather was half Korean and half American. They welcomed me and took me to Ben's band house located in North East Minneapolis. Ben did not have a car so they drove Heather's. In my typical Korean's understanding I wondered why Heather, who was pursuing her master's degree and had a car, wanted to be with someone like Ben, who worked at a restaurant as a server and didn't have a car. I knew he was a very nice guy for sure. That's why he was helping me, a homeless girl, whom he didn't know very well. I heard Heather's father was a medical doctor and her mother was a nurse. In Korea typical doctor fathers would not allow their daughter to date a band guy playing guitar at night clubs and working at a restaurant as a server. Ben was tall, handsome and very talented, but his qualification was not nearly good enough to impress typical Korean parents. To date a girl like Heather, guys should have at least the same or higher educational background, own a nice car, and have a professional job that can guarantee their daughter's happy life. But Ben did not have any of that. I thought it must be an American thing.

We arrived at Ben's band house and he introduced me to his roommates; Jason, Johnny and Ray. They were all Ben's band members. Jason played bass guitar, Johnny trumpet, and Ray drums. Ben played guitar.

Ben took me to the upstairs to show me where I would stay and put my luggage. There were two bedrooms upstairs. The first room was Jason's, the second one was Johnny's. There was an attic next to the second bedroom. It was for Ray. The ceiling was slanted and the wood floor made a squeaky noise. Ray put a mattress in the corner and used it as his bedroom. There was no natural light coming in at all and burnt candles were scattered on a small coffee table next to the mattress. The attic looked like a homeless shelter.

Ben's place, where I was going to stay, was not a room. He put a mattress on the floor and hung two pieces of fabric curtains around the space to make it look like a room. There was a small dresser and a television on it. I put my luggage in the corner next to the dresser and came downstairs.

There was a living room, a kitchen, and a bathroom downstairs. They had tons of CDs and records. Ben said there was one more place to show me which was the basement. We walked down carefully on the narrow stairs. There was a drum set and guitars. Burnt candles were scattered here and there. His band played jazz and experimental music that they created at local bars and sometimes they traveled to different cities in their mini-van. Ben said they played at First Avenue one time, which was the biggest night club in the Twin Cities. They received a big compliment from Prince, who had made First Avenue famous in his *Purple Rain* movie. After showing me the house and introducing me to the band guys, Ben packed some of his stuff and moved to Heather's. I was very sorry and also really appreciated him to let me stay in his place.

During the day time, the band guys went to work and I was home alone. After they were gone, I started cleaning the house. I washed the piles of dishes in the kitchen, put the scattered CDs away and mopped the floor. When all the house chores were done, I went upstairs and lay down under the blanket. I warmed up the cold blanket and the mattress with my body temperature. The band guys said that the winter had been warm and not much snow had fallen that year compared to the previous years and I must have brought the warm Southern temperature from Georgia.

I looked outside through the window. Big snowflakes were falling peacefully. I thanked God with tears rolling on my cheeks for the place to stay.

"My Lord, thank you. It is really quiet and peaceful now. I am still waiting for Your answer. I know You told me to be patient numerous times. I am and I will, but I am also worried about what's going to happen to me. Please help me.... You are the only hope that I have..."

Then, I turned around and lay on my stomach. I started reading my Bible and prayed. I cried a lot not because I was sad but because I thanked Him for being with me when I was so lonely and had fears of an unknown future.

Sometimes Ben invited me to go out with the band when they had a concert at night. Once in a while their parents came to the concerts to watch them too. The band wore the same shiny light silver color suits except Ray who was the drummer. I watched them playing music and singing on the stage. Wow! They were fantastic! I knew that they were talented but watching them on the stage was a lot different than I thought. I was really excited and very proud of them. I felt so lucky to be their roommate. I was especially impressed by Ray because I heard that he never took any music lesson or drum lesson. He didn't know how to read music notes at all. He just played by ear. He watched other drummers playing and copied the beat later. The band was awesome! After the performance I helped them pack their instruments, drank their complimentary beer from the bar and watched other bands play. I had seen guys playing classical guitar and singing at bars in Korea a few times but I had never seen that kind of group of guys playing at bars with people cheering loudly. In the mini-van coming home, Jason, who was the band manager divided the money for the night and gave each of them their shares.

When they didn't have a concert they came home after work, drank beer, and watched *The Simpsons* all together. They giggled and laughed like little boys. They didn't look like the guys who performed on the stage seriously.

Ben took me to his parents' house a few times. I met his

parents and was also invited to have homemade pizza together. Ben was the family chef. His mom asked him for advice on cooking. They made the pizza dough and tomato sauce from scratch. They made three different kinds of pizza and they were the most delicious pizzas I had ever had. Ben's mom said their family tradition was eating fresh homegrown tomatoes with pizza. His parents were always kind to me. They asked me if the band house wasn't too loud or uncomfortable for me to stay. I said I was just thankful that I had a place to stay especially in the winter time in Minnesota. We all laughed and had a wonderful time.

Usually when I finished cleaning the band house after the guys were gone for their work, there was no T.V. sound, no music practice, and no party. I enjoyed the quiet time alone. I read the Bible and my devotional books. I started reading a new book—*The Way of a Pilgrim* written by an unknown Russian peasant which was about the importance of constant prayer. In addition to the Bible, *The Imitation of Christ* and *The Way of a Pilgrim* were the two most important books that helped my prayer life to develop my relationship with God at that time. There were a lot of unfamiliar words and new vocabulary in the books so I had to use an English Korean dictionary to translate each new word for better understanding. If it was a fictional novel I would have skipped some words that I was not familiar with but this time I wanted to understand and meditate on the teachings, so I translated as much as possible although it took so long to read just one single paragraph. After the translation, I meditated on the teachings and tried to apply it to my life. I felt like living like a Christian monk devoted to God for the rest of my life; simple, humble and pure.

I couldn't pay the rent at the band house but wanted to contribute as much as I could. So I paid for their phone bill which was about $75. Since I did not have any income I had to spend the least amount of money to survive. I bought a whole box of the cheapest Ramyon noodle at a grocery store nearby and hid it behind the closet not to show others what I ate every day. One day I counted how many Ramyon packages to see how many days I could survive. I had no idea what to do after I ran out of the Ramyon. No matter how hard I prayed or meditated on the words, it was not easy to get rid of the fear of running out of money.

When I was walking to a bus stop from the church in downtown, where I had been with Ben's parents, some homeless people came to me and begged for quarters. I wondered why they had to live like that. If I were one of them who were born in the U.S. and didn't have to worry about a work visa, I imagined that I could do all kinds of different things and enjoy my life. They had what I didn't have and they were wasting it. I asked God why He let me be born in Korea and brought me to the U.S. I wondered what He wanted from me. I wished God would show me a sign or tell me more besides the *Be Patient* message. I prayed for His guidance and asked Him to talk to me every day.

Whenever the mailman dropped the mail I brought them in the house. One morning I went out to get the mail and accidently closed the door behind me. I was wearing summer sandals with no socks. I walked to the back door but it was locked. All the windows were locked too. I could not get in the house. I went to the next house and no one was home. It was only morning. I had to wait until the guys come back after work. It was cold and windy on a February morning in Minnesota. Snow banks were everywhere. I wished there was a police car driving by then I could ask for help but the police officer wouldn't be able to let me go in the house. I had no money and had nothing with me. I remembered that there was a Lutheran church several blocks away. Wearing a sweat shirt and pants and a pair of summer sandals with no socks, I walked fast to the church hoping that the door would be open. Thank God it opened! Some seniors were sitting around large round tables and there was a meeting going on. When I walked in quietly a pastor came to me. I explained my situation then he invited me to join the group. They were having a breakfast meeting and welcomed me. I briefly introduced myself and explained my situation to them. When the meeting was over late in the morning, an old man came to me and gave me a $5 Burger King coupon. He gave me his phone number in case I needed his help. The pastor was kind and let me stay at his warm office until he was finishing up his work then told me that I could stay at the church main sanctuary until I could go back to the band house. I read the Bible at the church and prayed. I didn't like much waiting for the work visa for such a long time but now I had to wait for the band guys to come home too. Waiting and waiting… Was I so bad at waiting all the time?

Is that why God was training me to wait for everything? I hated the feeling that I was stuck in one place and couldn't do anything. However, I thanked God for the church where I could stay inside, warm and safe. When I went back home I thanked God even more that I had the band house to stay. Whether I slept on the mattress on the cold floor or had to clean the house after the guys' mess, I was still thankful that there was a roof over my head to keep me warm and safe otherwise I was homeless with no other place to go.

Pretty much every day I went to either a community library nearby the band house or a church in downtown to study God's words and pray. I was desperate to hear from God. I read and prayed with tears. I faithfully prayed that whatever the outcome would be whether I would get the work visa or not, I decided that I would still praise Him because I surrendered to Him and He was in charge of my life. Then I was comforted and encouraged to be patient one more day.

When I came home one late afternoon, I saw Ben and Heather in the kitchen. They were having a large pizza and asked me if I wanted to have a piece of their pizza. I appreciated that they asked me but somehow it didn't sound like that they were sincere. I thought they just asked me to be nice. I said I was not hungry at all. I already took Ben's sleeping spot to stay and I didn't want to take his pizza. I hurried to the upstairs and buried myself under the cold blanket. I realized how poor I was and felt so insecure and miserable. I sobbed quietly under the blanket and asked God to help me be strong.

The band guys' girlfriends and buddies came over nearly every night. They smoked marijuana and drank in the basement. One of them asked me if I was a smoker. I said, "No." He said, "If you are going to smoke, don't ever start with garbage such as cigarettes but smell this kind of good stuff. Try this." He handed over a brown paper bag to me. It had dried leaves in it and I pushed my nose in and inhaled it once. They all cheered, "Yeah!" I did not feel anything good or bad. When I smelled the dried leaves it reminded me of the mulberry tree leaves at my grandmother's house. Grandma had two large utility rooms where my uncle used to sit and twisted rice straws to make ropes in winter. In summer, the rooms were occupied by thousands of silkworms on stacked shelves. When it was quiet I could hear the sound of silkworms biting the green leaves. It sounded very peaceful. I told the guys cheerfully that I was not that interested in smoking or smelling the weed.

Jason and Ray told me that I should go out sometime and have some fun. I asked them to take me out then since I didn't know where to go. So they took me to a night club called "Gay 90's" in downtown Minneapolis. We walked into a large dark room where a tall singer was singing on the stage. The singer had heavy makeup on and was dressed up as a woman but looked like a man. A bunch of guys holding beer bottles were watching the singer on the stage. I was not sure who were gays or straight. Jason and Ray led me into a different room. It was dark where I lost my total sense of direction. I did not know where we were going. I just followed them. I asked them, "Hey, by the way you are not gays, are you?" I met their girlfriends at the band house. Jason and Ray burst into a loud laugh and looked at each other. Then all of sudden they kissed each other for a second and laughed out loud again. I believe they did not kiss but just pretended to in order to tease me.

After the gay club, they took me to another night club nearby. It was a small bar where young girls danced almost naked. Guys were gathered around the narrow stage and they had a bunch of one dollar bills in their hands and put the money in the dancer's leg band. I asked Jason and Ray why they did not go closer to watch the dancer. They said they did not have money to give the girl. So we watched the dancer from a distance while sipping our beer. I wondered what the dancer's parents would think of their precious daughter dancing in front of those drooling guys. Did she run away from her parents like I did when I was in high school? If I were in her shoes, what would I do? I would do anything but I don't know that I could dance in front of other guys naked or become a prostitute. I had been to an interesting world that night—totally different from my world where I prayed and cried for God's help every day.

Although I appreciated very much for letting me stay at the band house, it was not easy to be there at night. The place turned into party central. Loud music was fine to deal with but when I was about to sleep at night I could hear one of the guys having sex with his girlfriend. They closed their door but it didn't matter. The house was old and one of the "walls" of my space was a fabric curtain. At the sound of them having sex, another guy turned his music volume up high obviously not to hear them and I also turned the TV volume high. The party was still going on in the basement well after one or two A.M. Guys were drinking, smoking, and playing electric guitar or banging the drums. The house was full of loud noise mixed with the moaning sound.

I covered my ears and cried out to God, "Not again, please! Oh, God, Please let me get out of this hell house as soon as possible. I cannot handle this anymore. This place is not for me. I can't stand it. Don't You see what's going on here? This is not a house. This is a hell. I am not asking for a nice fancy house. I just want a small quiet place where I can pray and study alone. I want to live like the monks from the books I read. I will be humble. Please take me out of this house. I can't deal with it anymore. Why don't You talk to me? I need You NOW! Please talk to me." I begged Him with tears.

Every day I went to either the church in downtown or to the library close to the band house. I read the Bible and prayed. I wanted to hear His voice. I could not pray without shedding tears. I knew no one else could help me but God and He was all I had. I asked Him to tell me something to comfort me but He kept telling me the same thing.

"Be Patient."

That's all. Honestly, I was sick of hearing the same thing all the time.

I asked Him back, "For how long?"

"Until the day comes."

Then I said to Him that I was sorry for not being obedient and promised that I would be patient until He gives me an answer.

One time Ben's parents came over to pick me up and we went to a Bible study at the Bethlehem Baptist Church in downtown Minneapolis. They introduced me to the group in the class and told them that I was staying at their boys' band house while waiting for my work visa. I never met them before but they welcomed me and prayed for me as if they had known me for a long time. I was amazed how they could pray for me like that. The prayer was full of love and sincere care. If I were God and heard those prayers, I would definitely want to answer to their prayers right away. That's how I felt.

Days went by and I still didn't hear anything from God. I could not control my tears when I prayed, "God, what do You want from me? Don't You know that I am nobody? What can I do for You? Nothing. I am just who I am and what I am. I am not a patient person at all and You keep telling me to be patient? I just want to get out of the hell house. My old American Dream has been lost. I don't want a fancy house or a fancy car. That's not what I want any more. I only need a small tiny quiet place where I can pray to You and read my Bible. Is that too much? If I forgot to confess any of my sins yet, please forgive me now. I need You. You are my only hope. I surrender to You. I surrender... No one can help me but You. Please..."

He was still silent. I felt that I was talking to a wall but I kept going to the church and prayed to Him. One day I asked God to show me something so that I could know that He was with me at least. I asked Him for a small sign even if it would be a small piece of dried leaf floating on water I would still hang on to it. I prayed and cried, prayed and cried. I started reading the Bible again and He showed me Psalm 40.

"I waited patiently for the LORD; HE TURNED TO ME AND HEARD MY CRY.

He lifted me out of the slimy pit, out of the mud and mire; he set my feet on a rock and gave me a firm place to stand.

He put a new song in my mouth, a hymn of praise to our God. Many will see and fear the Lord and put their trust in Him."

— Psalm 40: 1-3

I rubbed my eyes and read the scripture again. I read the whole Bible from cover to cover before but never remembered this particular scripture.

"My Lord, is this true? Are you really talking to me now and is this THE ANSWER TO MY PRAYER? REALLY? May I believe that this is YOUR ANSWER to my prayer? Really? Oh, Wow..... Wow..... Thank You! Thank You! Thank You!!!"

I marked the Bible not to lose the precious scripture ever. I felt so comfortable and my tensed muscles were relieved.

The "I" in the scripture was me. I waited patiently for the Lord; He turned to me and heard my cry. Who could ever describe my situation better than that in the whole world? I really waited patiently for the Lord with the uncontrollable tears and prayers every day and night then He turned to me and heard my cry, finally! I interpreted the rest of the scripture like this.

He lifted me out of the hell house and He set my feet on a rock and gave me a new place to stay. He put a new praising song in my mouth, a hymn of praise to my God. All the people who bullied me and mistreated me in my past will see and fear the Lord and put their trust in Him.

I could not help but keep smiling while walking through the cold wind. I came home from the church. Ben was home and casually said to me, "Hey Nami. You have a voice mail."

It was a message from Craig.

"Nami, it's me Craig. Your work visa is out. It was delivered to Bethel Printing and has been sitting there almost a week. You can start working now."

How long have I been waiting for this very moment? How many times have I practiced what to say when I get the news? One thing for sure, I did not want to just scream out of excitement. I wanted to thank God first.

I said quietly, "Hallelujah!"

All of sudden I felt the broken clock started ticking normal again, even faster. I had been in a slow motion dream for such a long time but now I had an urge that I needed to do something because I was running out of time. That's how I felt. I called the company and asked for the owner who hired me. He said the approval letter was delivered a week ago and it had been on his desk covered by other mail and he apologized that he could not inform me earlier. He said I could start working the very next day.

Next, I called Craig to get my office clothes that had been kept in his storage space for several months. I took some of the necessary items and came home. The next morning I was nicely dressed up and ready to go to work. I was a little bit nervous and excited to go to work after almost nine months of not working since I left Korea in July 1997. The band guys saw me right before I left the house for work and said, "Wow, Nami! You look very different! Congratulations!"

My waiting was over. I will never forget the miracles and angels God sent to help me through those difficult months. Although the band house seemed unbearable at times, I could never be thankful enough to those who helped me in my desperation.

4

The Land of Opportunity

I went to work and met the owner first. I appreciated him for waiting for me until I got the work visa for several months. He said it was not a problem and introduced me to Pam. She was one of the customer service representatives at the company. She explained to me overall the print production procedures at the factory and what to do. My duties were pretty much the same as what I used to do at the print factory in Korea but there was no need for interpretation for print buyers or ordering 40 feet containers for overseas shipments.

At the beginning I studied the previous job tickets that Pam wrote, pulled samples, and did whatever she told me to do. I expected that she would ask me to write up a job ticket after a month of training at least, but exactly a week after, she asked me to write a job ticket.

"Do you want to try writing up a job ticket now?"

I was nervous but could not say that I couldn't do it. She was always busy. That was why they hired me. I could not believe that they waited for me for six months to start working. I knew it was only because God let it happen for me.

The most confusing part besides communicating in English was switching the measurement systems from millimeters to inches. In the past, if someone said 10 by 10 at the print factory in Korea then I would picture a small piece of paper that was 10 millimeters by 10 millimeters in my mind but in America it meant 10 inches by 10 inches or 10 feet by 10 feet and the sizes were totally different from what I used to have in my mind. I just could not picture the large size. I also counted and calculated numbers in Korean then spoke in English. It was just absolutely confusing to think numbers in English. I practiced the abacus for many years and had a first degree certificate which was like a black belt in Tae Kwon Do. I used to have a perfect score in math when I was a student and I had pride in being good with numbers. But counting numbers in English was as if I was learning how to count for the very first time. I knew I shouldn't have been but somehow I was so frustrated when I didn't get the concept of a different measurement system right away and struggled with numbers in English.

When I went home after the first three days of work I was exhausted and could not think of anything else. Speaking English at home was just a simple thing. It did not require any intelligence to communicate. I just used the same repetitive expressions such as "Hi" and "How are you?" But at work it was different. I was glad that I started from Wednesday so the week went fast.

Friday afternoon Jeff said to me that employees were paid after a week of work, so I would not get paid until the next Friday. He offered to borrow me some money if I needed. It was very kind of him but I politely said, "No Thank you."

He asked me how my first three days of work had been. I said everything was fine except the confusing measurement system. He said, "I understand millimeters and centimeters are good." I thought he was agreeing with me however at the end he added, "But inches are better." I learned later that he never said "No" directly to anyone.

I had to do well at work. If not, it did not mean that I could quit and get a new job at a different company. It meant that I would not only get fired but would probably have to leave the country and go back to Korea. With my work visa I was allowed to work only for Bethel Printing in the U.S.A. There were no other alternatives so I had to do well no matter what. I was a little bit nervous about writing the job tickets but I did my best. Pam said I did a good job. Sometimes I had to interrupt her with simple questions but she seemed to be fine with that and was willing to help.

Before I got my first paycheck my mother told me that I

had to pay my uncle $500 back that he sent me to buy groceries while I was waiting for my visa. He was my mother's first younger brother. My mother insisted that even though he was my uncle, and he said the money was a gift, I must pay him back as soon as I got my paycheck. My paycheck of one week was not enough to pay him all at once so I sent him $250 each time. He said that he could not understand why my mother had to be so stubborn. Regardless, I paid him back the full amount of $500.

When I had my first job in Korea, right after college in 1993, my salary was $500 a month, but in America I made that much money in a week in 1998. I thanked God. I remembered how much help I had received from so many different people. Some of them I never met before. They were the angels whom God sent in my life. As soon as I started making money, I thought it's time for me to help others. So I started donating to charities. One of them was helping children in third world countries. I have been sponsoring children ever since.

I was getting better with my job. I wrote numerous job tickets, checked production schedules, pulled samples, organized files and other tasks. One day Jeff asked me if I would work for his brother Erick instead of helping Pam from now on. I heard from other coworkers how picky Erick was. Everyone was afraid of him. Each time Erick hired a new assistant, people bet how long the new assistant would last. The previous assistant could not survive for long and was let go after a month. I was reluctant to say "Yes" but said "Okay" and moved to Erick's office.

Erick did not say anything personal but work related only. He was always kind to his clients but when he talked to his employees he hardly smiled or joked except the plant manager and the receptionist. I did exactly what he told me to do, but a few days later he said the way I did was wrong. I told him I did exactly what he told me to do. He said he changed his mind and said not to do it that way anymore. He was never satisfied with what I did.

One day Jeff called me and said it would be more helpful if I assisted the prepress department instead of helping his brother Erick. He did not say Erick did not like me but I knew that Erick wanted to let me go and have a new assistant. It was kind of Jeff to give me a new opportunity to work at the prepress department instead of firing me and sending me back home to Korea.

Prepress was basically a computer team at a printing company. They took digital files from clients, developed proofs, films and plates for printing. Film was not popular anymore. Everything had been digitized. They showed clients digital proofs instead of print proofs. People who used to work with film had to learn how to use computers and electronic publishing software. If they didn't know how to use a computer they were let go and had a hard time to get a new job.

Apparently God put me under the picky boss, Erick, on purpose. When the unhappy boss wanted to get rid of me and hire a new assistant, it caused me to move to the prepress department. This would turn out to be a great opportunity and career builder. Scott, the prepress manager, showed me how to organize their scheduling board, how to handle disks from clients and organize electronic files in the network system. Downloading digital files was sometimes a time consuming job when the file size was huge. Some of them were over a gigabyte. I had to be very careful with the digital files not to overwrite or delete accidentally. I knew how to use a computer with basic office programs and how to send email but I had no professional experience with electronic publishing and printing prior to that. Scott said if I could download all the digital files from clients and make sure that they sent us everything we need for printing, it would be tremendously helpful for the team to save their production time and would be much more appreciated. Scott wanted me to do so-called "Preflight'.

"OK. No problem", I said.

After Scott showed me how to do preflight I had a terrible headache and lost my appetite to have lunch. I was overwhelmed.

There was a guy at the prepress department who was about 50 years old. He knew the basics of electronic publishing but was afraid of handling complicated jobs. So he only did preflight and other simple easy jobs. One day he called me quietly into a room where all the archived CDs and tapes were stored. He lowered his voice and told me not to touch the jobs for preflight. I said that Scott told me to handle those jobs to save their production time but he said he didn't want to be in trouble. I knew why. He was expected to handle more high level jobs but he was afraid of making mistakes and losing his job. I said I understood. But not long after that, he was let go and I continuously performed the tasks of what I was told to do.

Scott suggested to me that I take computer training on electronic publishing at a technical college. I thought it was a great idea. I was going to register immediately but I needed a TOEFL (Test of English as a Foreign Language) score. I called a test center right away. There was one spot available the following weekend. I took the test but it was too late to register for the semester. Scott suggested another idea to take computer classes. He introduced a computer institute where I could learn in a short period of time. So I registered to take three days of computer training. One program each day and I took three programs in three days; Adobe Photoshop, Adobe Illustrator and Quark Xpress. The company paid half of the tuition.

In the Photoshop class I was absolutely lost and felt miserable. I just could not follow what the instructor was talking about; layers, alpha channel, masking, cloning and etc. Was he speaking in English? I thought so. The level of my English was good enough to write up job tickets by then and I thought I could survive with it in America but now I was in a totally different world. I felt so dumb. I was afraid of what I had to deal with at work. I didn't seem to understand much of the class. After all the classes were over I now had a new fear rather than having a sense of accomplishment. On the way back home after the final class I thought about what I was going to do next. I knew that I would never say I couldn't do my job at work. So I decided to go back to school the next semester and learn the classes step by step. It wouldn't have to be three crazy days of fearing but I would actually learn something at least.

One of the employees in the prepress department was adopted from Korea when he was a baby. He drove a fancy sports car and always seemed to be knowledgeable and confident. I was glad to see an adopted Korean was doing well in America. I asked him a lot of job related questions every day. One day he was concerned and asked me, "Nami. If I am not here, how are you going to survive?"

Unfortunately, he was let go a couple of years later, but not me. He was really smart and had almost incomparable computer knowledge among the teammates. However, he trusted his ability too much and did everything too quick which often caused avoidable print mistakes. My biggest helper was let go but I was still there, did my best, and survived many more years even after he was gone.

I was not living at the band house anymore. Craig took me to an apartment search office and I moved into a small studio apartment. After work I usually had no one to talk to. Honestly, I did not want to talk to anyone at all. I was stressed out after speaking English all day long. When I went to my apartment I just sat in the empty room on the floor against the wall and stared at the opposite side of the wall for quite a while. No T.V. no radio. I did not have a phone either. I was all alone in the quietness. I felt lonely sometimes but it was way better than being at the loud band house.

I always liked rainy days since I was a little girl. On a rainy Friday afternoon I decided to take a long walk instead of riding a bus to get home after work. No need to rush to go home since no one was waiting for me. I walked in the rain and thought about all the things that had happened in my life. Every time I faced some unexpected situations God always sent someone to help me at the right time and at the right place. I could see clearly that He orchestrated everything to lead me out to reach the next stage. I thanked God for everything He had done for me.

I asked Him, "My Lord. Who am I? How could those people, some of them I never met until I came to America, help me unconditionally for nothing? I could not give them anything, yet they prayed for me as if they had known me for a long time. I was nothing but a homeless immigrant and totally broke. You know all that. With their help I am where I am and became what I am. Who am I? What should I do now to pay them back? And what should I do for You? I really want to know."

I kept thinking and talking to God all the way over six miles of walking. I had so many questions to ask but one thing for sure was that it was GOD who sent those guardian angels to help me and protect me.

I used to ride the bus to commute but I needed a car to go to school and to work. It was almost impossible to go to school and work without a car. The school and the work were located in two opposite cities, one in the North and the other in the South. I decided to buy a small economy car so I rode a bus one Saturday morning in search of a car. The bus was passing by Lake Calhoun, one of the popular lakes in the Twin Cities. People were running around the lake, inline skating, bicycling, and having fun. I looked at the people. They seemed to be enjoying their peaceful weekend with no worries.

"How lucky they are! Do they know they are blessed?" I wondered what the differences were between them and I. Why did God allow such a painful childhood and difficult times for me to go through? What kind of person does He want me to be? Is this my destiny to face obstacles one after another? What would be the next obstacle then? Am I ready to face it?

After the bus crossed over the Mississippi River and was passing by the University of Minnesota Twin City Campus, I noticed that the Econo Lodge and the Embers restaurant were gone; the motel where I stayed during my job interviews and the breakfast restaurant where I met Ben as my server. He let me stay at his place for two months without charging me rent. What a blessing that had been. I thought of the days at the band house. My experience there gave me such an invaluable lesson in my life. I learned how to be appreciative every little thing. To me, the band house was a hell and a shelter at the same time.

When I saw an auto dealer shop in St. Paul, I got off the bus and I walked into the shop. There were several cars displayed but I knew what I wanted to buy—the smallest car at the shop. A salesman came over to me and I told him that I wanted to buy the blue four door compact car. I did not want to lease but own it. The salesman took me to his office for paper work. He ran my credit history and said since I did not have much credit history in the U.S.A., two people should co-sign on the application in order to purchase the car. The next day I kindly asked my boss to co-sign on the application. He looked at the paper and signed right away. Then I had Craig sign on the paper too. When I was going to pick up the car, Craig wanted to go with me. He asked the dealer if the car was leased. He said, "No. She bought it."

We drove my first brand new car to Craig's house and gave Susan a ride. They were very happy for me. Before I purchased the car Craig let me use his car for a driver's license test. I had an international driver's license that I obtained in Korea but I wanted to have a Minnesota driver's license so I didn't have to carry my passport all the time.

It was my mother who told me to get a driver's license when I was in college. She had a Second Class driver's license that was for private automobiles but she told me to take First Class license test that was for driving commercial automobiles. At the driving school I saw most people, especially women, were sitting in the Second Class room. In the First Class there were mostly men, only three women in First Class including myself. Some people asked me why I wanted to take the First Class which was more difficult than the Second Class. I said it was my mother's idea and if I did not take First Class she said she was not going to pay for the lesson. My mother told me that I should do everything more and better than her for I was young and more educated than her.

It was hot and humid at the driving school. One day my instructor motioned to me to come over and said, "Do you see the student sitting in the pick-up truck over there on the S-course? He is having a hard time to get in and out of the course. Why don't you go help him to finish his S-course?"

"Sure."

So I guided the student how to get in and out of the S-course without driving on the yellow line. He made it. My instructor watched me instructing the student while standing in the shadow to cool off. When I went back to him, he said jokingly that I should not go back to school but be an instructor at his driving school. He said, "Driving the S-course is hard for the beginners but teaching the S-course is even harder but you did a great job!"

I got 97 on the written test for the driver's license and passed the driving test on the first try. I was excited and told my mother about the test result but she did not seem to be surprised or happy for me at all. She just said, "I am not surprised because I believed that you would pass and do better than me for sure. You are young and learned more than me, so it should be that way."

I appreciated her confidence in me but honestly I was disappointed. I wondered why she could not simply say, "You did a great job and I am very happy for you!"

When I was preparing for the written test for the driver's license in America I was not sure how many people would study for the test like I did. I highlighted the important parts with colored pens and studied as if I was preparing for a college entrance test. I chuckled to myself but thought it would be better than excusing myself that I failed the test because the test was in English. I did my best and passed the written test easily.

My new car had a stick gear but since I used to drive a pick-up truck with a stick gear at the driving school in Korea, it was a piece of cake to drive the new small car with a stick gear. The most convenient part to own a car was not only going to school and work but also going to the grocery store. Now I did not have to worry about how much I could carry. I drove the car to the band house one day and let Ben drive it around the neighborhood. I told him if he needed a car he could drive mine anytime. Also for his birthday I gave him a birthday card and $100 as a gift to show my appreciation for his generosity.

The job that no one wanted

The printing company had a lot of mailing projects such as periodical brochures, coupons, and flyers. They printed them at the shop but they sent the finished products out to a mailing service company. They sorted several thousands of mailing addresses, merged and purged the duplicated ones. Then they printed the automated addresses and bar codes on each mail piece. When it was completed the products were sent to the post office finally to be delivered to individual customers.

The owner wanted to save production costs. He walked into the prepress department and said he wanted to have the mailing jobs processed in the prepress department from now on in order to reduce the cost. After he walked out of the room everyone complained that they did not want to do the job.

Later the owner called me and said, "I know you are smart. Why don't you learn the program and do it yourself? I will raise your salary a lot if you do it."

I honestly told him that I did not want to do it like other guys at the prepress. I was afraid of making huge mistakes. That's why other guys didn't want to do it either. But I thought about the mailing job seriously while I was driving home. I was afraid of writing job tickets at the beginning but I got over the fear and did just fine. Next I was afraid of the preflight work and had a terrible headache but now I felt so comfortable doing it. Indeed I was doing way more different jobs besides the preflight. I learned a lot. I liked what I was doing. But now the company asks me to do something more. Why? Why God does not allow me to settle down here and enjoy my life once and for all? I was content with my small comfort zone and yet He was giving me more challenges. Why?

The next day, I went to the owner and told him that I was going to learn the mailing program and do the job. I thought he was going to be happy to hear that but he did not allow me to do it. I asked him why. He said if I worked on a job that I didn't like then I would want to quit and leave. I was surprised he said that. Did he really care about me quitting and leaving? Wow, I didn't know that. Maybe he said that for another reason but for me I was just happy to hear that. I asked him if he would not regret later that he did not give me the opportunity although I offered my service. He paused for a moment then said, "OK. Go ahead." He did not want to raise my salary a lot as he suggested initially so I had to negotiate to get $1 more per hour rather than his offer of 50 cents more per hour.

An instructor from the mailing company came to our company and started training me on how to use the program all day long. I heard that it cost $1,000 to take that private lesson in a day. The mailing program seemed to be challenging at the beginning but I picked it up pretty quick. At that time I had been already taking several computer classes at school. Among the classes I took that were the most helpful were *Programming Logics & Design*, C++ and HTML. I didn't have to take those classes for my job but I wanted to know how to make my personal website.

So I took those classes for my own curiosity. However, it became useful and handy now. First of all, those programming classes that I took helped me not to be intimidated by any new computer programs. Secondly, they helped me understand how the new software worked. The instructor helped me with several actual jobs to process. The more I practiced the more I felt comfortable doing it when the days went by.

One day Pam was passing by my work station. She saw my dual monitors and said, "Unbelievable! I remember you asked me how to use your check book when you just started working here and now you can handle that kind of program. Amazing!" Then she walked away. I felt really good about her comment.

Once I processed the data files for mailing I saved the final files and handed it over to Kim who was in charge of the mailing department. Everything went well until I found out that Kim was fired. One of the guys who worked at the mailing department told me that Kim made mistakes so she was let go early that morning. They said Kim set up the inkjet machine in order to print envelopes which had coupons inside. Each envelope was printed and lined up at the end of the conveyor. Then the girl sitting at the end of the conveyor collected the printed envelopes and put them in the trays. When she was collecting them she felt some of the envelopes were lighter than the others. She found out that there were no coupons in some of the envelopes. She brought the matter to Kim's attention immediately but Kim said just keep running the inkjet machine instead of stopping it. She didn't want to go through thousands of the printed envelopes to find out how many envelopes were empty. The girl who reported to Kim did not feel comfortable continuing so she reported it to the owner. So Kim got fired right away.

I went to Jeff's office and asked him to forgive Kim once but he said, "How embarrassing this is! When the customers open the envelopes, they will find nothing in it. I would be upset for sure if it was me!"

I almost begged him that the mailing department needed her to finish other jobs that had to be mailed out that day. But he did not give Kim a second chance even though I begged him with tears. He asked me instead, "Why do you need her? Are you not able to do your job without her?"

"No, I do not need her to do my job."

She did not know how to use the mailing program that I used at all. She just used the files that I gave her to print the envelopes. Kim never returned to work. Jeff wanted to set an example to let other employees know that that kind of irresponsible mistake would not be tolerated. One of the employees came to me when I got out of Jeff's office and said, "It was very kind of you stepping up and talking to Jeff for Kim."

After Kim was fired I knew that there were thousands of catalogues stacked on the pallets and they had to be sent out the very next day. At that time I worked the second shift as I had to go to school in the morning three days a week. No one told me to come to work early the next day but I got up really early and went to work at six o'clock in the morning. I punched in my time card then walked to the mailing department directly.

There were some people sitting around a table in the corner and they were putting some labels on the envelopes. As soon as I arrived there I kindly instructed them what to do with the catalogues and how to pack them in each tray according to the presorted lists that I processed a few days ago. I never worked at the mailing department before but I knew exactly how my processed data should be handled. They followed my instruction and we all worked together. Then I saw Jeff, the owner, was walking by. He was obviously concerned about the mailing jobs so he came in early to see what to do but there was me working at the mailing department. I bet that he did not expect to see me that early. He did not say a word to me but just walked by. When I got my paycheck that Friday, H.R. manager gave me an extra check of $500. I asked him what it was about. He said, "Oh, Jeff told me to give it to you."

I went to Jeff and asked him about it. He said, "It's not much but thank you. It's a bonus."

I knew what he meant. I appreciated him and also felt really good to be recognized even though I did not go to work for expecting any reward.

One day in front of other employees, the owner said,

"You guys expect pay checks will just come into your hands automatically every Friday. I would like people working hard without me telling them what to do. I wish all you guys are like Nami. Hey Nami, are all Koreans like you? Or is it just you?"

"All Koreans. Hahaha!"

"I wish I could have more Koreans working for me," he said.

A year at the printing company went by so quickly. Work, school, and homework were pretty much all I had. I walked around Lake Calhoun nearby my apartment sometimes. Everyone seemed to be happy and they had no worries what so ever. In the past, I used to think once I obtained the work visa, all my worries would disappear automatically then I would live my life happily ever after. But some new obstacle always seemed to pop up. Is it ever going to stop? When I was little I thought being special was a good thing. But now I did not want to be special. I just wanted to live a plain ordinary life with no adventure. Being special was tiresome. I wanted to be like other people running around the lake or walking their dogs. They all seemed to be happy to me. I really envied them.

Visitation to LaGrange Prison

I decided to visit Jenna in Columbus, Georgia over a weekend. She came to Atlanta to pick me up. We were so happy to see each other again. Jenna's first son, Ron, who came out of jail when I was in Columbus, was arrested again. He was sent to prison this time to serve 10 years. He stole a car and robbed a bank with other guys. Jenna said the other guys could afford good lawyers but she could not afford one. She said Ron would get his lesson this time for sure and would be molded by God while serving his time in prison. She visited her son every weekend and suggested visiting Ron while I was there. It was my first time to meet him in person. Before we departed Jenna told me to make sure that I was wearing pants, not a skirt. Wearing skirts was not allowed to meet inmates at the prison.

We waited for Ron at a meeting room. The room was full of other inmates and their families. There were some children and babies that came along too. Some inmates were holding the babies or put their kids on their laps. They seemed to be very happy to be with their families. None of the inmates looked like criminals to me. I wondered how they ended up there. I did not consider myself one bit better than those inmates. Only the difference between them and I was that they were in prison and I was not. However we were all sinners before God. Even though they were locked in the prison, if they confessed their sins and were reborn in Jesus Christ, they would be called righteous.

While I was in my own thoughts and looking at other people around, Ron came out to meet us. He was a good looking guy. I could not see any hint of a criminal. Jenna introduced us to each other. I said I saw him in the photos hanging on the wall at his parents' house. He said he heard all about me from his mother. He got some snacks from the vending machine in the meeting room. His mother asked how he had been. He said he had been doing great and started learning Spanish. He asked me about my job and I said that I was working for a commercial printing company. While we were talking, we came up with an idea that he would send me a photo of him in his prison outfit then I would do a photo retouch and send him a new photo of him wearing a suit. We chatted and had a good time. Before we departed we prayed together and said good bye.

Ever since I visited him at the LaGrange prison, Ron and I had exchanged letters for the next eight years until he was released. I thought maybe it was God's call for me that I encourage him by writing letters. In his letter he told me that when he got out of the jail before, he tried to join the army to be away from the gang members but they always chased after him and threatened him if he ever tried to run away from them they would kill him. However, while he was locked in the prison for years, none of the gang members sent a letter or visited him.

During the eight years of exchanging letters with him I probably complained a lot more about my life in the outside world rather than he complained about his prison life. We shared our friendship by encouraging each other. As far as I remember, he was originally sentenced to ten years to serve but was released after serving eight full years.

Before Ron was released from prison, Jenna went to a car dealer shop and was looking for a job for her son. The manager asked why she was looking for a job for him instead of him searching for himself. She said he was in prison at that time but he would be released soon. So she wanted to find a job before he was out of prison then he could start the job right away instead of wasting time and doing nothing. The manager gladly accepted her request and said he would hire Jenna's son when he gets out. Jenna was always positive and thinking ahead. I wondered how many mothers who had prisoner sons would do like Jenna did by visiting her son every Saturday for eight years and even looked for a job for her prisoner son. Ron got the job at the auto dealer shop and also started going to a community college.

Flying over the Hudson River

Greg called me once in a while to see how I was doing. He also visited me once in Minneapolis but we were no longer as boyfriend and girlfriend. We were just like good old friends. I showed him the band house and we drove around the Twin Cities to see houses like we used to do in Columbus, GA for fun. He spent a weekend and flew back to Georgia. It was the last time that I saw him and I heard from another friend that he moved to Germany for his job later.

Rich had been always like a good brother to me. I told him pretty much everything what I was doing in Minnesota. He always encouraged me and reminded me how smart I was and how much I had accomplished already by moving to a different country which was not easy for everyone. He told me to visit him some day when I had a vacation.

I flew to New York to meet him one weekend. He came to pick me up at the airport in his brand new SUV. I congratulated him on his new vehicle. I remembered his old car when he came to the greyhound bus station in Birmingham, AL to pick me up. It was an old junky car that had washed blue paint and close to 200,000 miles on it. He said he bought the new SUV with cash. At that time he finished his master's degree in aviation management and was a type rated multi engine commercial pilot but he was still working as an aviation mechanic for the time being. He usually worked long hours for several months then he took two to three months off to spend the summer in Puerto Rico.

I met his mother and half-brother. His mother seemed to be very young to have a son like around Rich's age. We walked around New York City for sightseeing and shopping. Walking among the crowd reminded me of my old days when I used to live in Seoul. My monotonous life in Minnesota felt so quiet and boring all of sudden; school and work. If I didn't have to be bound at one company because of my visa status I wished I could move to New York and live an exciting city life like New Yorkers.

I spent the night at Rich's small one bedroom apartment. The next morning when I was going to take a shower, hot water was not coming out. I turned the knob and waited for several minutes but still no hot water. I gave up and washed with cold water. When I came out of the bathroom I saw that he folded my blanket and put it away already. I was going to do it but he took care of everything while I was in the bathroom. His apartment was organized already. I didn't know when he had a chance to wash but he was nicely dressed up, packed, and ready to go. I asked him how he could organize everything so quickly. He said he got that habit and discipline from the military.

He took me and his brother to an airport to fly in a Cessna 172. We took off from the runway and flew along the Hudson River. I saw the Twin Towers of The World Trade Center and the Statue of Liberty standing just like the poster picture that I bought the day before as a souvenir. When we were flying over the river there was a helicopter flying not that far from us. Rich communicated with the helicopter pilot via the radio in the airplane. The helicopter pilot asked Rich what altitude he would maintain and how long we were going to fly in that area. Rich told him the altitude and about an hour or so for a tour.

During the flight I was a little bit nervous to fly in the small airplane but it definitely intrigued my curiosity in many ways. I wanted to know how the heavy aircraft could stay in the air while a small coin drops instantly when I toss it up. Rich encouraged me that I should learn how to fly and become a private pilot. It was quite a wild dream for me to even think of it. How could I become a pilot when I am still struggling with English daily? Besides I barely lived paycheck to paycheck. The money was always tight. Taking flying lesson was absolutely out of my comfort zone.

Rich was always busy, goal oriented, and focused on following his career path. He hardly talked about going out with his friends or any girlfriend. I appreciated that he took the time off to show me around New York City. It was the last time that I saw him.

Lonely life ain't so bad

I came back to my simple life in Minnesota. I was busy with school three days a week and worked from Monday to Friday. I missed hanging out with friends sometimes; having dinner together, drinking, shopping or simply chatting. I had not done it for so long. After school and work there was no one to talk with. Only homeless people came to me to beg for money once in a while. One time after I gave a beggar some money I thought to myself, "Thank you for talking to me."

I decided to try a bar next to the dry cleaner that I used to bring my clothes for dry cleaning once in a while. I walked into the bar one night. It was loud and smoky inside. Going to a restaurant or theater alone was a little bit awkward at the beginning but I got used to it after a while. So walking in the bar by myself was no different. I ordered a beer. The bartender greeted me and kindly asked me if I lived nearby. I said I lived only a few blocks away and it was my first time to the bar. He welcomed me and gave me a glass of tap beer. I looked around. People seemed to be having a good time. They were enjoying their worry free lives or at least they did not have to worry about two things for sure; work visa and speaking English. I thought, "You guys are so lucky…" I wished they would know that. Getting a work visa and speaking English comfortably were the most fundamental things that I desperately needed to survive in this country and they had the privilege by birth and I had not. I had to earn it.

I saw some people playing pull tabs. Underneath their tables were hundreds of opened pull tabs scattered all over. While they were smoking and tearing at the pull tabs I played my own *I-could-have-game* in my mind. If I were born in the U.S. like them,

I could have accomplished so and so and I would not have to sit alone at the bar. I could have had no problem with speaking English and I could have gone to a famous university in the U.S. or I could have had a better job or I could have made more money. But the fact was that I was not born in the country and the *I-could-have-game* was stupid and useless. Sigh… I sipped my beer.

Then I started thinking some positive thoughts this time. I thanked God, first of all, that I was not born in North Korea where the chance that I come to America for a job could have been impossible. I thanked God for my health, the people He sent to help me, opportunities that I had so far to learn at school and work. I felt better. So I ordered another beer. It was not so bad to drink alone, I thought. Work, school, and the bar became my regular routes ever since then. Instead of going to the grocery store and cooking at home, I skipped meals and started going to the bar more often. I was lacking sleep and nutrition. I weighed a little over 100 pounds.

I had dark brown long straight hair and used to wear a skirt and long boots which was a popular style among the Korean girls back then. At the bar, the bartender recognized me as one of the regulars now. Sometimes the bartender gave me a beer that I didn't order and said that it was from a guy sitting across the way. I nodded to thank him. Sometimes guys sitting next to me bought me beers. We cheered and chatted out loud. Maybe they wanted to spend a night with me but I ignored them and didn't care. However, I liked being surrounded by the guys. When I got drunk and walked home I thought, "Umm, life is not so bad after all. I think I can live like this. I don't feel lonely anymore." Deep down in my heart, I knew that I should not live my life like that.

My name is NOT ME

I had to behave before God put me in another training school for me to go through. I didn't want to go back to a situation where I had to stay at a place like the band house or even the depressing motels in Arkansas ever again. So I started trying different churches on Sundays to find a home church. I was originally baptized at a Presbyterian church in Seoul but the denomination of a church meant nothing to me. I believed that

God would not care about the man-made structure or so called "denomination."

Each church I tried had its own unique style of worship. At one church I saw people were jumping and dancing during the pastor's sermon. I did not feel comfortable to sit there while others were jumping up and down and dancing. After the worship they had fellowship time. Some of the church women tried to set me up with a guy at the church. They said the guy and I were both singles and it would be good to see us as a couple at the church. I did not feel comfortable to go there. I tried a few other churches but I hardly remembered what I heard.

Back in Korea I used to learn Korean sign language at a church where the pastor was hard of hearing and his wife could communicate by both speaking and signing. The pastor's sign language was too fast for me to learn but I learned some basic Korean sign language. I thought if I learned sign language I could communicate with all hard-of-hearing people in the world but that was not the case. Each sign language was unique and had its own letters like regular spoken languages. However, the sign for Jesus in Korean Sign Language and American Sign Language was the same. Left middle finger touched right palm and right middle finger touched left palm indicating the nails of the crucifixion.

I liked learning Korean Sign Language. The deaf pastor's wife made a sign language worship team and went out on busy streets. They brought a big boom box and played Korean worship songs loudly on the busy streets. Most of them were college students. They all wore white cotton gloves and put a donation box in front of them and signed with music. I wanted to be like one of them. People walked by and put money in the box sometimes.

After I moved to the U.S., I received an email from the pastor. He said he wanted to move to the U.S. and asked if I could help him out. He said his wife ran away with a man with the church money. He had been raising his daughter by himself and now he wanted to come to the U.S. I was shocked by the sad news and I had a deep sympathy toward him. But I didn't know how to help him. I was not in any situation to help anyone who wanted to move to America. Besides, I had no idea how to communicate with him except writing down each time. It was way beyond my capability. Regretfully, I kindly apologized that I was not able to help him.

It was my mother's idea for me to learn Korean Sign Language and be an interpreter when I was in Korea. I thought it was a cool idea but was never good at the language so I admired others who were good at sign language. One day I searched if there was any church that had a sign language worship service. I found one in Edina nearby my apartment. I visited the church.

The leader at the hard of hearing worship service was able to talk. He said he used to hear and speak like other people but lost his hearing ability significantly when he was very young. So he spoke as if he had no problem. Since he had difficulty of hearing, he spoke really loud. His wife who was also hard of hearing told him to lower his voice. I liked him speaking really loud and signing at the same time.

They asked my name so I spelled my name in English and also spoke my name.

"N-A-M-I"

They read my lips and said, "Ah, your name sounds like Not-Me!"

So they gave me my American Sign Language name as "Not-Me."

In order to sign "Not," I touched my chin with my thumb from inside toward out. In order to sign "Me," I pointed and touched my chest with my index finger. In order to sign my name, they made "Not" sign with an alphabet "N" then touched their chest to make "Me."

Since then "NOT ME" officially became my American Sign Language name. What an honor to get a real American Sign Language! They said it was a tradition that hard of hearing people give speaking people their sign language names instead of speaking people give themselves their own sign language names.

Although I wanted to learn American Sign Language very much and took an A.S.L. class for one semester at a technical college, it was not easy for me to communicate with them and I had a hard time to understand the sermon messages. So I switched to the contemporary service which was at five o'clock in the afternoon on Sundays. I felt comfortable there. So the church became my home church—Grace Church, Edina at that time and now in Eden Prairie, MN.

Roommates

I hardly cooked at all. I always stopped by a coffee shop to get a bagel and coffee in the morning and had fast food for lunch. I went to a bar at night. If I cooked at home, brought my own lunch to work and had dinner at home I could have saved a lot of money. But I was tired and getting lazy. I wanted to have everything easy and I thought I deserved something better.

Handling everything in an easy way was convenient but I was always running out of money and I couldn't wait until the next Friday to get another paycheck. So when the apartment lease was up I wanted to move to a house where I could share rent with other roommates in order to save some money. I was tired of living on pay checks week by week. I made one month salary in Korea in one week in the U.S. but I had a hard time to keep up with paying the bills. The biggest expenses were apartment rent, school tuition, car payments and ridiculously expensive auto insurance. The auto insurance company charged me $150 a month for one small economy car. I expected to pay less than half that.

The insurance company said that it was high because I did not have any driving record in the U.S. One day I met a guy at a bar. He was sitting next to me and we started chatting. I don't remember what we were talking about but somehow the topic ended up being about the expensive auto insurance. He said a buddy of his ran an insurance company and gave me the guy's number. When I called his friend, he said he heard about me and gave me a price of $67 per month. Oh, thank God! I thought going to a bar wasn't that bad after all. If I did not go to the bar, how could I meet that kind of people? I tried to justify myself going to the bar frequently so that I would feel less guilty. A funny thing was that I never saw the guy who introduced me to the insurance company again. It was a bar I went probably two or three times only and I didn't have his phone number so I couldn't even thank him after I got the generous fee for the auto insurance. He was just another great helper whom I would not ever forget.

I told Craig that I wanted to move somewhere and have roommates to save some money. He said there was a convenience store in his neighborhood where people put their ads on the board so he would check into it if there was anyone looking for a roommate. He found one. It was a duplex located a couple of blocks away from his house. Three guys lived downstairs and two girls upstairs. The one who was looking for a roommate was Lisa. She was looking for a third roommate to share the rent. It was a tiny bedroom, right between a bathroom and a kitchen. I liked it and agreed to move in by the end of the month. The other roommate, Amy, usually stayed at her boyfriend's house and came to the house once or twice a month and she paid the rent. She was the oldest among the three of us. Lisa was next and I was the youngest. But Lisa acted like a big sister, always more mature and logical. Amy was like a little sister and I was in the middle. We got along pretty well.

Lisa had a cat named after a French fragrance in a women's magazine, Fracas. I never had a pet for myself and did not see many cats around. So I liked the cat as if she was my own. Fracas visited my room everyday and loved sitting on my bed. She slept with me too. One day I discovered that her claws made hundreds of tiny needle holes in my blanket. I washed the blanket right away and sent her out of my room. She had to sleep in Lisa's room but she came to my room very early in the morning. She pushed the unlatched door and came in. When I closed my door not to let her in, she started banging her head on the door and made a constant banging noise until I let her in. She got up so early but I still wanted to sleep more, so I put a thick yellow book and a heavy backpack against the door. She banged her head against the door but she could not make any noise. So she started mewing in front of the door. I felt so sorry for her but I had to sleep and didn't want her in to ruin my blanket with her claws.

Lisa knew that Fracas was very smart and clever. So she trained her like a circus cat. Every time when we had guests over, Lisa brought small fur balls and put them on high places. Fracas looked at them for a moment. Then she jumped on chairs, tables or book cases and knocked them down. We all cheered for her and she got her treats. I liked living with them.

When I had a little bit of extra money available since I shared the rent with roommates, I decided to try some new hobbies. So I took swimming lessons for the first time in my life to get rid of a phobia of deep water. My class at the high school went to a camp in a mountain one summer and all the students rushed to the water in the valley. When I was in the water other students pushed me under the water and did not let me come up. Whenever my head was about to get above the water, several girls laughed and pushed my head down again. They thought it was funny but I had a hard time to breathe. I couldn't stand up in the water and lost my balance. I started to panic. I screamed really hard, out of fear. Then they stopped. Ever since then I was afraid of deep water and hated the girls who pushed me under the water. I wanted to get over the fear so I decided to take swimming lessons. I was probably the oldest student at the swim school. After two months of private lessons, I was able to swim free style and back stroke. But I was still afraid of going into water without anyone nearby me to catch me in case I needed help right away.

After the swimming lessons I started taking horseback riding lessons. It was not cheap but I thought I could come up with the money by not drinking alcohol every night. Horseback riding was the most fun hobby I ever had. I enjoyed the beautiful autumn trees and clean fresh air in the forest. I felt a sense of peace outside the city life. I bought a cowboy hat, riding boots, and riding pants. I followed rodeo shows or horse shows in different cities on weekends and watched horse races on television. I imagined if a cowboy ever proposed to me, I probably wanted to give up the crazy city life, go marry him and settle down in the peaceful country.

Debbie and Arnie at the bindery department owned a farm and they had many horses. They drove about an hour and a half from their farm house to work in the city every day. Debbie was a manager at the bindery department and Arnie was a cutter. They invited me to their farm house on weekends and let me ride on one of their horses. Debbie's daughter trained horses and showed them at competitions. I did not ride her good looking horses. I rode a farm horse. Not like the slow walking horses at the ranch where I took riding lessons this farm horse was fast and I could have a chance to actually gallop. I rode the farm horse for about an hour in the gated grass field. It was a little too fast for me at first. I had to hang on tight not to fall off. I was a little bit scared by the unfamiliar speed at the beginning, but once I gained my balance and confidence, galloping on the back of the farm horse felt almost like flying. When I got off the horse, Arnie said he saw such a big happy smile on my face that he had never seen when I was at work. Debbie fixed dinner for all of us. The menu was hot dogs, slow cooked pork, smoked red beans, B.B.Q. sauce, pickled cucumbers, potato chips, cold beer and apple cider. It was like heaven to me. They showed me genuine farmer's hospitality each time I visited their farm. I drove home full of happiness and gratitude.

When I visited the farm one time I noticed Debbie and Arnie's old white blind horse in the barn was missing. I asked Arnie where she went. He said they brought her out to the field when she was still alive and shot her with a rifle. She was too old and blind. She could not do anything and they expected her to die sooner or later. So before they could not move the heavy dead horse out of the barn, they walked her to the field and shot her. I was so sad and so sorry to hear that.

Trip to Korea

Before the three years of my work visa expired I wanted to prepare an application and supporting documents to extend my visa. One of the salesmen at the company said his wife was an immigration lawyer. So I decided to get some help from her this time instead of bothering Craig again.

I met Sonia, the immigration lawyer. I explained that I needed to extend my work visa to three more years and I also wanted to visit my family in Korea. She looked at my approval letter issued by the immigration department with which I was able to work legally in the United States. She said, "Fantastic! You can visit your family at any time and enter the country with no trouble."

I said I had the approval letter but I did not have a sticker of work visa glued in my passport because I switched my status from a visitor's visa to a work visa while I was in the U.S.A. She assured me that I would have no problem at all to travel with the approval letter and re-enter the country. She also gave me her business card and said, "If you have any trouble to get into the U.S. have the INS officer call me. I will explain. You just enjoy your trip."

Then she asked me if she could copy my passport and all my other documents that I brought to her. So I let her do it.

I flew to Korea during my two weeks of summer vacation in August 1999. I arrived at the Kimpo International Airport in Seoul. Everything seemed to be different somehow. I remembered that while I was going through my own difficult time in the U.S. waiting for the work visa, the entire nation of South Korea had to go under financial struggles called the IMF (International Monetary Fund) crisis in 1997.

The IMF crisis happened throughout Asia and my mother told me that I should stay in the U.S. until I get the result of the work visa. If I went back to Korea at that time there was nothing for me to do. I heard that a lot of companies had to lay off employees so it was almost impossible to get a new job. Whether I went back to Korea for nothing or stayed in the U.S. as a jobless person, there would have been not much difference but at least in the U.S. I had a job waiting.

People in Korea lost their jobs and suicide stories were common on the 9 o'clock prime time news. It was almost like the entire nation declared bankruptcy. Korean money became like tissue paper. A lot of Korean students who studied abroad had to give up and return to Korea because they could not afford tuition and living expenses. If I did not waste money on drinking alcohol every night but sent U.S. dollars to Korea, I could have gained a lot of profit from the currency rate. But I had no spare dime to invest at that time because I was busy to pay the bills and to live a drunken lazy life.

I took a limousine bus going from the airport to Gang Nam Express Bus Terminal to catch an express bus to go to my hometown. It was the same bus terminal that I arrived at when I ran away as a teenage girl in 1985. The bus driver saw my big luggage and asked me where I was coming from. I said, "America." He was in awe and asked me if the life was good in America. I said it was good but I missed my family in Korea. I felt a little bit strange to see so many Korean people all of a sudden and hearing people speaking in Korean.

I leaned my head against the window and looked outside. The bus got out of the terminal and was driving on the highway. It was cool to see the mountains on both sides of the highway since there were no mountains in Minnesota. I recalled the old days when Hanna and I used to hang out as crazy party girls at the pub in Itaewon. Two drunken girls at the pub thought they were cool and enjoying their lives. Those G.I.s at the pub probably thought that we were hookers. Who knew? I chuckled. I thought that I could have worked at one of those bars or night clubs for foreigners in Itaewon during the IMF Crisis since I could speak English well. And who knows that I could have become a total lost child forever. I could have done anything if I were in such kind of difficult financial situation in Korea. I imagined all kinds of dirty jobs that I might have tried but I thanked God that He placed me somewhere thousands of miles away where I could do nothing but pray with tears. God let me avoid the unthinkable sins that I could have committed. I used to think that I was the only one in the whole world having the worst time in my life while all other people in the world were enjoying their lives. I felt so sorry and thanked God again and again.

Five hours of bus riding went fast while I was thinking of all kind of memories in the past. I took a taxi from the bus terminal to my parents' house. I was excited to see my parents for the first time in two years.

I walked in the house and said, "Hi! Mom and Dad. How are you?"

My father said, "Ah, here you are. Come in! Must be tired from the long hours of traveling, aren't you? Why don't you take a shower and go to sleep early tonight?"

We just saw each other for the first time in two years. There was no kiss or hug. That was all. But just by looking at his eyes I could feel how happy he was to see me again. The way he looked at me and the tone of his voice told how much he had cared about me. No words could ever express his heart! I could also tell that my mother was excited to see me again. She took my heavy bags and prepared dinner for me. She was no longer the same woman whom I hated when I was younger. She still showed serious depression and anxiety once in a while but she was truly not the person in the past who tortured me and my brothers. She came back to me as my mother. I would never forget what she told me when I was in college. She said that she deserved to go to hell for what she did to me and my brothers. I used to believe that Satan manipulated my mother to torture me when I was little. But I didn't know that God allowed everything to happen on purpose.

I questioned myself if I were born in another family, could my mother in the other family help me go to America for English language training even though she had a tight budget for groceries then encourage me to get a job in the U.S.? I doubted. I thought other moms probably would say to stay in Korea, marry a nice guy and settle down here. But my mother was different. It was her who convinced my father,

"We don't have any fortune to give our children but here she has a great opportunity to take right in front of her. Why should we be the obstacles for her pursuing her dream? Let's allow her to go to America." So my father approved.

My mother always wanted to prepare us for unexpected situations to survive. One winter she told me and my first brother to sell sticky rice buns at night. They were made of sticky rice and sweet red bean paste inside. Roasted nuts, wood grilled sweet potatoes and sticky rice buns were the most popular night snacks in the cold winter. My mother purchased the buns at whole sale price, put them in a large bag and gave them to us to sell at night. She put nice winter jackets and hats on us to make sure that we were warm and did not look like poor kids. The whole purpose of selling the buns was to get us prepared to survive just in case my parents died all of a sudden. We did not have any life or disability insurance. If we were trained well in advance, then it would not be too hard for us to survive. That was what my mother told us before she let us go for selling the buns. She told us not to drop our heads at any time in front of people but be confident. She reminded us that we didn't sell the buns because we were poor or didn't have parents. She added even if we didn't sell any we did not have to worry about it because we could just eat them all at home. So we went out to an apartment building and knocked on each door. I don't recall any people being mean to us. Some of them told us, "Hope you would sell a lot tonight." We thanked them and went home after a couple of hours of selling. We met our revenue and also had some buns left over. We told our mother how it went and showed her how much money we made that evening. We were happy to see that my mother was happy.

My mother was born in Jinju-Si. That was the city where I grew up. It was a small developing city and was also known as the City of Nongae who was a female entertainer. When Japan invaded Chosun (the country name before Korea) in 1592, Jinju was attacked and claimed by the Japanese. They held a big party by the Nam Kang which was the river that ran through the middle of the city. Nongae, the entertainer, was standing on a large rock in the river. The Japanese general at that time was attracted by her beauty and jumped on the rock hoping to seduce her. She was wearing jade rings on each of her ten fingers. When the Japanese general approached her, she put her two arms around him and locked the fingers with her jade rings then jumped into the fast running river. The rock still remains these days and there is a shrine built next to the river to honor her. She is viewed as a hero for giving her life to eliminate the Japanese general.

My mother experienced the Korean War (1950-1953) when she was about seven years old. My grandmother was pregnant at that time. My mother was the first child and she had a sister who was a couple of years younger than her. My grandparents, my mother and her younger sister had to evacuate their village and go somewhere else to hide. They became war refugees. They walked day and night to go hide deep in the mountains. My grandmother was always kind to my aunt but not to my mother. Grandma always compared my mother to her younger sister and gave my mother harsh comments on pretty much everything. She verbally and mentally abused my mother. She gave my aunt piggyback rides while they were on the road but never my mother. Maybe my mother was too big to have piggy back rides, but grandma let my seven-year old poor mother walk over five to six miles every night until they reached the mountain they were heading for. My mother cried and begged her parents to stop for a moment and get some sleep whenever she saw dimmed lights in a village but my grandmother harshly scolded her to keep walking without complaining. They tried to walk at night usually to avoid North Koreans. After experiencing the war, my mother became extremely obsessed with the thought of surviving for her entire life.

My mother grew up in poverty after the war. Her dream was becoming a teacher someday but she had to give up her education and get a job right after middle school to support her family. She worked at a textile company for many years. Whenever she had vacation time from her work, my grandma told her to go to their rice field and work so she had to work all the time and never dated any man until she married my father by a match maker. The match maker set a wedding date and they married after meeting only once to introduce each other.

My father was from Sakok-Ri which was in the deep countryside where people could see buses running twice a day, one in the morning and one in the afternoon. He was raised in a very traditional and conservative family. His family used to have servants helping them with their farming and household work. My father always reminded us to be humble and polite to others, especially elders. He did not allow us to greet elders casually. We had to bend our upper bodies 45 degrees to bow to them and show our respect. If we met them in their house we had to give them a traditional full bow that was gently kneeling down on the floor, putting two hands together in front of us then bow our heads almost touching the two hands on the floor. We could not think of waving, chewing gum, wearing earphones or wearing sun-glasses while talking to older people. Those were all considered very disrespectful.

My mother told me that I should visit my grandparents' grave sites first then relatives next, to greet them while I was in Korea. So I spent most of my vacation for visiting relatives in different cities and most of my spending money for transportation on the road. Then I visited the printing company where I used to work and met the old co-workers. They welcomed me and took me out for a drink. The guys ordered beer constantly with some side dishes. After the first round of drinking beer we moved to a different place to eat some food and drink more. I was used to drinking beer but never had that much to drink in my entire life. Each person offered me a drink. I should have said I could not take it anymore but I could not refuse their hospitality. Then we moved to a song room (Karaoke). They ordered more beer. I was totally trashed and it was impossible to go home by myself. One of the girls took me to her apartment that night. She had to go to work the next day but I passed out and slept all morning. I barely got up and made it to the bus terminal to catch a bus to go home. While waiting for the bus, I could not stand or sit up straight so I found a bench and laid down on my side.

I thought about the day when I arrived at the bus terminal after I ran away from home when I was in high school. I was afraid of kidnapping. Ten years had passed since then and I thought about what I should do if someone tried to take advantage of me now. I had a hangover and laid down on the bench like a homeless person. If a bad guy told people that I was his crazy wife and ran away so he was trying to bring me back home, what was I going to do in this situation? I was hardly capable of anything. How could I defend myself in the situation? People might believe the bad guy. I had to come up with an idea to defend myself. I decided that I would start speaking in English, then people might be curious how a crazy drunken wife could speak English then they would suspect him and might help me instead. I thought speaking English might be useful if that kind of situation really happened. It was all nonsense running through my half-conscious mind.

While I was imagining the ridiculous thoughts in a half asleep on the bench, the bus finally arrived at the terminal and I got onboard. I wanted to take a five-hour nap all the way to the final destination without even getting off the bus for a bathroom break but it was too cold because of the air conditioner. I kindly asked the bus driver if he could turn it off just for a little while but he refused and said if he turned it off other passengers would complain. I did not have a blanket or a long sleeve jacket. My body was getting extremely cold and I had a splitting headache. Sitting in the cold bus gave me goose bumps all over my arms and legs. I felt like I was being tortured in the bus. I regretted that

I had too much to drink and was disgusted by my alcohol breath when I exhaled.

When the bus stopped at rest areas twice, I dragged my body out of the bus and really appreciated the over 100 degree humid hot summer weather outside. The short 10 minutes of bathroom break ended soon and all the passengers got onboard again. I did not like the bus driver at all. He could at least turn the air conditioner down a little bit but he never showed any kindness. I suffered the total five and half hours by shivering. As soon as I arrived at home, I passed out.

My whole body ached as if someone beat me with a baseball bat from head to toe. I had a high fever. My mother took me to see an oriental medicine doctor the next day. He checked my pulse and said I was very weak and needed to avoid any stress. I was always amazed how the oriental medicine doctors could tell if someone had internal medical problems by touching someone's wrists. In old days, when a queen was ill and a doctor had to check her pulse, he could not see her directly or touch her wrist. The queen's assistant tied a silk thread around the queen's wrist and the doctor who was sitting behind a bamboo screen held the other side of the thread extended from her wrist and checked her pulse. I watched it from a Korean traditional drama. If the queen recovered then the doctor was promoted and gained wealth. If the queen died, although it was not his fault, he was exiled. It was totally unfair and ridiculous. Though it could have been complete fiction as far as I knew.

Oriental medicine was mixed of all kinds of dried herbs. My mother used to boil the dried herbs in a clay pot for several hours until the hard dried herbs became tender then she poured the medicine on a large burlap piece placed in a china bowl then squeezed it with two long wooden sticks. It tasted really bitter and I did not like it at all. But these days' oriental medicine clinics boiled the prescribed herbs really quickly in a machine and put the liquid in each plastic pouch to drink easily. My mother and I received the medicine and came home. I was recovered after taking the medicine and resting for a couple of days.

My trip was too short. All I could remember was visiting my grandparents' grave sites, relatives in different cities, and drinking heavily, then being sick to death. I packed and headed out to the airport. I said good bye to my parents and brothers. I was not sure when I was coming back again.

No visa to enter the U.S.A.

I arrived at the Seattle Tacoma International Airport. Almost 400 people came out of the Boeing 747 and lined up to enter the country. I had my passport and the letter of approval notice from the immigration department in my hand. At my turn, I walked up to the immigration officer and gave him my passport and the letter.

He looked at them and asked, "Where is your visa?"

"I don't have a visa but my immigration lawyer said that I should have no problem to enter the country since I have the approval notice from the INS."

I handed him her business card as she instructed me. He took the business card and glanced at it for a second. Then he said with no particular expression on his face, "You need to get a new lawyer. Follow me."

He stood up and got out of the booth! What's going on? People standing behind me obviously wondered what was going on with me. I could feel that the hundreds of people were staring at me. I followed the officer. He put me in an empty office and said, "Wait here."

Then he walked away to resume his duty. I just prayed, "Lord, please be with me and help me." A few minutes later, another immigration officer, an Asian, walked in the room.

"Hi! How are you?"

"I am Fine. Thank you." I was a little bit nervous but forced myself to smile.

"No, you are not fine! I can tell from your face!"

I could not help but laughing when he said that. Well, I guess I was not fine then. I felt much more relieved by his friendly tone of voice. He sat down across from me and started asking questions.

"Let me see what we have here. Are you a Korean?"

"Yes."

"An Nyung Ha Se Yo?" he said in Korean which meant "How are you?"

Since I was an Asian, an Asian officer came in to interrogate me in my native language, I thought.

He examined my passport and the approval letter from the immigration department. Then he asked what my occupation was and why I did not have the visa. I explained that I was already in the U.S. so I converted my status from a visitor to a temporary worker. I also told him that my lawyer assured me that I should have no problem to enter the country since I had the approval letter.

The officer told me that I should have obtained my visa BEFORE I entered the country. However, he was going to let me get in this time but I had to pay the fine—$300 in cash. No credit card or check was accepted. I thanked him and paid $300 out of the $1,000 that my parents gave me as a gift before I left home. If they did not give me the money, I had no $300 cash in my pocket and they didn't accept credit cards. I couldn't be thankful enough to my parents. I knew very well how hard and how long it would take for my parents to save up that much money.

I walked out of the room with a big smile on my face on purpose because I knew people who saw me going in the room would be looking at me again with curiosity or they might think that I was an illegal immigrant and was caught. I did not care much about what other people would think of me but I kept thanking God that I had the cash ready to pay and also could defend myself with English this time, not like the day at the University of Alabama way back when I was attending at the E.L.I. I hurried to the next gate to catch my next flight going to Minneapolis.

Now my thoughts were entirely occupied by the anger and disappointment against the lawyer woman. How could she do that to me? I needed my $500 back that I paid her up front for her future service. As soon as I arrived home, I called my parents to let them know that I arrived home safely and thanked them for the money again. I did not tell them about the visa and the penalty at the airport. Then I called the lawyer and told her everything. After listening to me, she said that I gave her misinformation. I was absolutely speechless for a moment and did not understand why such a thing was happening to me. She was the one who said that I should have no problem to enter the country and if there was any trouble, she told me to show her business card to the officer. I did exactly as what she told me to do. I told her that the officer said that I needed a new lawyer.

"I gave you everything I had. You copied my passport from cover to cover and the approval letters from the Department of Labor and the INS and yet you could not recognize what was missing? You confirmed several times that I should have no problem to enter the country. I was so embarrassed at the airport in front of the hundreds of people. Besides I had to pay $300 penalty in cash. I don't want to hire you as my lawyer for my next visa extension. Please give my money back."

She blamed me that I gave her misinformation and she would not return the $500 that she charged me up front before she even started anything for my visa extension. She said she gave me a special discount since I was her husband's co-worker. How could I give her misinformation when I gave her everything I had? She copied my passport and there was no work visa but she could not tell what I needed to enter the country. Yet her business card said that she was an immigration attorney. "What a joke!" I thought. I was very upset with myself and felt like I had been duped into giving this attorney $500 for nothing.

I started questioning myself why the unexpected situation happened to me. Why? I thought everything would go smoother this time since I hired an immigration lawyer. Last time it was just Craig and I who completed the application and submitted it. Why did God allow it to happen? For what purpose? What was He trying to tell me? I wanted to know, so I started reading the Bible because I knew He usually gave me some new thoughts while I was reading the Bible so that I was able to understand His will better. But I did not know which specific book or verse would help me in that particular situation. I just decided to read it from the beginning—Genesis. The Lord showed me this.

"After Abram returned from defeating the enemies, the king of Sodom said to Abram, "Give me the people and keep the goods for yourself.

"But Abram said to the king of Sodom, "I have raised my hand to the Lord, God Most High, Creator of heaven and earth, and have taken an oath that I will accept nothing belonging to you, not even a thread or the thong of a sandal,

"so that you will never be able to say, 'I made Abram rich.'"

— Genesis 14:21-23

When I read that, I knew exactly what God was telling me. I understood the scriptures like this.

If I hired the lawyer as my immigration lawyer to extend my work visa and get my green card afterward, I would always say that the lawyer (the king of Sodom) helped me (Abram) get my extended work visa and green card. (I made Abram rich.)

Then the priceless time that I shared with God through the prayers, tears, fasting and devotion would disappear and His glory would be replaced by the lawyer's name.

At the very moment, I decided not to hire ANY lawyer from now on to extend my work visa or to get a green card but I would do it alone with help from God only. That was it! That was what God was trying to tell me. I got the clear answer from God that I did not need any lawyer to stay in the country. I knew that it was Him who brought me out of Korea and to the U.S., like He brought Abraham to a new land. It was going to be God only who was going to provide me with what I needed as He did to Abraham. I just had to find the purpose of Him why He brought me to this country. I wondered what my true mission is in this life.

I received a set of applications by mail from the immigration department to extend my work visa for another three years. It was basically applying for a brand new one so I had to start the process all over again. The two major differences from the first time were that I had a job to buy groceries and had my own place to stay this time. The situation was much better than the first time. However, since I was no longer a customer service representative but a prepress operator at the prepress department I had to get a new approval from the Department of Labor which would be used as one of the supporting documents to the immigration department.

When I submitted the application to get approval from the Department of Labor, they informed me that since they did not have the specific data on how much salary a prepress operator should make, I must contact at least 10 different companies that were similar in size of the company where I worked, then get each prepress manager's signature in order to prove that they all agree on my suggested income for my position. I didn't expect to get that kind of letter but I was thankful that it was not a rejection letter but they just asked for some information, ultimately to give me their approval.

I knew there were many printing companies in Minnesota but I did not know which companies to visit, so I went to our plant manager. When I explained to him that I had to visit ten different companies to get prepress managers' signatures, he chuckled and said, "That's it? Bring me a more difficult question next time."

Then he took out a thick Yellow Pages book and started writing down the company names and their phone numbers on his note pad. It was more than ten companies. I thanked him and got out of his office where his radio was turned on 24 hours a day 7 days a week.

Some companies were located outside of the Twin Cities. While I was driving to those companies, I thanked God that I could handle the matter because I was able to speak English to explain and that I had a car to visit the companies. I visited a dozen companies. 10 would have been fine but I visited two more to make sure that I got enough approval signatures to prove to the Department of Labor.

I called first to set up an appointment with each prepress manager then I explained why I needed their signatures. When I met them in person, they were all very kind to me and one of them jokingly offered me a job. After I received all the signatures, I submitted the evidence to the Department of Labor and received their approval right away. Then I applied for the work visa extension to the immigration department with required documents including the approval notice from the Department of Labor. I did not receive any letter from the immigration department asking for more supporting evidence but I got a notice of approval right away that I was allowed to legally stay and work in the U.S.A. for three more years.

When I got the notice of approval from the immigration department I wondered why I wanted to hire the immigration lawyer by spending money while God just let me have it with no sweat. I just wasted my $500 to the attorney and $300 at the airport as a penalty. I regretted that I wanted to do it my way and did not seek God first.

VISA SEEKER

I wanted to have a work visa sticker glued in my passport so that I could travel outside the U.S.A. and re-enter the country freely. What I had was just a letter of approval. In order to get the work visa I had to go out of the country. Korea was too far and Mexico was near but I did not speak Spanish so I decided to go to Canada. I searched for a U.S. Embassy where work visa service was available. I found one in Calgary and I set up an appointment. First come first serve did not work. They only accepted people who made an appointment ahead of time. My plan was flying in on the first day, having an interview on the second day, getting the visa and fly back on the third day.

I arrived at the Calgary International Airport. The immigration officer asked me the purpose of my trip to Canada. I said I had a visa interview appointment and showed him the appointment schedule sheet. He stamped on my passport, "**VISA SEEKER**"

I arrived at the Youth Hostel Calgary to spend the next three days. I checked in my room. Everything was clean and it was just the right place for me to stay for a short period of time. I saw an Asian guy with a jar of Kimchi in the kitchen. He was eating Kimchi with white sandwich bread. I knew right away that he was Korean. What he needed was not the white sandwich bread but white steamed hot rice to eat with the Kimchi.

I told him, "You must be Korean. I can tell by your Kimchi jar."

"Hahaha! Yes, I am. Are you Korean too?"

"Yes."

"Do you want to try this Kimchi with my sandwich bread? They don't go well together but it's edible."

"Oh, no thank you. I am fine."

We introduced each other. His name was Min-Ho.

Min-Ho was a runaway groom. He was supposed to marry his girlfriend. They set a wedding date but he was not sure whether it was the right thing to do. So he just left with no plan what so ever. He did not know when he would go back to Korea. I told him that I was going to stay at the Youth Hostel only for a few days until I get my visa and had nothing else to do besides the visa business. He said he was invited to a Korean pastor's house for dinner that night and asked me if I wanted to join him. I was not invited but he said he was going to ask the pastor if it would be okay to bring a guest.

Pastor Lee came to pick up Min-Ho. He introduced me to the pastor and asked him if it would be okay to go with me. He gladly said okay. When we went to Pastor Lee's house, his wife, Samonim, welcomed us. Sa-mo-nim was a generic title for wives of respected men in Korea. I apologized for being an unexpected guest that night.

Samonim said, "Don't mention it. It is just adding one more spoon on the table. We are glad to have you here."

Samonim made us Bi-Bim-Bab, which was a famous Korean dish of mixed vegetables and rice with hot chili sauce. I could tell right way that Pastor Lee and his wife were very humble and good servants of God by the way they talked and how they treated us. They knew that we were staying at the Youth Hostel and would leave the country soon. We were not going to stay there long and become their church members but they still showed us their warm hospitality and shared the Gospel. Min-Ho suggested that he was going to sing a song to Samonim to thank her for the delicious dinner. He sang a famous Korean gospel song—*You are born to be loved.* Samonim wiped her tears and thanked him. Pastor Lee prayed that I would get my work visa with no problem and go back to the U.S.A. safely. We exchanged our contact information and he gave us a ride back to the Youth Hostel.

The room at the Youth Hostel had bunk beds. I used the lower one. Before I went to bed I set the alarm clock that I brought for 6:00 A.M. I went to sleep early to get up early. I wanted to be on time for the visa interview. I woke up early, double checked what I needed to bring, and headed out to the consulate. It was extremely windy and icy cold to walk. I wondered how Canadian people survived in that kind of extreme weather every winter. But the weather was not my main concern at the moment. The center of my entire world was focused on my visa interview. I could not think of anything else.

I arrived too early—30 minutes before the consulate opened the door. I anxiously waited outside. They opened the door on time and let me in. I was the very first person who arrived. I took a waiting number and sat down. Everything was all set. It was just a matter of time. After a couple of hours I would get a brand new work visa in my passport and my true American Dream would start from that moment! I was excited and prayed to God that I would have no problem with speaking in English for the interview. I thought that I might want to go and have a couple of beers to celebrate later.

When my number was called I walked to the officer at the window and submitted my visa appointment letter, passport and the notice of approval from the immigration department. He checked the documents carefully and told me to wait for a moment. He walked away with my documents and came back.

He said, "It seems that you have all the required papers in order. However, we cannot give you a visa at this time because of your passport."

All of sudden I could not believe what I just heard.

"Excuse me?"

He opened my passport and said, "Do you see the lamination on the photo here? This corner is damaged. I am sure this is your photo and your passport but other people can replace the photo when it is damaged like this. You need to get a new passport."

Are you kidding me?!! Where and how in the world could

I get a new passport all of sudden? I need the visa today or tomorrow afternoon at least so that I could catch a flight going back to Minneapolis in the evening. I had no money and no place to stay in Canada until I got a new passport. I booked the Youth Hostel only for two nights. Why is this happening to me? Why does it have to be NOW? I was so full of confidence that I could get the visa right away. I had all the approval notices. It was already a done deal. But now, because the lamination of the photo was slightly cut, he would not give me the visa? Who in the world could ever imagine that the transparent lamination would cause a big problem in my life especially when I was broke and had nothing? I just could not accept the reality. I could feel that my face was turning red and getting hot.

The officer said, "Don't worry. There is a Korean Embassy nearby, just a few blocks away from here. Here's the address and a phone number. When you have a new passport, come back. Then I will give you a visa."

All of sudden, I had a tiny hope. I thanked the officer and walked out of the building.

"Thank you, God. At least there is a Korean Embassy nearby!"

It was easy to find the office. I walked to the receptionist and forced myself to smile.

"Hi! Is this the Korean Embassy? I need to get a new passport."

The receptionist kindly replied, "I am sorry. We are not a Korean Embassy. Some people misunderstand that we are a Korean Embassy but we are not. We help Koreans with their international business in Canada. You need to go to Vancouver to get a passport."

"Vancouver?"

"Yes, there is a Korean Embassy in Vancouver."

"How far is it from here? Can I go by bus?"

"Yes, you can but it is a little too far to go by bus. You might want to fly. There are many commuter flights from here to Vancouver."

Then she handed me a piece of paper on which she already wrote the Korean Embassy address and phone number. Since many people mistakenly visited them, she probably wrote down the Embassy information in advance and gave it to people like me. I thanked her and came out of the building. It was still cold and windy outside. I didn't know where I was going but just walked.

I already figured out why it was happening. I knew from my previous experiences that Satan always tried to jeopardize me when things were going well with me. I knew I was going to get the visa for sure but Satan was not happy about it at all. He had to do something bad to stop me from being happy because it was his pathetic job.

"Satan replied, "But stretch out Your hand and strike everything he has, and he will surely curse You to Your face."

"The Lord said to Satan, "Very well, then, everything he has is in your hands, but on the man himself do not lay a finger."

"Then Satan went out from the presence of the Lord."

—Job 1: 11:12

So Satan had God's permission to jeopardize my visa matter and see how I become miserable and blame God for what's happening.

I asked myself, "What should I do now?"

First, I decided to go take a picture for the new passport. So I found a nearby photo shop. I did not want my passport picture to remind me that I had a sad moment each time I saw the passport photo for the next five years. I smiled on purpose when the photo was taken. I took care of the photo business easily. Then, I found a public phone booth nearby and called an airline to see if there were any seats available. Luckily I didn't have to worry about a seat. So I called the Korean Embassy in Vancouver next.

A young woman's voice came out, "Hi. This is Korean Consulate, Vancouver. How may I help you?"

"Hi. I need to get a new passport. How long does it take?"

"It takes about two weeks."

I tried to be calm but felt Satan was punching me in the gut. I explained to her my urgent situation and what I heard at the U.S. Consulate that morning.

"I have no place to stay for two weeks and have no money. I need a new passport by tomorrow. Could you please help me?"

There was a little pause then she said, "Let me ask Mr. Consular. Could you please hold?"

"Yes, of course. Thank you."

While holding I kept praying. "My Lord, Please help me. Satan is crazy now trying to jeopardize my life again. You heard what the officer said to me at the U.S. Consulate this morning. I need a new passport. The Korean Embassy says it takes about two weeks but I need it by tomorrow. This is impossible without Your help. You are my only hope. Please help me. I believe You will. I pray this in the name of Jesus. Amen."

"Hello. I explained your situation to Mr. Consular and he said if you could arrive here by 8:50 A.M. tomorrow morning, we will try our best to issue your new passport by the end of the day. Can you come here by 8:50 A.M. tomorrow morning?"

Thankfully there was one hour time difference between Calgary and Vancouver. So even if I would take the 7:00 A.M. first flight it would still be 7:30 A.M. in Vancouver when I arrive there. Then I calculated another hour from getting out of the airplane to riding in a taxi and arrival at the Embassy building. I could arrive there at 8:30 A.M. at least.

"Yes, of course. Thank you so very much. However, I need your guarantee that you will give me the passport by the end of tomorrow. I need to change my flight ticket right after talking with you here, so if you don't guarantee, then I cannot book the flight coming back tomorrow evening. I have no place to stay in Vancouver. I know I am asking you too much but could you please promise me that you will give me the passport by the end of tomorrow for sure? I am really sorry but I have no choice. Please."

She paused for a second and said, "I understand. But you

must arrive here at 8:50 A.M. at the door. You cannot be late. Otherwise, I cannot guarantee you."

"I swear that I will be standing at the door at 8:50 A.M. tomorrow morning. Thank you so much." I hung up the phone. I felt that I talked with an angel who was sitting at the Korean Consulate.

Then I called an airline company to book a flight. The air fare was about 300 Canadian dollars. I did not have a credit card with me which I regretted so much that I didn't bring one. I never dreamt of going to Vancouver to get a new passport. I called home to see if my roommates were able to help me with some money. If they were, I was going to ask them to deposit in my checking account so that I could spend it in Canada. Lisa was not home but Amy answered the phone. She said she was broke and did not have any spare money to lend. She said she was so sorry. I said I understood and hung up the phone.

My checking account was pretty much dried out because I spent all my money to buy the round trip tickets between the U.S. and Canada and paid for the Youth Hostel. But I wanted to check my savings account just in case although I did not remember when I saved money last time. The balance of the savings account was a little over $280. I was surprised that I had the money in the savings account. I wondered how come I did not spend the money. Somehow I totally forgot about the money up until now. The round trip airfare between Calgary and Vancouver was about $300. However because of the different currency rate between the U.S. dollar and Canadian dollar, I was able to come up with $300 Canadian dollars with the money from the savings account. What a miracle I just had! I said, "My Lord, did you put the money in the savings account for me?"

So I booked the flight going to Vancouver the next morning and coming back in the evening of the same day. Then I called the airline company to adjust my return flight schedule to the U.S. Thankfully there was no penalty fee to change the flight. After I made all the necessary phone calls, I came back to the Youth Hostel and sent an e-mail to my company. I explained my situation that I would return to work as soon as I get back to the U.S. after the visa matter was settled. I also extended my stay at the Youth Hostel. I felt much better and relieved after taking care of everything. There was nothing else that I could do more. I just thanked God that everything was in order now.

I did not see Min-Ho and there was nothing to do at the hostel. So I went out to kill time. I found a sports bar and walked in. I ordered a beer and looked around. Everyone seemed to be having a good time. They had no idea what kind of crazy visa matter I had to deal with that morning. I felt that I just got off of a crazy roller coaster and wondered why my life had to be stuck with visa matters constantly.

There was a woman sitting next to me. We said "Hi" to each other. Her name was Joanne. She was in her 40's and talked really loud. She asked me where I was from.

"Originally from Korea but now I live in the U.S."

She asked me if it was my first time to Canada. I said "Yes." She welcomed me loudly and we cheered with our beer. She told me that she had breast cancer and had surgery to remove both of her breasts.

"Oh, I am so sorry to hear that."

"It's okay. I didn't like having breasts anyway."

Joanne and I instantly became drinking buddies after drinking a couple of beers.

"I got two tickets for the hockey game tonight. You want to go with me? You should go with me. I like you", she said.

"Why do you have two tickets? Were you going to go to the game with someone?"

"Yes, but the loser didn't show up. It's better. I want to go with you."

Joanne and I walked to the hockey arena as if we were long lost friends. The game was between the Calgary Flames and one of the U.S. hockey teams. Everyone screamed loud to cheer for the Calgary Flames. Although the U.S. team was not from Minnesota, I wished the U.S. team would do well and cheered for them quietly.

As soon as the U.S. team scored, the Canadians booed all together. Then the Flames scored soon after. The Canadian fans were all up and became so wild. They seemed to be almost getting out of control, especially Joanne. She held her beer can high up and talked to the people next to us ever so loudly.

"Hey, my friend Nami is from America. She is here to get her visa!"

I did not understand why she was telling people about me all of sudden. When the Flames got another score, Joanne was totally out of control. She pulled her sweatshirt high up as if she was going to take it off. I became so nervous but she actually showed people her breastless chest that showed obvious scars. She stood up and shouted.

"Hey guys! I don't have breasts! Look at me. Yeeaah!!!"

People were disgusted by her unexpected behavior and started leaving their seats. Some of them threw garbage at her and cursed. I pulled her shirt down and helped her to calm down. I apologized to the people and tried to excuse her that she was pretty drunk.

People told us, "You two should leave."

She acted as if she was so excited but somehow I felt so sad. She was mentally unstable. She should have taken some psychological help before or after having the breast cancer surgery. I did not feel like watching anymore of the game. I persuaded her to leave with me and we got out of the arena.

We went back to the same bar and had more drinks. I did not eat hardly any food all day long. The shocking news at the U.S. Consulate that morning made me lose my appetite. I did not feel like eating anything. Joanne and I were both quite drunk. I knew that I had to go back to my room and get ready for the important trip to Vancouver the next morning but I could not just leave her alone. I felt so sorry for her. I asked her if she could go home by herself. She said no problem. She and I exchanged our addresses and phone numbers. Then we said good bye.

It was a little after midnight when I returned to the hostel. As soon as I entered the lobby I felt my muscles were loosened by the warm temperature inside. If there was no wall, I either could have gone all the way to the left or all the way to the right. I hit the left wall and bounced back to walk in the isle then I hit the right wall and bounced back to walk. When I walked in my room, I crashed on the bed. I had to get up at five o'clock in the monring to get ready and catch the seven o'clock flight going to Vancouver. I had less than five hours to sleep.

Did I set the alarm? Maybe Yes or maybe No. I was not sure. Let me set the alarm now. I set it at 5:00 A.M. OK. Now I can really go to sleep. I was dizzy and hungry but the sleepiness overwhelmed. What I experienced that day felt absolutely like a bad dream. But the bad dream was only beginning.

I did not know how long I had been sleeping. I did not hear the alarm go off. I was not sure if I was sleeping or half awake. I kept telling myself I should not miss the flight. What time is it now?

It must have been really windy outside. I thought I was still sleeping but somehow I was able to hear a rattling noise caused by a couple of small pebbles in an empty can rolling from side to side. I thought I was dreaming but the constant rattling noise became irritating and I could not sleep any more.

I slowly opened my eyes and felt my own body was so heavy like soaked cotton. I felt sick. I barely got up and dragged myself to the shower room at the Youth Hostel where I stayed. It was a little after five o'clock in the morning. I was glad that I heard the annoying can noise. If it was not there I probably was not able to get up. I did not know what happened to the alarm. I did not hear it or maybe I was unable to set the alarm properly the night before. I wondered how the can ended up tossed right under my window with the pebbles in it. I believed God woke me up that morning.

I called a cab and headed to the airport. I was so sick and could not sit up. I was lying on the back seat. Then all of sudden, I wanted to check if I brought my old passport. Although I was going to get a new one, I still needed to show it at the airport in Canada. I was a foreigner there. I realized that I forgot to bring my old passport. I felt so dumb and stupid. I did not know how to apologize to the taxi driver.

"I am soooooo sorry. I did not bring my passport. Would you please go back to the Youth Hostel? I need to grab my passport. I am really sorry. I made a terrible mistake. I had too much to drink last night."

The female driver said, "Not a problem. I understand. We all make mistakes sometimes."

She could have thought that I was a stupid drunk girl but at least she did not show any unpleasant manner to me. I ran into the room and found my passport then ran back to the taxi.

"Thank you so much for waiting. Thank you."

When I was checking in to get my boarding pass, the airline ticket agent kindly asked me, "Excuse me. Are you okay? You look so pale."

I was hardly able to stand up. The lack of food all day long the day before and drinking too much made me sick. My head was spinning and I collapsed right in front of the check-in counter. I was so cold and shivering. I just wanted to sleep forever. I did not want to go anywhere. I was not sure why I had that much to drink the night before. I drank more than usual and it was too late for regret.

The ticket agent asked me if I could travel in that condition. I said I must go. Soon a wheelchair was brought and they put me on the wheelchair. While I was being pushed on the wheelchair to the gate, I felt people were staring at me. I was ashamed of myself that I was sick because I had a hangover. So I had my head down and pretended that I was really sick. As soon as I was seated in the airplane I covered myself with a blanket but a thin blanket was not nearly enough. I was still cold. I asked for another blanket. The flight attendant brought me two more blankets. I felt like vomiting. I had the sick bag ready but since I had no food, nothing came out. I was glad that no one was sitting next to me. I laid down on the three seats and closed my eyes to get some sleep.

Million Dollar Passport

When I got off the airplane I felt a little bit better after sleeping for an hour at least. I got out of the airport as soon as possible then took a taxi going to the Korean Consulate. I wanted to make sure that the driver was not taking a longer route to charge me more so I told him that I had an appointment at 8:30 A.M. He said it was not that far from the airport and soon we arrived in front of the Korean Consulate building. I walked in the elevator with a few other people. When the elevator door was closing, I saw myself in the reflection of the metal door. I was ashamed of what I had done the night before by drinking heavily and thanked God so much that He let me make it to Vancouver that morning. I felt warm tears spring up. *Thank you, God. I made it!*

I was early but I was glad that I made it as I promised to the woman on the phone from the previous day. As soon as the door was open I told the woman at the consulate that I talked with someone yesterday regarding my passport. She said it was her and handed me an application to fill out. There were a few other people who looked like students. I bet that they didn't have to have their passport in one day. They didn't seem to have a hangover either. I felt that I was the only one whose destiny was bound with visa and passport in this life. When I gave my application to the woman, she said she was going to ask Mr. Consular to take a look at it, so I should go somewhere and come back around 3:00 P.M. I thanked her sincerely and went to a coffee shop nearby.

At the coffee shop I was so sleepy but I could not sleep there. I stayed there only for a couple of hours by fighting with sleepy eyes and a heavy head then went back to the consulate building. I went in to the women's bathroom and tried to take a nap sitting on the toilet. I was nervous that I might snore and someone might come in to check. I regretted again and again that I drank too much but it was too late.

I kept looking at the clock. The other people who came in with me were all gone and even some of the employees at the consulate were leaving for the day. I was the only one left and waiting. Where is my new passport? Are they going to give it to me today or not? The clock was ticking. I had to catch the returning flight as soon as I received the new passport. The woman who was helping me came out of Mr. Consular's office and called me finally.

She said, "Mr. Consular approved. Here is your new passport."

Oh, my Lord! I wanted to bow down to her right there. I

wanted to give her whatever I had but I had nothing. I thanked her so many times. I also thanked Mr. Consular although I did not see him. I asked God, "My Lord, did you put the angel lady in the office for me?"

I walked out of the Korean Consulate building with a brand new passport issued in less than eight hours then took a taxi going back to the airport. I felt like I was holding a million dollar passport in my hands. Although I had a smiling photo in the passport, God and I knew the true story behind the smile and I was not so thrilled to see the photo. I finally came back to the Youth Hostel but there was no celebration for the new million dollar passport.

"No more drinking, you stupid!"

I went to bed early that night.

"As a dog returns its vomit, so a fool repeats his folly."

— Proverbs 26:11

I arrived at the U.S. Consulate early the next morning. I took a waiting number and walked to the same officer when he called my number. I gave him my brand new passport. I felt like yelling at him.

"HERE IS MY NEW PASSPORT THAT YOU ASKED FOR!!! NOW GIVE ME THE FREAKING VISA!!! SO I CAN LEAVE!!!"

But I lowered my voice and kindly told him, "You told me the other day to get a new passport because of the damaged lamination. Here is my new passport. The address you gave me was not the Korean Embassy by the way. There is no Korean Embassy in Calgary. I had to fly to Vancouver to get this passport yesterday."

He paused for a moment and looked at my eyes straight then asked, "Do you mean that you went all the way to Vancouver and got this new passport in one day?"

"Yes, Sir!"

He could not believe that I obtained a new passport in such a short period of time. He examined the passport and looked at me again with a hint of a smile this time. He seemed to be thinking, "What a crazy Korean woman!"

"Your visa will be ready tomorrow morning."

What?

He told me that he was going to give me the visa when I bring a new passport. Why did he need another whole day to give me a visa? I really wanted to ask him, "Could you just give me the visa now?"

But I did not want to argue with him and have him upset. I hid my boiling emotion inside and kindly responded with a forced smile on the face.

"OK. Thank you."

I was glad that I booked my return flight leaving the next day.

I returned to the U.S.A. with the brand new passport and the brand new work visa. I had no trouble at the airport. I did not need a lawyer. God helped me with everything. I did not have to worry about a visa for another three more years.

Dubliner

Amy said there was an Irish bar not that far from where we lived so we should check it out. The bar was pretty packed and my eyes had a burning sensation as we entered the smoke filled room. We ordered beer and blended in with the loud crowd right away. I didn't know what the Irish band was singing but it was something about whisky in the jar. People were clapping and singing out loud as if they were a choir.

Amy asked me with her high pitch, "So what do you think? Do you like this place?"

"Yeah, I like it. I really like the Irish music."

A guy next to us said "Hi" to us. We started chatting, drinking and played darts together. The Irish bar did not have a kitchen so they did not serve any food but had free popcorn in the corner. We were getting hungry. The guy suggested moving to his place next for more drinks and food. Amy and I didn't want to go home yet but wanted to continue our party so we decided to follow him and his buddies. I don't remember his name but he said he was a chef for his work.

The guy's house was messy. CDs, video games, DVDs, and beer bottles were all over. The chef guy brought us shots. "Bottom up!"

We drank it up right away. He said it wouldn't take too long to make us spaghetti so have a seat and drink more beer while waiting. His friends watched football on television and sipped beer. I did not like watching football so just sat there drinking. Amy was really drunk especially after the shot. She could not sit up straight. She leaned on the couch with her face down. I had a bad feeling when I saw Amy was totally trashed and could not even speak. I thought we should go home. I didn't want to let Amy be like that.

I excused to the guys and said, "I am really really sorry but I think I should bring Amy back home now. She is not doing well."

The chef said, "Spaghetti will be done soon. She can sleep on the couch."

But my thoughts were, "No, no, no. Get out of here right now. Take Amy home."

So I said, "I know, but once she falls asleep then it will be too hard for me to bring her home. I am responsible for her. I need to bring her home now. I think she is sick. I am really sorry. We gotta go. Thank you for the spaghetti though."

I had Amy stand up against my body and walked out of the house. I put her in the back seat of my car and drove away from the guy's house. While driving I realized how stupid I was to follow a guy to his house whom I did not know. Amy and I came home safely that night but we were very lucky. Thousands of different things could have happened that night not only at the guy's house but also on the road when I was driving drunk. I only had to drive a few miles but nonetheless, we were so lucky that night.

I used to sit at my old studio apartment and stare at the blank wall for hours in the past. But now I did not like sitting in a quiet room alone at all. I wanted to be surrounded by people. It didn't have to be with someone but just being among people was better. While sitting at a bar, usually my thoughts were trying to decide whether I would stay in the U.S. or go back to Korea after the expiration of my work visa. I did not want to go through another visa process. I was tired of dealing with visas. I missed my family and wanted to settle down in Korea. I thought six years of job experience in the U.S. would give me some open doors to get a job in Korea at least. So my thoughts were leaning toward going back to Korea.

I got excited by the new plan that I was finally going back to Korea. I ordered another beer and kept thinking more. I remembered the sexual discrimination and bullies that I experienced in Korea. At least in the U.S., I didn't have to worry about sexual discrimination. I never felt that I was sexually discriminated in the U.S. I always felt that the men I worked with treated me fair. Besides no one asked me how old I was or if I was married or not while in the U.S. In Korea I had to mark my birth date and whether I was married or not on my job application. I really appreciated the U.S. system. However I thought I might be able to avoid those issues of my age or sexual discrimination in Korea because of my unique job experiences in the U.S. Nothing was confirmed. I just kept thinking back and forth between staying in the U.S. and going back to Korea.

I tried several different Irish bars in the Twin Cities but I liked the one nearby my house because I did not have to drive long after drinking. One night I saw a bunch of guys as a group. Among them there was an Asian guy. He looked like a Korean to me. I thought he might have been adopted. Next to him there was an American guy wearing a newsboy hat and he kept smiling at me.

Do I know him? I don't think so. Whatever… I ignored him first but I noticed several times that he kept looking at me and smiling. Then he came over to me finally and introduced himself.

"Hi, I am Matt."

"Hi!"

He asked me if I came to the bar often. I said "Yes." He said he came often too but never saw me before. We drank together and chatted. He said I was an interesting person to talk with and asked for my phone number. He was a few years younger than me. I was not interested in dating such a young guy but I gave him my phone number just to hang out for a drink sometime. He gave me his phone number on a dollar bill. I thought that was clever. There had been a number of guys who gave me their phone numbers before but I never met any guy who wrote his number on money so I kept the money.

The very next day I had to drive up to Detroit Lakes, MN. That was about 200 miles to the Northwest of Minneapolis. I wanted to see my favorite Christian gospel singers at a three-day gospel music family event. There were thousands of people gathered on the camp ground. I brought a tent that I borrowed from my co-worker and tried to set it up but did not know how to do it properly. After struggling with the tent for a while, I just decided to sleep in the car. I parked at a less crowded site. Everyone seemed to be with their families and friends but I was alone. I did not have any Christian friends to come along with. Sometimes I participated at a single's group at church but most of them were younger than me. After worshiping I went out with them to socialize several times but I did not feel comfortable or that I fit in the young group. Rather I felt much more comfortable chatting with drunken guys at bars.

At the gospel music festival I felt really isolated and lonely. I had no one to talk to among the thousands of people for three days. I thought about the guy, Matt, whom I met at the Irish bar the night before. I wondered if he was Christian but I could not ask him to come with me to the festival. He could have thought that I was a desperate crazy woman to go out with him. I wished to go home soon but my favorite band, *Avalon,* was scheduled to sing on the very last day. I drove 200 miles to see the band. I had to stay.

Everyone was with someone but me. I was a little bit embarrassed when other people glanced at me wondering what I was doing alone at the family festival. I hardly saw any Asian people either. I parked my car in a somewhat remote area from other people not to be noticed. I lowered the car seat and pushed it back to stretch to get some sleep. I wished that I would not go sleepwalking among the campers in the middle of the night. I didn't know how long I fell asleep or what time it was but I opened my eyes after having an awful dream then realized that I was sleeping in the car behind dark trees to hide myself from others. I was so scared. I couldn't see other campers around at all. I could not stay there any longer. I wanted to go home but it was too late to drive 200 miles back home and I had not seen my favorite band yet.

Nonetheless, I had to move my car and be closer to other people so that I would not to be scared in the dark remote area by myself. I slowly drove and parked right in front of the restroom and shower area. There was a super bright light hung up high. It was too bright to get some good sleep but I was not scared any more. How could I have a bad dream in such brightness and with so many people walking by? Well at least I felt much better and safe there.

On the very last day, my favorite band *Avalon* came out on the stage. I was so excited to see them. My scary and uncomfortable camp nights finally paid off. I thought I was so lucky to see them in the U.S. If I were in Korea, it could have been almost an impossible dream. I really enjoyed their music and was glad that I stayed until the last day of the festival.

Matt called me to see how my trip to the festival was and wanted to get together. We started getting together for drinks. Since I was still considering going back to Korea, I didn't feel obligated that I date anyone. One day he sent me a card. He said how happy he had been since he met me and enjoyed talking with me. It was very sweet of him but I did not feel comfortable to develop our relationship without letting him know that I was married and divorced once in Korea. I told him about my past and said that a lot of girls would love to date him because he was a dental school student and would become a dentist someday. I was rather more interested in finding a cool looking cowboy as I really liked horseback riding quite a bit. He said past is past and give him a chance to get to know me.

I called my father and asked him what he would think of

me if I dated an American guy. He said, "Why don't you just pack and come back to Korea right away!"

He was not happy about my idea of dating an American guy at all. But when my parents visited me in the U.S., I introduced Matt to them. After spending time together for about a week, my father said that Matt seemed to be a very nice young man. I knew my father would like him. So I got my parents' approval of dating him officially.

Matt also invited me to his parents' house for dinner. When I arrived there he was busy with preparing the dinner. He made lasagna. It was unusual to see a guy cooking in the kitchen. In Korea, usually mothers would prepare dinner especially when they had guests. I met his parents and one of his sisters. They were kind and asked me about my background in general and my family in Korea.

When Matt had to study for his upcoming exams we did not get together until it ended. One time he had to travel to Northern Minnesota for clinical volunteer work for two weeks but he visited me over the weekend. I was very impressed that he drove all the way to see me. Our relationship was going well at the beginning but I had a weird feeling that he was going to ditch me as soon as he graduated from school. The more I spent time with him the more I became insecure somehow and I was not sure whether I should return to Korea or not.

One day he pointed to a bar when we were driving by and asked me if I had been to the place. Instead of saying yes or no, my response was "Why? Have you? Who did you go with?"

I became ridiculously insecure, jealous and, unreasonable. We were at the Irish bar one evening with his friends. Matt was talking with his friends. I hated him talking to his friends and not paying attention to me. I thought he was ignoring me and I got upset again for no reason. I said, "I want to leave. You are interested in talking to your friends but not me. I guess you don't like me anymore."

I stood up on my feet and walked out of the bar. I was expecting him to follow me and take me back but he did not like that at all. He said, "If you leave now I am not coming after you.

You want to leave then leave. I don't care."

So I went home and was very upset. I knew I should not act like that but I did not know why. My jealousy and insecure attitude were getting worse every day and I felt that I was going crazy. When Matt did not call me, I had nobody to talk. I felt so stupid about my action and became so miserable. So I called him and apologized.

His final board exam was coming. He was going to hire an assistant but she could not find a baby sitter, so he asked me if I could be his assistant. *Are you kidding me?* How could I become his dental assistant when I had no idea about dentistry? He said that other students were going to have their mothers, sisters, or girlfriends as their assistants and he was going to show me what to do during the exam. So he took me to his dental school where his exams were going to be and showed me what to do.

On the day of the board exam he brought in two patients who had not seen a dentist for a long time. Their treatments were free and Matt also paid them for participating in the exam. When Matt started cleaning the teeth for his first patient I saw lots of bleeding. Obviously the patient never flossed his teeth. I was disgusted to see it. My job was holding the suction tube for Matt. Once a procedure was completed, I took the patient out to have an examiner take a look, then I brought the patient back to him for the next procedure. Matt told me that I could go out and have lunch during an hour lunch break, but I could not eat anything after seeing the bleeding mouth. After the lunch break, I saw some students packed and leaving already. I was glad that I could leave soon too. But Matt and some other students showed no sign of leaving. I wondered if Matt was not doing his tasks in time so he was being delayed. I worried if he would fail the exam, so I asked him why he should stay longer when other students were going home. He said those students were hygienists and their exams were over now. Only dental students were left for more exams. I was relieved to hear that. It was not the first time I doubted him out of ignorance.

I remembered when I went to his hockey game one night. I had no idea what the hockey game rules were. Matt played as a goalie in a local amateur hockey team. All of his teammates were playing awful. I understood that they played hockey as a hobby but they just hit the puck from one side to the other back and forth all night. Matt was the only one who was so busy to block the pucks from the other team. The other goalie was doing nothing but standing on the ice or sipping water once in a while. I was so bored to watch them playing. It was so cold in the arena and I wanted to go home. All of sudden I saw Matt was leaving the goaltender position. *How could he give up now!!* His net was empty and the other players were rushing toward the goaltender to score. They easily scored and cheered. Matt gave up because his team was playing terrible and he did not want to play anymore. *How disappointing…* I was so disappointed in him. I saw him being upset and throwing his gear on the floor. *He is showing his temper now!!* I started thinking that I had to break up our relationship. *I should not be with someone with no responsibility and so impatient. He would betray me someday for sure…*

I walked to my car as soon as the game was over and waited for him to come out. I wanted to say good bye and leave. I was preparing what I should say to break up with him. Then a guy whom I knew through Matt walked out of the arena first. He recognized me and said it was a good game and the goal they scored with a minute left helped at the end. He said his team was nervous at the end when the goalie was pulled. They were concerned Matt's team might tie the score. I said, "Oh, yeah, it was a real fun game to watch. Congratulations! Hahaha! Have a good night!"

Then I thought *"Why would they be nervous with no goalie on the other team?"* Fortunately, I figured it out that it is a team's strategy to put an extra skater on the ice to try to tie the game when little time is left. When Matt was walking toward my car with his heavy bag on his shoulder, I felt so sorry that I was upset and disappointed in him out of my own ignorance. He was sweaty and steam was coming out of his hat even though it was freezing cold outside. I just said, "You did a great job!"

Matt was raised in a Catholic family and attended Catholic schools until his dental school. I still remember that I asked him if he was Christian before we started dating. He said, "Yes."

I wanted to make sure that I was dating a guy who had the

same faith in God. I didn't want to force a guy I was dating to become a Christian or argue about our two different religions for the rest of my life. We started going to our non-denominational evangelical church where I initially started attending the American Sign Language worship services. We dated steadily even though I was awfully ridiculous for silly reasons from time to time and caused arguments because of that. It was me who usually ended up apologizing and asking for forgiveness. Thankfully, he accepted my apology each time and we moved on. The more we spent time together I realized how much I relied on him, emotionally. With no family on my side close by, he was probably the closest friend I ever had for a long time. He proposed to me to marry him about seven months after his graduation from the dental school.

Green Card

I submitted an application for a green card based on employment sponsored by Craig's publishing company. Craig's business was heavily related to the print factory in Korea where I worked as a project manager. So this time Craig became my sponsor for my green card. I had to get a green card before my H1B work visa expired. Sometimes I had to go visit the immigration office in Bloomington, Minnesota to ask some questions. I tried to call the customer service number but I had to hold for so long, sometimes over 20 minutes. It was enough time to cook a pack of Ramyon noodles and eat while I was on hold on the phone. So I decided to visit and ask in person.

I went to the immigration office at eight o'clock in the morning expecting that I would speak to one of the officers and get some help but the guard at the gate said that I was too late. How could I be too late when it was only eight o'clock in the morning? He said the people waiting inside arrived there a couple hours earlier. Next day I went there before the business hour started and it was still dark outside. The door was closed and there was no one waiting at the door so I was glad that I was the very first person to arrive this time. I stood there and waited for the door to open soon. Then a guy showed up and told me that I should sign on the waiting list he handed over to me. There were numbers and names. About a hundred people's names were already listed on the yellow note pad. He said since it was too cold to stand and wait outside everyone was sitting in their cars and waiting. I asked him if it was a policy that the immigration office requested to put people's names on the list. He said "No" but they did it voluntarily. I looked around the parking lot and noticed that the parking lot was quite packed, indeed, and people were sitting in their cars looking at us to see what was going on.

I was upset that I was still too late even though I arrived there before the office was open. I went home again instead of putting my name down on the long waiting list. It would take forever to get in and talk to an officer. At my third attempt, I decided not to go to sleep but went to the immigration office around 1:30 A.M. I was the sixth person who arrived. I could not believe that there were still five people ahead of me already. When the office door was open and my number was called finally, it was already close to 8:30 A.M. I had to go to work by 9:00 A.M.

Next time when I had to visit the immigration office, I arrived there at 11:45 P.M. While I was driving to the office I thought what kind of crazy woman in the world would go to the immigration office at midnight to talk to an officer but I was glad that I was able to do it. Talking to an officer in person, showing the documents that I prepared, and getting their advice on what to do next was definitely helpful and beneficial to me. So I didn't even bother calling the customer service number anymore. There was another ambitious woman who arrived a little after midnight. She said she had the same experience that I had before so she decided to come really early. After 1:00 A.M., a few more people arrived.

This time I brought a spread sheet that I made as I expected that I would be the one arriving first. The list had a table of two columns for numbers and names. After writing down our names on the list, we could go in the cars and wait. Each time new people arrived, I asked them to write down their names on the list like what I was told before by other guys. I had to be in charge of the waiting list and make sure not to lose it as I was the first person who arrived there and I made the list, but there was a guy whose name was Mohammad. He was the third person to arrive there and he said to me, "It is cold here. Why don't you go in your car and get some sleep. Let me take care of this."

It was very kind of him to say that. His English was pretty good and the way he dressed was just like other American guys. I asked him what made him come to the immigration office. He said he was a student at a state university, majoring in computer science. He had some complicating cultural issues with his last name so he was often questioned about his legal status in the U.S. especially after 9/11. I wanted to chat with him more but I thanked him and went in my heated compact car.

Numerous cars constantly arrived at the parking lot as time went by. When I saw people who were arriving after 5:00 A.M., I thought, "You must be newbies and have no idea what's going on in this Immigration Parking Lot World. I doubt if you guys can talk to an officer today. You know what time I arrived here? 11:45 P.M. last night!"

I used to be frustrated and upset when I was told that I arrived there too late. This time I was so excited and wanted to enjoy every hour and minute at the parking lot because I was the very first person to get in!

About two hours before the office door was open, people started getting out of their cars and were lining up. So was I. It was still freezing cold and windy. If I had to use the bathroom then I told people behind me where I was going and would be back soon. I went to a gas station nearby, used the bathroom and got a hot coffee too. People who could afford immigration lawyers or people born in the country never had to experience that kind of thing. But to me it was not just a matter of financial reasons. If I wanted, I could have used a credit card and pay the lawyer fees but I promised God that I was not going to hire any immigration lawyer neither for work visa nor for a Green Card after the incident with the previous lawyer that I was almost going to hire.

Standing in the waiting line, I looked at the snow falling from the dark cobalt blue sky while sipping the coffee. Snow landed on the coffee cup and melted right away. I thanked God that I was able to visit the immigration office and talk to an officer for the next step to follow. Standing in the icy cold and sometimes below zero windy weather was not a fun thing to do but it definitely became one of my priceless memories in the U.S. and I thank God that He was with me all the way through.

The immigration office door was finally open and we all went in the warm heated building. It felt like all the hungry and cold refugees were finally saved by the good guys. We all passed through the security gate and took our number to be called. I saw a guy carrying a heavy suit case was called and bypassing us. I thought he must have been a lawyer and had a prescheduled appointment for his clients. But I did not envy his clients who didn't have to stand in the waiting line at all. I liked my way better and treasured my way because I believed that Jesus was my immigration lawyer.

5

The Last Birthday Party

Matt and I got married at our church a little less than three years after first meeting. My parents came over from Korea. My uncle and two cousins flew from California. Amy was my bride's maid and Lisa helped me with flowers, gifts, and other arrangement at the wedding. I wore a Korean traditional dress and Matt wore a nice suit and tie. I invited some of my close coworkers, a couple of church friends, Craig and Susan, Ben and Heather and Ben's parents. Most guests were from Matt's side. Although I did not have many family members, the entire guests made our wedding look a lot bigger than I expected and that made me feel special and blessed. Matt and I really enjoyed ourselves on our wedding day and we were truly happy to see our guests were having fun when we presented our wedding slide show at the reception dinner.

A few days after the wedding Matt and I drove 200 miles up North to Beaver Bay, Minnesota along with my parents to stay at a cottage house for three days. The cottage was a two story house with two bedrooms, a living room, a kitchen, a fire place and a Jacuzzi. It was the middle of March but still cold. We set the fire and enjoyed a beautiful view of Lake Superior. The next morning my mother got up early and urged me to get up and come to see something immediately. I wondered what it was about. There were several deer walking through the front yard and one of them was right next to our kitchen window. It was really quiet and calm outside. The birch trees were covered with thick snow and it was absolutely gorgeous. My father couldn't help but write a poem in the guest book about the magnificent scenery in the Minnesota Winter.

I prepared him a special dinner for his upcoming 60th birthday. I wanted to celebrate while he was with us in the U.S. We went out for snow shoeing, visited a light house and put our hands in the cold Lake Superior. We had a wonderful time. But somehow once in a while my father said he had an ongoing splitting headache. When we went out for snowshoeing once, we had to come back because his headache was getting worse. We stayed inside by the warm fireplace and enjoyed looking at the snow falling on the peaceful Lake Superior.

When we returned home my father had to get one of his decayed teeth out. I noticed that he had unusual bad breath which he did not have before. Matt said the decayed tooth might cause the bad breath. So he took my father to his clinic and extracted the decayed tooth easily with no sweat and advised my father to floss his teeth regularly. When we came home, I offered my father that I was going to give him a shoulder massage. I started massaging his shoulders and rubbing his back then I was so shocked how small he became over the years. I didn't realize it until then because he was wearing bulky winter outfits. His body had significantly shrunk and he was like a little teenage boy. He became so small and skinny. I felt so sorry that he had to work for his entire life, laboring long hours at construction work to support his family.

After four weeks of visiting for our wedding, my parents went back to Korea. As soon as they arrived home, my father was hospitalized the very next day at a university hospital. He was diagnosed with late stage lung cancer. The cancer was spread all over and there was not much to do to save him but he started taking chemotherapy.

When I called him I was not sure whether he was aware of his condition or not. He said after the treatments he would recover soon. Maybe he didn't want to scare me so he tried to sound positive. My brother, Woo, asked me why I did not send him back to Korea immediately when he was in such bad condition. I told him that I had no idea that his condition was that bad. I thought that he had headaches. When he complained that he had the constant headache, my mother and I both agreed that it was because he could not drink alcohol as much as he used to while he was staying with us. He used to drink every single day for most of his life. I believe that he knew something was wrong with him before he came to the U.S. for my wedding but he forced himself to come and tried to hide his pain.

Ever since my father was hospitalized my mother stayed at the hospital 24 hours a day to take care of him. She slept next to him on the floor and had a hard time to find time to go to bathroom in case he needed her. My mother told me that the hospital said to her and my dying father to pack and move to different rooms numerous times because other patients were constantly checking in and out. I did not understand why the hospital didn't check new patients in to other empty rooms but had to rotate the dying patients constantly. My mother was suffering from lack of sleep and was exhausted. I felt so sorry for her. If I were in Korea I could have visited them often but I could not go anywhere because I was thousands of miles away from them and I was told that I'd better not leave the country while my Green Card was in process. I learned that getting married does not make immigration issues magically disappear. A Green Card or work visa does not show up in your mailbox right after getting married. There is still an agonizing process of paperwork and waiting to go through.

Craig showed me a newspaper article one day which was about a new drug for lung cancer. It was really convincing news and I thought the new drug might save my father so I cut the newspaper article, highlighted the important parts and sent it to my father's doctor at the university hospital through express mail. I said that I would absolutely understand how busy he would be and probably did not have time to read my letter or the article especially written in English but I asked him if there was any chance that he might want to try the new drug to treat my father.

When I called my mother to see how she was doing, she asked me, "Did you call the doctor at this hospital?"

"I did not call but I sent him an article about a new lung cancer drug for father. Why?"

"The doctor came to our room with a group of medical school students last night. He asked how we were doing and apologized for how inconvenient it had been to move from room to room. He said we did not have to move anymore but we could stay in this room now. He also said, "You raised your children very well." He met One and Woo before to discuss what to do to treat your father. And he asked me if I had a daughter in America. It was very kind of him to visit us like that."

I did not expect the doctor would visit my parents but not only he visited them but also replied to me as well that he already knew about the new drug and he had been using the drug for his patients including my father.

I went to the immigration office again at midnight one night to line up. Standing in front of the office in the middle of the night was not a new thing anymore. I felt it became a part of my life now. When my number was called I walked to the officer and said in tears, "I need to travel to Korea right away. My father is dying."

I didn't mean to show tears but couldn't help it. I was desperate and frustrated whenever I thought about the feeling that I was stuck in the U.S. while my father was dying in the hospital and I couldn't do anything for him. The officer granted me permission to travel and re-enter the country. I had to book a flight right away to go to Korea. As soon as I got the traveling permit by mail from the immigration office, I was going to fly to Korea. When I came home after work I saw the answering machine blinking with number one. I always wished the answering machine would show number zero. I knew by instinct what the number one meant without playing the message. It was my brother One.

"Sis, father passed away not long ago. He went to heaven in peace. He did not struggle with pain. He was sleeping. So, don't worry. I am just calling to let you know."

Too late. He was gone already. I thought I was going to see him in a few days. Matt was there when I played the voice mail. He swallowed his tears and hugged me. When I thought that this moment would come eventually, I thought I would cry frantically but somehow I could not cry. I felt a total emptiness and became speechless. I could not say anything and I could not cry. My eyes lost focus. It was something beyond my ability or my control. I could not do anything. I should have been there with my father but I was thousands of miles away. I wanted to run fast but my feet were stuck on the ground and moved ever so slowly.

He was gone forever… It was too soon. He just turned sixty years old a couple of months before.

I arrived in Korea after his funeral was over. It was already getting hot and humid in late June. My parents' house looked like an abandoned house outside. The light blue paint on the entrance door and the front wall had been peeled off and looked so dirty and ugly. Other houses next to my parents' looked clean and well maintained. I walked in the house and met my widowed mother and my brother, Woo.

My mother looked so old and skinny since I saw her on my wedding day three months ago. I felt really sorry for her. I could understand how hard it must have been to sleep on the floor in the small hospital room night after night and had a hard time to find time to go to the bathroom. There was another patient besides my father in the same room. They shared the tiny room together. My mother had to let the other patient's family know where she was going. One time my mother had to get out of the shower room in the middle of washing her hair. She had endured really exhausting days and nights but she had pity on her dying husband and she prayed that he would go to a better place and rest in peace. She was so sorry that he had lived such a hard, restless, laboring life and ended up at the hospital at his early age.

When I walked in the house, there was my father's framed photo on a table. My mother talked to my father in the photo, "Your daughter is here."

I sat in front of the table and closed my eyes. I quietly talked to him in my heart.

The next morning my mother, my brother Woo, his family, and I went to the mountain where my father was buried. None of my uncles expected that my father, who was younger than them, would die before them so there was no grave site prepared until my father was hospitalized by the late stage lung cancer. My uncles and two of my older male cousins in the family gathered together to have a family meeting to discuss what to do for my father's grave site. My two younger brothers didn't know what to do for the burial site so they waited for the decision from the family meeting. My grandparents used to own some land and my first uncle inherited all of it. My uncles and cousins decided to have a family grave site on part of the land my first uncle inherited. The site was full of bushes and pine trees all around. They called in a crane, a dump truck, and hired some people to make a family grave site immediately. They decided to have eight graves on the top row for my uncles and their wives including my parents. The bottom row was for their sons and their wives. For the next generation, my uncles said it was not their responsibility.

When we were driving to the grave site, rain was pouring down as if the sky had holes. I was worried how we could get out of the car. The window wipers were busy to keep up with the infinite pouring rain. When we were getting closer to the grave site the sky was clearing and all of sudden the strong sun came out. The newly made walking path to the grave site was completely wet from the monsoon rain. The red clay road was really sticky to walk on. Our shoes were stuck in the wet mud pit and it was not easy to pull our feet up to step forward.

I saw my father's fresh grave from a distance. It was covered with new grass. My mother walked toward the grave first and said, "Your daughter came here to see you."

Father, I am here to see you. I wanted to see you before you went to heaven but I came too late. I am so sorry. I believe that you are in a better place now. No more pain. Thank you for everything that you have done for me. I will do my best to live my life and will not disappoint you. I will make you proud of me. Please rest in peace with God. I will see you again when I go to heaven.

My mother and my brother burned my father's old clothes there. My brother brought my father's old camera. He dug at the edge of my father's grave and buried the camera underneath. He said, "Dad used to like taking pictures. Dad, I brought your old camera. I am sure you would enjoy taking pictures in heaven."

Then he looked at me and said, "Hey sis, I think Dad stopped his tears as soon as he saw you. Look at the clear sky. I can't believe that we had such pouring rain on the way here."

When we returned home my mother was busy to cook for me. She wanted to feed me something special before I went back to America. While she was cooking, I went to a paint shop and bought two gallons of light blue paint and brushes. I started painting the entrance door and the front wall. It was unusual for a young Korean woman to paint her own house in Korea. Korean people usually hired professional painters or carpenters to paint or fix their houses. Men fixed small things for their houses but hardly any women did, especially painting the entrance door or the house wall. People who walked by stopped and watched me painting.

An old man stopped and said, "You need to finish the painting by the time I come back after I take care of my errands. The line at the bottom of the wall looks crooked. You need to fix it."

I responded, "Hahaha! OK. I will make sure that I will fix it and finish the paint job when you come back later."

When the door and the wall were painted with fresh new paint, the house looked much better and I felt much better too. I wished I lived closer to my mother then I could take good care of her.

My father had some pending invoices from his business. My brothers went over his notebooks and visited each person or company to pay the bills on behalf of our father with the money people gave us for condolences. Woo's wife worked for an insurance company for a few years back then and she suggested to me about getting insurance that would cover my parents' hospital fees in case they were hospitalized later and said it might be helpful someday. So I had been paying for the medical insurance for my parents for a few years. When my father was hospitalized with the lung cancer we were able to get the benefits from the insurance company and paid the hospital bills and the funeral fee with it. If God did not prepare us we could have had no money to pay for the expensive hospital bills and for the funeral. I thanked God countless times that He knew all and prepared us in advance.

While my father was in the hospital taking the chemotherapy, there was a pastor who used to visit my father. The pastor baptized him before he passed away. I asked my mother which church he was from. My mother and I visited the church on Sunday and expressed our appreciation. The pastor actually had me stand up and introduced me to his congregation that I came from America. I also sent a thank you card to the doctor who took care of my father. After visiting some of my close relatives I returned to the U.S. It was a bittersweet six week journey back to Korea.

How to use chopsticks

I submitted two different Green Card applications; one employment based and the other relative based. Although I was married to a U.S. citizen, it did not mean that I could work in the country automatically. The fiancé visa simply meant that I was allowed to stay in the U.S. legally. That's all. I had to get an approval from the Department of Labor separately. Neither of the two Green Cards came out before the H1B work visa expired. I had to quit my job at the printing company. I informed the company that my Green Card had been delayed and I was not sure when I was going to get it. Then the company gave me 100 days of a waiting period. I was told that they were going to hold my position for 100 days. When the 100 days were up I got a letter from the company notifying me that they no longer were holding my position at their company. I was sad but also grateful that they valued me so much that they would allow a waiting period like that.

The spousal based Green Card came out first. Since I had an approval to work from the Department of Labor, I started working at Craig's company part time while I was trying to find a full time job. In the meantime, I wanted to get another part time job so that I could support my mother in Korea. She had no income source after my father passed away. In Korea most parents supported their children financially for their education, spending money and living expenses until their children get their jobs. Living with parents until children get married was not a strange thing in Korea. Parents expected their children to live with them. Children didn't have to pay for rent or groceries. However, once children had a job and were married, it was their turn to take care of their parents. It was not required and not everyone did it but it was considered as a virtue to take care of their parents.

Matt and I were doing alright but he was still recently graduated and had a hard time getting consistent hours of work at a couple of different dental clinics, and he had considerable student loan debt to pay back.

I went to a hotel for a cleaning lady position but they never called me. I applied for a server position at a sports bar but they never called me either. I went to an Italian restaurant and bar where I used to go for drinks once in a while. I chatted with the manager a few times while I was drinking there as a customer. So I asked him for a serving job. He asked me if I knew about wine. I did not know any particular wine names or how to differentiate their tastes at all. I only drank beer. Not only was my wine knowledge lacking, I was not good at reciting Italian menus to customers. It was like a third language to me. I couldn't get the serving job there but the manager told me to check the Japanese restaurant right across from his restaurant.

I walked into the Japanese restaurant and saw the servers wearing Kimonos and serving customers. I met the restaurant manager. He asked me one question.

"Do you know how to use chopsticks?"

"Yes."

"You can start tomorrow."

So I got the job at the Japanese restaurant. He introduced me to a server. She was a Korean American. She spoke Korean fluently and gave me basic training for a week. Most servers working there were college students. They were Japanese, Chinese, Thai and Korean. They all spoke two or three languages fluently.

One girl spoke four languages. When Japanese customers came, I thought she would speak in Japanese but she spoke in English although her Japanese was very fluent. I asked her why she did not speak Japanese to them. She said sometimes Japanese customers were not polite to her when she spoke in Japanese but when she spoke in English and Japanese customers who could not speak English well were intimidated and were not rude to her. She seemed to know when she should speak which language depending on each customer and each situation. I heard there were Japanese pro baseball players coming and I saw their photos hanging on the wall. I also got one of the baseball players' autographs although I was not sure who he was. I brought it to Matt and he told me who the baseball player was. Since then I started watching the player with more interest when his team was on T.V.

Although I did not have to know much about wine I had to memorize Japanese sushi names in Japanese! I was so confused to distinguish which one was which. Raw fish meats on the steamed rice looked the same and the sushi names sounded the same. I just wished that the sushi chef would not make mistakes by making extra or less sushi from the lists that I gave him. Often I had to cook at the customer's table. That was why the manager asked me if I knew how to use chopsticks. Everything was new to me but I learned little by little. I prayed that I would not drop anything in front of the customers or trip on my Kimono and fall with my tray on the wet floor. I tried my best to serve my customers. I always had a cheerful smile on my face and shared some funny jokes to have my customers laugh and have a good time. One time when I was walking away from my customers after giving them their bill, I heard them saying, "I like her. She was more than just a server." Then I received a big tip. One time a guy gave me a $50 tip after having a bill just a little over $100. I thought he tried to impress his lady friend who came with but I appreciated him anyway.

Although I tried my best to serve my customers well I couldn't completely get rid of the sadness deep inside. I kept thinking that I did not come to America to be a waitress at a Japanese restaurant. When I was in Korea, I strongly felt that God was telling me to study English. I did not know why He was giving me the thoughts constantly. I didn't want to forget the calling so I wrote down in my diary, "I don't know why but I just feel that God is telling me to study English for some reason."

I went to college and got my B.A. degree in English and I had jobs using English all day long at work. I even attended an English Language Institute after work. Wasn't it enough to get a job for a living? Back then I had no idea that I was going to move to America, get a job and live there. I knew God had a plan for me and that's why He let me go through all the waiting periods and difficult times for my work visa and Green Card but I did not think that God let it happen so that I could wear a Kimono and serve customers at a Japanese restaurant. It was not a part of my American Dream. There should be something else. Then what was His ultimate plan for me? I did not know. I never thought the serving job was bad. I just thought there should be something more than that.

On-going Training

I finally got a new job through a manpower company. It was an investment banking company in downtown Minneapolis. The manpower company told me briefly about the job descriptions of the position but I had no idea what the company was doing specifically. I found the company with the address that the manpower company gave me. The office manager took me to the main conference room and let me meet with a managing director, an associate and a financial analyst in turn. The managing director summarized what the company did in a single sentence. He said, "We buy companies and we sell companies."

Their clients were corporate companies rather than individual people. No wonder why I never heard of the company name before. They were looking for someone who was good at desktop publishing for their business presentations. The office manager said they wanted to see what I was capable of first so they gave me one month of a trial period. If I did well then they were going to hire me after a month of the trial.

The team that I worked for was busy all the time. I asked the financial analyst how many average hours he worked per week. He said probably from 70 to 80 hours a week. I did not work for 80 hours like he did but often stayed really late since I was the only person for desktop publishing which they called *word processing*. My duties were creating business presentations, marketing materials, and converting or fixing files for financial officers.

The associate in my team gave me a thick book one day which had close to 150 pages. He told me to recreate the entire book from scratch. I asked him if he had an old file but he said the file did not exist anymore. The original file was deleted from the server so I had to recreate the book. There were so many logos, pictures and charts to collect or recreate. I did not know about a text converting program yet so I had to type up the texts as well.

My right wrist was getting weak and numb by the time I was coming home after work.

Three weeks had passed. Friday afternoon. The associate asked me if I finished the book. I said, "Not yet."

He said, "Why don't you print the book as much as you did and bring it to me."

Then the office manager came over and told me to come into the associate's office with the printed book. I still had one more week to work there but wondered if I did anything wrong.

The office manager asked the associate, "So what do you think?"

"I think it looks good."

"The book you worked on was a test. We wanted to make sure that you are capable of doing the job. I know you still have one more week for the trial but we wanted to congratulate you a week early 'cause we know your birthday is next week. This is your birthday gift," the office manager said.

"Welcome aboard! Congratulations!"

So I got the job. I remembered what Mr. Park, one of the managers at the international trading company, said to me many years ago: "I think you are brilliant and talented but if you don't have any connection with any powerful man who could help you it would be really difficult for you to be successful in your future."

Well, I moved to the U.S. without knowing any powerful man and I got the job without any powerful man's help. I didn't need a powerful man. I had God on my side! How much more power could I ask for?

I worked overtime pretty much every day or was called in to work even on holidays. When I requested for a vacation day one time, it was not approved. The office manager emailed the team that I supported and asked if it would be fine with them that I would take a day off.

They replied, "No. We need her to work for an upcoming pitch next week."

When I read the email the first time I did not feel like talking to anyone at the company but soon I thought about the opposite side. I did not have to be down or upset at all. They wanted me to come to work. In the past, I wanted to work desperately but I did not have a job or I could not work because I was not allowed to work without a proper visa. All of sudden I became excited and happy again. I cheerfully emailed them, "You guys love me so much and don't want to let me leave. I like that. OK, I will come in to work. But next time, I am going to take two days off instead of one day. Thank you."

Soon after, every single one of them in the team sent me emails to thank me. One of them said, "Thank you. Yes, we love you very much. We can't live without you. Next time you can take a whole week off!"

A friend of mine who used to work at the same printing company in Korea asked me once if I enjoyed my new life style in America going home on-time after work from Monday through Friday and no work on Saturdays. At the printing company in Korea I ate Ramyon and coffee as breakfast, free lunch and dinner at the company cafeteria and worked really late every single day. I went to work on Saturdays too. There was no overtime pay. I worked for a fixed salary. Once in a while when I left work on time, I felt guilty and had to sneak out of the company so that no one would see me leaving on time. Although I lived in America I worked an average of 50-55 hours a week at my full time job at that time, then I would go to Craig's company for a few hours at night for about three to four months at the beginning of each year for his calendar projects.

North Koreans had a slogan of "An exercise to see the moon." North Koreans went to work before the sunrise and went home late at night. They worked all day long and called their intensive laboring day as an exercise to see the moon. When I looked at the beautiful full moon brightly shining, I thought of the slogan but I felt good inside. I was glad that I was not driving from a bar after drinking and being drunk but was working hard. I thanked God that I was not born in North Korea. I thanked God that I had the opportunities to work. I thanked God for the knowledge and training that I had since I moved to America. I said to God numerous times while driving home late at night, "Father, thank you so much for everything. You are not physically with me but You have raised me and taught me as if You were right next to me. How could you do that? Wow... I remember the days that I had no idea how to use a computer but look at me now. What I do all day long is a computer job. All I know and all I can do are all because of You. Thank you. Thank you and Thank you...I love you so much."

I thought the investment banking company was a perfect place to work and no one would ever leave the company but I had seen numerous employees come and leave over the years for various different reasons. When I encountered some of the old co-workers who left the firm they always asked me one same question, "How could you still work at the company for so long?"

Then my response to them had always been the same. "I am not working for any particular person but I work for God."

There were several times that I also wanted to quit the job but I always ended up going to a church in downtown during my lunch break and prayed until I was comforted by the Holy Spirit. A lot of time I cried and complained to God why my life had to be miserable but sometimes I just sat there and cried in my quiet prayer, "My Lord, I am here again. I didn't know where to go but You. You don't have to say anything to me. I just want to be with You. That's all." Then I sat there and stared at the cross. In my meditation I asked myself, "Jesus died on the cross. What does that mean to me?" The answer was always the same. *He will do anything for me.*

Although I knew that there were girls at the company who gossiped behind my back and treated me cold and rude, I believed that God was in control and He knew everything that was going on with me at work. After sitting at the church for a while I went back to work and lived another day. There was a great opportunity once that I could have gotten a new job. The salary was good and the H.R. manager at the company even called me if I could start right away. It was really tempting to get the new job but it didn't seem to be right that I was running away from the problems and do it my way instead of trusting God and wait for His answer. So I kindly declined the H.R. manager's offer. I didn't know what God wanted me to do exactly at that time so I decided to be patient, obedient, and wait for His next call.

Solo Flight

Nearby our church there was an airport—Flying Cloud Airport. I saw some small airplanes were flying over. The loud engine noise reminded me of the sightseeing flight that I had around the Hudson River when I visited Rich in New York. He always encouraged me to become a private pilot but flying solo in a small airplane seemed to be scary and probably too expensive to take lessons.

One time I went to a bar in downtown after work and happened to sit next to an airline pilot. We chatted and I told him about my sightseeing flight experience in New York. After chatting with the pilot the idea of learning how to fly intrigued me this time and I felt that I wanted to challenge the impossible dream. At that time I was taking Tae Kwon Do training after work and used to hang out at a bar with friends after the training pretty much every night. Going to work, Tae Kwon Do school then going home was my daily routine. I wanted to have something different and more challenging so that I would be able to have a sense of accomplishment. I was sick of drinking every night and wanted to get out of that bad habit. Flying had always been my fantasy and I was always excited whenever I saw airplanes flying by. So I decided to learn how to fly.

I visited a Cessna Flight Training School in late December. The C.F.I (Certificated Flight Instructor) suggested that I take a scenic flight first and see if taking flight training would be comfortable for me or if it would be too overwhelming. When I sat in the captain's seat in the cockpit for the first time I was overwhelmed by the complicated instruments. It was not the first time seeing these kinds of instruments but I was indifferent when I looked at them as a passenger before. The instructor read my mind right away and told me not to worry about the instruments because an instructor would teach me about each one later. Then he taxied the airplane out of the parking lot and called the tower to get a clearance to cross the taxiway and get to the runway for take-off. The instructor and the air traffic controller both spoke so fast by using phonetic alphabets. I heard those phonetic alphabets in some old black and white World War II movies. I had no idea what they were saying. Immediately I felt that it was too much for me to do it. The dream of learning how to fly seemed to be just a dream.

We took off Runway 28 Right and flew over the countless lakes in Minnesota. Everything was covered by snow and looked the same to me. The instructor pointed out some of the lakes one by one; Lake Minnetonka, Lake Waconia and so on. He said I should be familiar with the shapes of the lakes and be able to tell which lake was which on the aeronautical map. To me, they all looked the same; irregular shapes and sizes covered with snow. I saw some people parked their pickup trucks on the lakes and were ice fishing. They looked like tiny toy trucks. After about twenty minutes of flying on above the hundreds of lakes the instructor said he would turn around now and return to the airport. I looked at the instruments and saw the needle on the heading indicator was moving around. I totally lost my sense of direction and had no clue which direction was North, South, East or West.

As we flew close to the airport he asked me, "Can you see the airport? Can you see the runway?" Everything was covered by snow and it was not easy to find either one of them. I wondered what would happen if I couldn't find the runway right away when I fly alone. I would fly around like a dog chasing his own tail, run out of fuel, be scared to death and crash somewhere. Until he landed the airplane smoothly I did not even think of having to land the airplane someday by myself. I was just stunned and intimidated. I felt so small and asked myself why I came there. While he was taxiing back to the parking lot I started thinking that flying an airplane was meant to be for someone special, not for someone average like me. When we were back to the school he asked me if I would like to start the training. Even after the overwhelming sensation and anxiety for the past thirty minutes I spitted out, "Yes."

Before I started the flight training I had to register as an Alien Student to get an approval from TSA (Transportation Security Administration). I was a legal resident with a Green Card but was considered as a foreign student taking flight training in the U.S.A. since I was not a U.S. citizen yet. All foreign students had to register and get an approval from TSA with no exception, especially since the 9/11. I reported who I was with my original nationality, what kind of airplane I would train in and how long the flight training would last. Then I took a Third Class Aviation Medical Exam. First and second class medical exams were for airline and commercial pilots.

After I got the approval I started ground school first, which was done in a classroom. The actual flight training in an airplane had been delayed because of the snow. I followed the Cessna Pilot Training Program on a computer as a part of the ground school. Learning the specifications of how an airplane could stay in the air, fly, and find its destination was fascinating.

One of the most intriguing parts in aviation was that there were a lot of invisible variables which played big roles in flying; air density, temperature, wind speed, wind direction, magnetic forces, radio signals and so on. There were no markings in the sky like the stop signs or speed limit signs on the road but there were designated air spaces and rules to follow; some I could fly in and out but some I was restricted. They were all invisible but I had to apply all of those invisible variables into each and every flight. There was one more invisible and powerful being—GOD. I always remembered Him and prayed for my safety before I started the engine of the airplane.

English was the official aviation language. Radio Communication was one of the big obstacles that I had to face but once I started the training I did not want to excuse myself that I couldn't do well because English was not my native language. Everyone spoke so fast; the pilots and the air traffic controllers. Communication in aviation was like learning a new language. Everything was abbreviated and had its own meaning to interpret. Without studying hard and memorizing them there was no quick easy way to master what the markings or codes meant. However, I was surprised to hear that some English native speakers also had the same fear and had a difficult time to talk on the radio. I heard a couple other guys speaking really slow on the radio. They must have been in training too. I was not the only one. One day I read a funny story. There was an old man who was waiting for his clearance from the tower. The controller spoke to him really fast. He was supposed to read back to the controller what he just heard so that the two parties could understand each other. But the old man could not catch a single word what the controller said to him. After a pause the old man asked the controller, "Is what you just said so important?" It was a really funny story and I was glad that I was not the only one who had struggles with the radio communication.

In order to get familiar with radio communication, every time I started my car I pretended that I was talking to an air traffic controller. Before I made a left or right turn I made a position announcement and pretended that I was flying in an airplane. It really helped me a lot. My instructor was very impressed with my improved radio communication. Because of my unique non-native English accent all the air traffic controllers at my home airport; KFCM—Flying Cloud Airport, Eden Prairie, MN; recognized my voice and said to me to enjoy the flight when they gave me the clearance to taxi or take off.

I usually flew to the practice area with my instructor and practiced based on the Cessna Pilot Training Program. Before I started the flight training, I merely thought that I would fly in an airplane in the beautiful blue sky, have fun and feel good about myself. But most of my training at the beginning stage was preparing myself for emergency situations such as simulated stalls when taking off or landing, how to recover from the stalls with power on or off, how to proceed in case of engine failure, what to do when some of the instruments were not working properly and so on. While people on the ground were enjoying their lives I put myself in the simulated emergency situations and sweated by paying my own money. I wondered when I could actually fly peacefully and enjoy myself.

Landing was the biggest challenge ever!!! It seemed to be absolutely never ending training and required a great deal of focus and dedication. The very first day when I was introduced to the landing practice, I felt like quitting. Up until then my flight instructor landed the airplane for me and now I had to do it. I was scared to death and cried after the training. I started the flight training to accomplish something but all I had was more new fears. When I got over one fear then there was another one waiting. After spending so much time and money I had to make a decision whether I was going to continue the flight training or not. I didn't want to give up but I thought I might have to. I was disappointed and discouraged. I was losing my confidence every time I couldn't land by myself. I did landing practices during the hot summer time with no air conditioner in the airplane. I was always covered with sweat.

My first flight instructor was hired as an airline pilot after training me for about three months. Before he left he encouraged me to join the AOPA (Aircraft Owners and Pilots Association). So I joined the group and applied to have an aviation mentor. I was matched up to a Mentor who lived not far from where I lived. We met at Lake Elmo Airport where his hanger was. He owned a small experimental airplane that he put together from a German airplane kit. The manual he used was at least two inches thick. My mind was absolutely blown away that there were people like him who not only enjoyed flying but also put thousands of the bolts and nuts together to build his own airplane as a hobby. It would probably take a hundred years for me to put them together.

I told him where my training stage was at and I felt like quitting. He said what I needed the most at the moment was not flying but gaining my confidence back. He said I did not have to force myself to do something I was not digesting at the moment. Rather he suggested taking a short break from the flight training but in the meantime, prepare for the FAA Aeronautical Knowledge Test. If I passed the test, it might help me change my mind of quitting but continue the training. His advice sounded convincing to me. I did not want to excuse myself that I had a disadvantage because I was a non-native speaker. So I studied really hard and got 93% in the Aeronautical Knowledge Test. The required score was 70%. My Mentor congratulated me and asked, "The written test part is done and out of the way. Do you still want to quit the training?"

I said, "No. I will continue for sure."

One time I was practicing landings at KGYL, Glencoe Airport and he was flying over 21D Lake Elmo Airport, which was about 70 miles apart but we both used the same radio frequency (122.8). He recognized my voice and we greeted each other over the radio. It was a really fun and exciting day.

On Saturday August 25th, 2007, the weather was beautiful.

Wind 5 knots, sky clear, visibility 10 statute miles. My second instructor who trained me mainly on landings was also hired by an airline company and left. My third instructor said that I was going to practice landings with him a couple times then I would fly with the Chief Flight Instructor for a stage check later.

We came back to the parking lot after practicing landings then he said, "Now, you are going by yourself."

I thought I was going to fly with the Chief Flight Instructor. All of sudden I got so excited and nervous. My heart was pumping rapidly. I said to myself, "Okay. This is it! You have done this so many times. Just calm down and do it exactly as you have been trained."

I walked to the airplane. I prayed to God for my safety and a successful SOLO flight!

Everything became a first time now; my radio calls without an instructor, my taxi, take-off and landing without an instructor. I was about to taxi to the runway. Suddenly the air traffic controller's voice sounded ten times faster than usual. I could not even understand if the controller was talking to me or to other pilots. I said, "Flying Cloud Tower, Warrior 523 Papa Uniform, I am a Student Pilot and this is my first solo. You speak so fast. Say again please."

Then, the controller spoke to me again slowly and kindly. I taxied out. At the runway, the controller spoke slowly and clearly again and gave me the clearance to take off Runway 28 Right. I took off from the runway by myself! I must not be freaked out and must not give up while in the airplane in the air. I had no choice. I was airborne alone. I talked to myself what to do for each procedure. I almost could hear my instructor's voice as if he was sitting next to me but there was nobody! The seat was empty!

Ohhhhh my God! Am I flying this airplane or is this plane taking me somewhere? No, you cannot think like that. Focus! Focus! Total Focus!

I concentrated on flying the airplane and maintained the desired airspeed and the altitude. I landed safely the first time. I felt great! I gained confidence after the first solo take-off and landing. I had to do it two more times in order to officially complete the solo flight. Second attempt, I took off from Runway 28 Right again. While I was climbing I noticed the needle on the airspeed indicator was significantly increasing. I raised the airplane nose up ever so slightly to reduce the rapidly increasing airspeed and when I was closer to the traffic pattern altitude, which was 1,000 feet above the ground, I reduced the power to maintain the altitude. It's called, "Pitch for Airspeed, Power for Altitude."

I was on the Runway 28 Right Base. If I turned to the right one more time then I was going to face the runway to land but the tower had not cleared me to land yet. It was a really busy day at the airport. Maybe the controller forgot my position. I couldn't wait any longer so I called the tower to get the clearance to land.

"Flying Cloud Tower, Warrior 523 Papa Uniform, am I clear to land, Sir?"

"Warrior 523 Papa Uniform, Flying Cloud Tower, Clear to land. 28 Right."

The second landing was not that great because I was holding some power just in case I was not getting the clearance to land and had to do a Go-Around.

The third attempt. I said, "Okay, forget about the second one. Just focus. You can do this!" I took off smoothly. This time I watched the airspeed indicator and everything was fine. I maintained the traffic pattern altitude. 90 knots on the downwind, 80 on the base, 70 on the final, flaps all the way down. 65 knots on the short final. I killed the power completely as soon as I knew that I was going to make the aiming point on the runway. Then I saw the end of the runway. Flare the airplane and hold the ground effect—another invisible thing to remember right before landing. The two main wheels touched down on the runway gently then the nose wheel slowly came down afterwards. The last landing was the best landing I had ever made in my flight training! It was incredible! My instructor was monitoring my entire solo flight. When I completed the third landing the air traffic controller at the tower said over the radio, "Congratulations!"

Thunderbird Aviation, where I took my flight training, was having an open house that day. When I got out of the plane at the parking lot, people who were watching me land applauded and congratulated me. I felt great!!! I had a huge smile on my face. I really had a strong sense of accomplishment that day. The fear of radio communication and the fear of landing were gone a million miles away. I gained nothing but confidence after my solo flight.

Once I completed the solo flight successfully, the rest of the training went smoother. I did a night flight as well as short and long cross country flights. The best part of flying at night was not just that I could see the beautiful moon and the stars real closely but I could turn on the runway lights by pressing the radio button. It was really cool and fun. I could even control the brightness of the runway lights by pressing the Radio Button. For the long cross country I visited three different airports and got a stamp at each airport to prove that I landed there then flew a minimum 100 nautical miles to meet the requirement. It was hard to believe that I flew 100 nautical miles of the long cross country flight all by myself. I found my way back and landed safely. An interesting thing was that when I was flying I never remembered any of the worries or bad memories that happened on the ground. I loved my own little space in the sky. When I was driving back home after the long cross country flight, walking on the ground felt different as if I could almost feel the gravity that was pulling my feet.

Before the final check ride there was an oral test—questions and answers. The examiner was a pilot trainer at a major airline company. He looked like the movie star Tom Hanks, so I called him Mr. Tom Hanks. He flew with me a few times as my Stage Check Examiner before and I did babysitting for his baby a couple of times. On the oral test day, he said to me seriously, "I know you. That means I need to make sure that you know all these questions and answers. I cannot just let you pass because I know you."

He made me nervous but I understood what he meant. However, he gave me so many mechanical questions and I did not do well in answering those questions. It was like as if I had to know how to put an airplane together instead of knowing how to fly one. It was taking too long. I felt that I would never be able to finish the pilot training ever. I dropped my head and started sobbing. He saw me wiping my tears then he said, "Why are you crying?"

"It is just so hard. I will never be able to finish this."

"You are going to be a pilot! That means you will have moments to make critical decisions. When you face that kind of situation, are you going to cry?" he said.

I could not say a word. Then he added, "I will say that I did not see you crying. Let me go and have lunch. When I come back, we start from scratch. Sounds good?" "OK."

Before the oral test I heard some people saying that if people got a high score in the aeronautical knowledge test then the examiner wouldn't give them a hard time with difficult questions. Since I got 93 on the test I thought it would be a piece of cake to pass the oral exam but it was nothing like what I expected. While the examiner was gone to have lunch I checked the parts that I was not able to answer and when he came back we started all over again. The oral test took almost two hours to finally complete.

For the final check ride I had to demonstrate everything I had learned so far; normal take-off and landing, soft field take-off and landing, short runway take-off and landing, traffic pattern, stalling the airplane with power or without power, recovering from the stalls, slow flight, 45 degree steep turns to the left and to the right, declaring emergency, emergency landing procedures, finding destinations, maintain certain airspeed and altitude, instrument flight and so on.

I completed my final check ride after attempting three times. The first time it was too windy and the cross wind was just too strong for me to handle when we went to an airport to land. The examiner landed for me. The second time I was so nervous and did not do well. The third time I went to the airport early in the morning when the wind was calm and not many airplanes were flying yet. I demonstrated all three required take-offs and landings pretty well and completed all other procedures successfully.

When I taxied the airplane back to the parking lot, I was anxious what the examiner was going to say this time. He said, "Congratulations! You are a Brand New Private Pilot!"

WOW!!! I FINALLY DID IT!!!!!!!!!!!!! I DID NOT GIVE UP!!!!!!

Fear of God's Punishment

Two years after we got married Matt purchased a small dental clinic from a retiring dentist with his ambitious dream of running his own business but in the slow economy his business didn't generate the revenue he was expecting. There were not enough new patients coming in and even the existing patients didn't come to see the dentist regularly in the slow economy unless they had an uncomfortable toothache which needed urgent care. He had to face the uncertainty of his career and started experiencing awful depression. He drank alcohol pretty much every day. I found a bottle of brandy hidden in his closet on more than one occasion when I was cleaning the house. He did not take care of himself, overslept for work, or called in sick often, and was more or less falling apart. Our relationship was becoming increasingly frustrating. Substance abuse was tearing us apart. We used to pray and read the Bible together but we no longer lived as a happily married couple. We became total strangers to each other and lived like college roommates. Our marriage was gradually falling apart.

We hardly spent time together except seeing each other at the Tae Kwon Do school right after work. We had been in Tae Kwon Do training for years. After Tae Kwon Do class Matt had Hop Ki Do class so he stayed at the martial art school another hour but I usually went to a bar across from the school and drank beer almost every night. Most of the time I hung out with other Tae Kwon Do friends but when I didn't go to Tae Kwon Do I stopped by a liquor store on the way home and drank alcohol at home. I didn't understand why I wanted to drink constantly but it became a very bad habit. I used to drink two or three glasses of beer a day but my alcohol consumption was increasing and I could finish a cheap bottle of wine by myself in one night. Then I got drunk and hungry so I ate junk food or bar food. There were countless times that I drove home after I got drunk. I knew I should not live that way but I kept doing it because I thought I could handle it. When I was driving I asked God for His forgiveness but my relationship with God was nothing like what it used to be and all I had inside of me was the guilty feelings that I walked too far away from Him.

Guys whom I met at bars were impressed that I was a

private pilot and wanted to hang out with me more. Although I told them that I was married, one of the guys flirted with me and wanted to date me. If I were not married all those guys could have been the opportunities for me to date but since I was married they were all nothing but temptations. The temptations were strong considering how disappointed I had become with my husband. One time a guy whom I met at a bar invited me to his apartment for a second drink. I didn't need another drink because I was already quite drunk but I followed him. The guy gave me a bottle of beer and he said he needed to use the bathroom. I knew his apartment was not that far from the bar where we left but my head was spinning and I had no idea where the exact location was. I felt like vomiting a couple times and had fear that I might pass out. I looked at my cell phone then dialed 911. The operator answered but I hung up the phone without saying anything. In my heart, one voice said, "It is okay to stay" then the other voice said, "No, you need to get out of here NOW."

Soon after I hung up the phone, my cell phone rang.

"Hello."

"This is 911. Did you just hang up the phone? Are you okay? Do you need help?"

"Yes. I don't know where I am. I am at someone's apartment. I want to go home."

"Do you know the address?"

"Just a second please. Let me ask."

I asked the guy in the bathroom loudly, "WHAT IS YOUR ADDRESS?"

He told me his address. I gave the operator the guy's address. After I hung up the phone again I sat down on the couch. I felt miserable and started regretting that I followed the guy to his apartment after meeting him at a bar. Several minutes later, a police officer showed up and knocked on the door. He came in and asked the guy if he called 911.

"No."

"I did. I want to go home."

I could not look the man in the eye so I looked down on

the floor. I heard him saying to the officer, "I don't know why she called 911."

"I am sorry. I meant to call a taxi."

The police called a taxi and helped me leave the guy's apartment that night. I hated myself acting like that. When I came home I saw Matt sleeping on the couch. He asked me where I had been. I lied to him that I hung out with the Tae Kwon Do friends. I felt guilty and was sorry to him. I knew that I had no right to blame him only for our marriage falling apart. We had both given up on the marriage and were making poor efforts to make it right. I concluded that my life in America had failed after all.

The more I watched Matt fall apart the more I became less interested in the marriage. I was tired of watching him sleep all day long. Tired of him letting his business fall apart. Tired of there never being any money in our checking account, despite the fact that we should have made more than enough to pay the bills and then some. I felt betrayed. I could no longer trust him. I told Matt that I wanted to go back to Korea and called a lawyer to ask about how to get divorced. The lawyer said that since Matt and I had no children together it would be easy to get divorced. Matt did not want to get divorced so he suggested getting a marriage counselor instead. I agreed to meeting with a marriage counselor because I didn't want to be blamed that I did not even try to save our marriage. However, I thought meeting with a marriage counselor was useless and wasting my time because I believed that God didn't grant my request to bless us. I clearly remembered the day when I was driving back home after church. I was driving and Matt was dozing off in the passenger's seat. When I saw him I prayed to God that I didn't want any materialistic happiness but just wanted to live a happy life with Matt for the rest of my life and kindly asked God to remember my prayer and bless us. But I wandered around from bar to bar and blamed God that He didn't listen to my humble prayer. I thought to myself when God didn't bless us how could a marriage counselor save our marriage?

We met at the marriage counselor's office and talked quietly about what we thought of each other. The counselor suggested doing something together as a married couple such as cooking or having a hobby together. My biggest fear was that I might not be able to love Matt as I used to ever again. I was afraid of being doomed and trapped in the unhappy marriage forever. We went to a pastor at our church to ask for prayer. Craig and Susan also tried to reconcile us. I knew all those kindnesses and efforts were nothing but nice gestures for me to show to others that at least I tried but I knew it was not going to work in the end. I was still going out to drink and chased after temptations. I felt deep inside of me that I walked away from God, way too far this time and all I had was fear of God's punishment.

One day Matt and I decided to try something else. I moved out of the house and rented a room in a house which was close to our church in Eden Prairie. Matt called me or texted me every night. We pretended that we just started our new relationship all over again.

The landlord was a lesbian. She lived on the first and second floor and I lived in the basement. She told me that she and her partner not only owned the house together but they also purchased their burial site together to be buried next to each other after they died. But they broke up not long ago and she needed someone to share her mortgage payment. The landlord was a flight attendant but she wanted to change her career so that she didn't have to travel a lot. We didn't see each other very often but sometimes when I went home early I helped her with her college algebra that she took at a community college.

The landlord asked me one morning right before I headed out to work, "Which road do you take to go to work?"

There were a couple of different routes to take and I told her that I took the longer route. She asked me why. I said, "Well, I could take the shorter route then I have to drive by my church. I have not been attending the church for a long time and I feel guilty."

I felt guilty and dirty to go nearby God. She chuckled and said, "Oh, nonsense! I did not know you went to that church. The woman next to my house, she goes to that church too. I hate her. She came to me and Melissa and told us that being a lesbian is a sin. She said we shouldn't live together."

I thought the lady was quite brave to say that straight forward to her next door neighbors.

"Because of this, God gave them over to shameful lusts. Even their women exchanged natural relations for unnatural ones.

"In the same way the men also abandoned natural relations with women and were inflamed with lust for one another.

"Men committed indecent acts with other men, and received in themselves the due penalty for their perversion."

— Romans 1:26-27

There were a few gay and lesbian friends at the Tae Kwon Do school. I was confused how to understand them at first. They were all nice people and I got a long with them. But the Bible clearly showed in Romans that it was a sin. After thoughts and thoughts I concluded that I am not God. I am not in the position to judge others. I have my own sins to deal with. Let God handle the matter. It's His job not mine.

From Monday through Friday I stayed at the rent house but weekends I usually visited our house briefly to get something I needed. One day I started feeling awful. My throat was itching and I had a constant runny nose. The night before, I should have gone home early after work rather than rushing to a bar after the Tae Kwon Do training. I thought I could ditch the cold after drinking and eating some food. When I went home late at night I decided to take a bath. In the hot tub I closed my eyes. No matter what I did the heavy guilt always lingered on me and I had nothing to say to God. I was just speechless and ashamed of myself. On the other hand I said to myself, "He doesn't listen to my prayer so why should I pray to Him? He doesn't love me anymore."

I was getting dizzy and could not concentrate on work at all. I felt like vomiting. I sent a message to the office manager if she could come to my desk. She replied that she was on the phone. I started vomiting in a trash can under my desk. The office manager was informed and rushed in and said I should go home right away. I called Matt but he was with his patients and could not get out of the office to pick me up. He sent his receptionist instead. She was going to take me to our house but my body temperature was getting too high and she did not want to leave me alone. So she took me to a hospital emergency room. My fever had spiked to 105. I had an IV injection and took a nap for a few hours. The chain of drinking alcohol, staying up late every night, and going to work early in the morning caused me total lack of sleep and I became exhausted. When my high temperature went down under 100 degrees I was discharged to go home.

Matt came home after work and was glad to have me back home. We lived apart almost two months. Although I visited our house on weekends the feeling of coming home was different this time. Matt gave me a glass of protein shake to gain some energy back. Without him I could not do anything. He had to help me sit up, eat and walk to the bathroom. I missed four work days. Matt came home right away after work and stayed home to take care of me. When I was sick and could not do anything without him I realized how precious he was to me and how mean I had been to him for my own selfish reasons. I shed regretful tears and felt really really sorry to him. I realized that I did not try to understand his situation or his depression but accused him instead that he was lazy and had nothing to do with me. I was sorry... truly sorry... for everything I had said and done to him.

I appreciated him deeply when he was taking care of me for those four days. He was my only family I had. I said to him sincerely, "Thank you..."

"For what?"

"Thank you for taking care of me."

"It's my duty!" he said.

I told the landlord that I wanted to move out of the house and go back home. She said, "That's totally fine and I understand."

Matt came along with me to pack and we drove back to our home together. Everything started feeling different. Matt did not spend his weekends sleeping on the couch all day long anymore. We said "Thank you" more often and appreciated each other. We started praying again.

I had to go through the repentant process first but I just could not say a word. I didn't know where to start. I realized how far I walked away from God.

Is it possible to go back to Him as who I am and ask for His forgiveness? How am I going to tell Him everything I have done?

Although He knew all, I had to confess my sins through my mouth. I saw Matt was changing and our relationship was getting better day by day. I did not want to fail our marriage. So I started confessing all my sins one by one. I was truly sorry to God…

"Therefore, there is now no condemnation for those who are in Christ Jesus, because through Christ Jesus the law of the Spirit of life set me free from the law of sin and death."

— Romans 8:1

I had a dream one night. I was not sure where I was but it was dark and I knelt down on the ground with my face toward the ground. I heard a voice saying to me, "Get up. Lift your head up."

"My Lord, I am a sinner. I cannot see Your face." I responded nervously.

I put my face down lower almost touching the ground. Then the voice said to me again, "Lift your head up. I forgive your sins."

I was so nervous to see His face but I lifted my head up slowly toward the voice. It was dark and hard to see His entire figure but I saw the eyes. I said, "My Lord, I have sinned against You too much."

He said, "I forgive you."

His eyes seemed as if He knew all my sins in the past and already knew my yet uncommitted sins in the future. However, His eyes were very much forgiving, gentle and understanding. I felt that I had a new life again.

Matt eventually got on the right track to better health. Through pressure from his work and disgust he had in himself from disappointing so many around him, he committed to a substance abuse rehabilitation program. He was hospitalized for three weeks as part of the program. He has lived a much happier life ever since and the strength of our marriage improved immediately. He had a true spiritual awakening and mended his relationship with the Lord as well. After cleaning up his emotional and spiritual problems he was determined to get his physical health back. He started a nutrition program and shed close to fifty pounds in just less than three months. It was this kind of determination and willingness to change that has made him the man he is today.

I was going to be on the diet program with him too but started exercising and decided to run a half marathon instead. I ran on a treadmill when it was cold outside then gradually started running outside either early in the morning or after work. I followed a training program and before I ran for the half marathon I was able to run 13 miles without a pause. On the half marathon day Matt and I booked a motel which was about 40 minutes driving distance from Duluth, Minnesota. There was no room available for one night or it was too expensive because of the crowds of people running for the half or the full marathon. We got up at 4:00 A.M. in the morning and he made me a protein shake to drink as a breakfast. We drove to the gathering place to catch a bus which took runners to the starting point.

I was all set and started running among the hundreds of runners for the half marathon. I felt great to run along Lake Superior. A lot of local people got up early in the morning and came out to cheer for the runners. People made loud noises with cowbells or played boom boxes really loud at six o'clock in the morning. Some were sitting on their porch drinking coffee in their pajamas. Running a half marathon was a great experience but looking at those cheering people was also so much fun. I finished 13.1 miles in 1 hour 58 minutes. I felt great! Matt was waiting for me among the crowds but missed me at the finish line. I received a medal after the race and a bottle of water then went to the meeting area where Matt and I had set ahead of time. He congratulated me then we went to watch other runners coming in.

Matt used to say that he was not interested in running much but he was inspired by the runners and the exciting atmosphere. He said he was going to start training and run the half marathon the next year and he did it. I was there to see him coming in across the finish line. I was so proud of him and glad that we both ran the half marathon. We also continued our Tae Kwon Do training and got our black belts.

Anonymous Phone Call

My mother called me at work one day. It was usually me who called so I wondered what the urgency was about that made her dial at her late night in Korea.

"Hello. Hi, Mom. Is everything okay?"

She started sobbing so hard and couldn't talk. I never heard her like that before.

"I think your brother Woo became insane."

"What do you mean by insane?"

She cried so miserably, "My life is over…"

My heart sank and didn't know what to do or say. She kept crying and could not speak for a while. I saw her crying before but not like this.

"Please tell me what happened."

My brother called my mother twice in the past two nights and the content of their conversations was shocking and unspeakable. Although she knew that she should not continue the conversation with him, she thought she was helping him. She cried and wept. It was a total shock to hear the whole story from her. Not only her life was over but I also felt that my life was over too!

Oh God, Why do You do this to me? Aren't my sad childhood and the painful memories in the past enough for me to endure? How many awful things should I go through more? This is beyond my ability to handle. I cannot take it anymore. Are You really my God? Are You really there for me? Then why is this happening to me? My mother and I have already experienced sad and bitter memories more than enough. Please tell me something. What is this for? And how am I going to handle this unthinkable situation? Is my brother really a crazy man now? Or is it my mother who became insane and heard from a ghost? Which is the truth? Please tell me. What do You want from me? I thought You forgave all my sins. Then what is this about? Is this some sort of punishment for my sins? Please say something to me!!!

My mother said, "I asked God if He was going to punish Woo for whatever he did wrong, punish me instead. He is still too young and has little children to look after. The punishment for him is just absolutely unbearable. I want to be punished instead. I have lived my life long enough. I would take whatever on behalf of him." Then she wept again.

"Mom, are you sure if the voice was really him?" I asked.

"I knew you wouldn't believe me and would say that I am crazy. How could I not recognize his voice? It was him!!!"

I knew that God would never allow any trial that I could not bear beyond my ability. I knew that God always gave me a way and knowledge to handle the trials that I had to face in the past. But this one was nothing like that at all. None of the trials that I had in the past could be compared to this one. I had no clue what God had in store for me this time. I felt as if God abandoned me. I cried with my mother on the phone.

I finally told her, "Mom. Please don't worry. Everything will be okay. I am coming. I will catch a flight as soon as I can and see you soon. Just hang in there until I come. Okay?"

"What could be changed even if you come over here? Everything has happened already. Nothing can be reversed."

I kindly reminded her that she did not do anything wrong. She was scared but tried to save him as a mother. Although it was an awful story to hear I was deeply moved by her. She did not care about her dignity or pride but threw herself to save her son. She was no longer the awful mean mother who abused me when I was young. If God asked her if she would die on behalf of my brother in order to save him, I believed she would definitely say, "Yes!"

I requested two weeks of vacation time to the company and flew to Korea immediately. I did not even have time to buy any gifts for my nephews and niece. All my concerns were about my mother and my brother.

My mother was happy to see me. My brother Woo, who lived nearby from my mother, came over to see me with his family. I was not sure if someone called by mistake and my mother lost her mind momentarily and thought it was my brother. I asked my brother cautiously how he had been doing. He said he was fine. I could not read any sign on his face that he had any trouble what so ever! I wondered if he was acting or if nothing had really happened. I could not ask him directly about the weird phone conversation with my mother. I was totally confused and not sure whom I should trust.

I saw my mother's cell phone lying on the floor in her room. I picked it up while she was in the kitchen. I saw number 1 in her SENT message box. I opened it and read. It said,

"Woo, I can help you. I have money."

That was all. There was no reply in the Inbox. I thought about checking the phone numbers in her recent call listing. Then a voice sprang up in my mind, "Can you handle the truth?"

I was so nervous and afraid of knowing the truth. I could not open the recent call listing. I just closed the phone.

Woo's wife told me that my mother had a medical check-up scheduled at a university hospital in Dae-Jun where One, my first brother lived. When Woo was not around, I asked his wife how he had been doing lately and if she knew about any argument between my mother and my brother. She said,

"Your mother told me that she needed to take Woo to see a doctor. She said something about a phone call but I remember that he came home really late that night and he was heavily drunk. He went to sleep right away. I don't think he had energy to get up and make a phone call to anyone. I am very sure that he went to bed early that night."

The next day my mother and I took an express bus to go to Dae-Jun for her medical check-up. I asked One's wife why they set the schedule in Dae-Jun, not at the town where my mother lived. She said they talked about my mother hearing something lately and they wanted to have my mother see a psychiatrist. But they did not want to offend my mother so they just told her that it was a regular medical check-up to see if everything was okay. They did not want to tell my mother to come up to see a psychiatrist so they arranged an overall medical check-up including counseling with a psychiatrist.

My sister-in-law and I took my mother to the hospital. All the check-ups were completed. She even took an endoscopy test. When she woke up after the test, we finally went to see the psychiatrist. The doctor asked us to come in individually. When my mother came out of the room after talking with the doctor, her eyes were red. I could tell that she probably cried more than she talked.

I knew that there would be no immediate answer for her. How could my mother tell the doctor her entire life in a half hour session? When it was my turn to see the doctor, she told me that my mother was experiencing serious depression and might need to consider having her see a doctor on a regular basis. The doctor suggested listening to my mother more often and trying to understand her from her perspective. I said I understood.

On the way back to One's apartment, One's wife suggested that we all stop by at an OBGYN clinic and have me checked to see if my health condition was normal to conceive, as Matt and I had no baby even after four and a half years of marriage. It was actually my mother's idea but she thought that I would be stubborn and would not listen to her so she had One's wife ask me instead. I told them that I had an annual physical check up every year and I was very healthy. But they both insisted that as long as I was in Korea, it might be better for me to have a second opinion at least. So I agreed and the three of us walked into an OBGYN clinic. No appointment was needed. The doctor took an MRI and the result came out right away.

The doctor said that I had a tumor in the uterus. I could not believe what he said. I had no physical symptoms at all. There was no pain, pressure, or bleeding and I took an annual physical exam every year and the results always came out normal. The doctor gave me a copy of the image and said it was common to see that kind of tumor at my age. He said I did not have to remove it if I didn't want to but my mother insisted that I should take the tumor out before I go back to the U.S. She said there was no reason to keep the tumor which was not going to help me at all.

We came back to my mother's house and went to another OBGYN clinic in her town. I explained to the doctor about my situation and I needed to have surgery as soon as possible as I had to go back to the U.S.A. He said he understood and scheduled the surgery date two days later at 11:00 A.M. and I took all the required tests the very next day before the surgery. He said it was going to take about two weeks to recover after the surgery. Before the surgery I emailed the office manager at my work and explained my situation. She said she understood and let me take time off as much as I needed. I appreciated her for her generous consideration and favor.

On the day of the surgery, my mother and I walked to the clinic together and I checked in for a surgery called myomectomy. I could not believe that I was the one who needed medical attention instead of my mother or my brother. I never imagined that I was going to lay down on the surgery table when I was flying to Korea. All my thoughts were about my mother and my brother, but IT WAS ME who ended up on the surgery table. How could it happen like this?

I started having question after question. I was so confused. I felt the whole thing was just a dream. Did God intentionally set this whole fiasco for one purpose? Were these bizarre and mysterious phone calls to my mother a way to get me to Korea? To have me get the surgery? If so it had to be done in Korea where my mother was. If I had to have the surgery in the U.S. there was no one who could stay next to me during the surgery or the recovery. Everyone had a job and had to go to work.

When my mother told me that she was not feeling well in the past I just told her to go see a doctor. I never attempted to fly to Korea when she was not feeling well. Even when my brother, One, had a car accident I did not go to Korea. I just believed that his wife would be there for him and he would be well treated at the hospital. In order for me to fly to Korea with urgency it had to be something totally and absolutely shocking and Yes, It Was!!! After I got the call from my mother I even thought about quitting my job in the U.S. and moving to Korea for a while to take care of my family. It was just utterly beyond my understanding. I was totally blown away. I could not understand why God was giving me that kind of unimaginable test at that time. I couldn't concentrate on anything. I had to go to Korea and do something for my family if there was anything in the world that I could do for them. So I went there to help them but it turned out that I was the one who may have been in danger and my mother was there to take care of me!!!

On the surgery table, I asked a nurse to take a picture of me with my camera. I heard her counting one, two, three then I did not remember anything after that. When I opened my eyes I was moved to a recovery room already. My mother came and told me that the doctor stepped out of the operating room in the middle of the surgery and told her that my appendix had become enlarged and might burst sooner or later so he asked for her approval to remove it. My mother approved it, of course. I ended up having two different surgeries in one day.

The doctor visited me and said the surgeries went really well. I told him that I had a terrible headache. I had to put my hands around my head as if I was trying to hold the splitting scull together. He said it's because I shed blood more than they planned initially because of the additional appendectomy. After his visit a nurse came in and gave me something in an IV bag. I asked what it was and she said it was like fake blood and it would reduce the splitting headache pain.

While I was in the recovery room my mother sat next to me and stroked her fingers through my hair as if I were a little girl. It reminded me of the days when I envied the girls who lay on their mothers' laps to catch lice from their heads. When I had lice once, my mother scolded me harshly and questioned whom I hung out with to get the lice from. Now my aged mother whom I once hated with all my heart was taking care of me. She had the horrible phone conversation, whoever it was with, but because of that I flew to her right away in order to help her but it was her who was taking care of me instead. Was it truly God who orchestrated everything like that? Who in the world could say, "No, it was not God!"

My belly was cut for the surgeries and stitched with medical staples. I was not able to get up or pee by myself yet so a nurse changed the plastic urine pouch connected to me. A few days later the doctor finally took out the tube and the urine pouch. I had to bite my teeth so tightly to fight the extreme pain when the tube was being removed. I could not eat or drink for a few days until I had to pass gas. I didn't realize having gas was such an important thing until then. I remembered the days at the band house. I hardly had anything back then. The mattress on the floor I slept on and the foods I ate were far from fancy but they were the only ones that I was allowed and I thanked God for them every single day. When I had nothing or was incapable of anything, I could learn more how to appreciate God and humble myself.

I tried to get up to go to the bathroom but I could not walk straight up alone. I hung on to my mother's arms and walked slowly to the bathroom. She stood next to me holding the IV bag up until I finished peeing. I thought, "Who else in the world could or would do that kind of thing for me except my mother for over a week in the recovery room? Nobody…" I needed my mother so badly. The surgeries had to be done in Korea where my mother was.

Then I realized one hundred percent that it was God who caused everything. He let the unimaginable phone conversation happen to my mother so that I could come back to Korea immediately. Then I ended up having the surgeries!!!

I could not believe that I did Tae Kwon Do and flew in an airplane as a pilot in command while I had the tumor inside of my body besides carrying the inflamed appendix which was about to explode. It was really scary to even think about the appendix exploding while I was flying in the air. I could not imagine what kind of tragic accident I could have had.

I thanked God a thousand times and at the same time I feared Him more than ever who knew all these things ahead. I asked God so many times if it was my brother or someone else. But the answer was always the same—"Try not to get every answer for every situation. Focus on what it is now and focus on Me."

Seven months after the surgeries I became pregnant. We found out a day before we were leaving for California for vacation. The news made the trip that much sweeter. Matt and I were thrilled to have a baby. Until then we thought we were not able to have one and almost gave up. We had been considering adoption. However, nine weeks after the pregnancy I miscarried the baby. When the nurse practitioner told me that there was no sign of a heart beat I was totally shocked and devastated. I didn't know what to do. I was afraid of telling Matt and his family that I lost the baby. I left work early and went to a church nearby our house. I sat there and cried out to God for hours to show me a miracle.

I called my doctor in Korea who did the surgeries on me. I told him that I miscarried a baby. He said,

"I am very sorry to hear that but don't be too sad because now we know for sure that you are able to conceive and you can try again."

Reborn

We did try, though unsuccessfully. We decided that God's blessing for us must be to adopt a baby. We found an agency where we could begin the process of adopting a boy from Korea. We went through our background checks and had some of our friends write recommendation letters. We had even paid some of the fees already. After completing some classes we were ready to have our home study.

In late October 2010, I was pregnant again. Matt and I were so excited. We could not help but admit that we wanted to have a baby boy. The main reason why I wanted to have a boy was because I did not want my baby girl to live a sad life like I did. The night before the ultra sound test to find out whether it's boy or girl, I could not feel any movement of the baby at all somehow. I was so afraid that I might have miscarried again. All of sudden a fear covered me and I realized that my attitude to have a baby was not right. I should have prayed for a healthy baby regardless of the baby's sex. So Matt and I both repented our wrong attitude and prayed for a healthy baby. We promised God whether it was a boy or a girl we would raise the baby with love and teach His words.

At 2:15 P.M. July 11, 2011, we had a beautiful healthy baby girl. She was born three weeks early by caesarean section. When I heard her crying sound for the first time it was surreal. Matt repeatedly asked me, "Can you hear that? Can you hear that?"

The crying sound never existed in the world before and we were hearing the fascinating sound for the first time ever. When I saw her she looked exactly like her daddy. She was absolutely adorable. I couldn't believe that we had such a beautiful and precious baby together, finally. I could not be happier than that and her birthday instantly became the best day ever in my life! We named her Reena that was originally from Rena in Latin which means Reborn. Matt and I were reborn in Jesus Christ!

When Reena became ten month old we went to Korea for a week and brought my mother to the U.S. to spend the summer with us. During this time, my mother and I prayed together in the name of Jesus Christ and she accepted Jesus as her Savior. I believe that God forgave all her sins. While she was staying with us there was not a single day without laughing out loud and being happy together. It was a true blessing from God and we treasured our time together.

Stepping out of the Grave

Years ago I blamed God that He did not bless Matt and I and that's why our marriage was falling apart. Now I realized how unwise and rebellious of a person I was against God by my own choices. I repented all my sins and thanked God for giving me the second chances. I had lived half of my life by wandering around but now I decided to live the rest half of my life for Him. No more regretful mistakes.

Whenever I tried to be closer to God I always experienced that Satan tried to jeopardize me at the same time. Something always seemed to interfere, or test me. Sometimes I had awfully scary dreams. I felt like I had been in hell. Those dreams were gross and shameful and sometimes I was chased by a dead person. I would be so afraid of going to sleep at night. I needed prayers and awareness that I was in God's hands.

There was a woman whom I helped at the citizenship ceremony when I became a U.S. citizen. She introduced me to a Korean woman who was visiting her daughter from Korea for a month. So the woman came over to our house and helped me for a week after Reena was born. She cooked for me and gave me massages as my hands and feet were swollen so much after the delivery. I had to go to an urgent care to see a doctor because of the swelling. We shared God's love and grace. She was a wonderful Christian woman. Her son-in-law was a Korean pastor who came to the U.S. for his master's degree in theology. I called the pastor and asked for prayers after I had those scary dreams. The pastor's family came over and prayed for me. I thanked God again that He always sent me all those kind people who helped me at the right time and the right places.

Matt and I knew that drinking alcohol caused us a lot of sadness and troubles in the past. We didn't want to waste time and repeat the same mistakes any more so we promised that we would avoid drinking alcohol as best we could for the rest of our lives. He already had been sober several years already. Matt diligently continued on his diet and exercise. We both abstained from drinking alcohol.

We promised three things—No divorce, No alcohol, No smoking for the sake of our child or children in the future.

We wanted to be obedient to God and continue to help others. We tried our best but there were some people who misunderstood us and tried to take advantage of. When we were helping them they were friendly and kind but when we said "No" to them they accused us and blamed us that our faith and the way of our living didn't go together. It was like as if everything had to be their way otherwise we were considered as hypocrites. Ironically, those people were Christians and claimed that they read the Bible everyday and prayed to God all the time.

I was deeply hurt and offended. I had so much pain and anger by their selfish attitudes but I knew that I had to forgive them because of my faith in Jesus and I did. When I asked God why those things happened to me and it was not fair, the Holy Spirit gently reminded me in my heart, "Let it go... Let it go... because I KNOW everything. So let it go..."

"Get rid of all bitterness, rage and anger, brawling and slander along with every form of malice. Be kind and compassionate to one another, forgiving each other, just as in Christ God forgave you.

— Ephesians 4:31-32

"But I tell you: Love your enemies and pray for those who persecute you, that you may be sons of your Father in heaven. He causes his sun to rise on the evil and the good, and sends rain on the righteous and the unrighteous."

— Matthew 5: 44-45

"And when you stand praying, if you hold anything against anyone, forgive him, so that your Father in heaven may forgive you your sins."

— Mark 11:25

"Do not judge, and you will not be judged. Do not condemn, and you will not be condemned. Forgive, and you will be forgiven. Give, and it will be given to you. A good measure, pressed down, shaken together and running over, will be poured into your lap. For with the measure you use, it will be measured to you."

— Luke 6: 37-38

Matt had been mentoring students at the *Minnesota Adult and Teen Challenge* for a while. It is a one-year Christian recovery program for alcohol and drug abuse. I wanted to help students at the program too so I applied to be a volunteer for the computer learning program but the hours didn't work out for me. They wanted someone who could help during the days but I had to work. So they suggested that I be a mentor instead and meet with a student once a week after work or on weekends. I was not sure if I was qualified to be a mentor.

Being a mentor sounded like I had to be a role model and I felt that I was far from being a role model to someone. However, I had seen Matt how he was mentoring his students. When I asked him what I should do to be a mentor he said, "Being a mentor doesn't mean that we have to be Jesus. We don't need to lecture them what to do. It's His job. But what we can do is be good friends and encourage the students to do well."

He also read his Bible before meeting his student. So I asked him, "Are you reading the Bible?"

His response was "I need some spiritual ammunition before I meet my student. Otherwise I don't know what to say."

Then we laughed together. Matt and his student usually went out for hockey and baseball games or to a movie theatre. Sometimes he invited his students to our house. We ordered pizza and watched football together. One of the students was a highly talented musician. So we asked him to play the piano for us and he played his own music that he composed and sang for us. It was such a blessing to all of us. We thanked God for the opportunity to share God's love and prayed for the students.

I decided to be a mentor and went to a mentor orientation class. When I was waiting for the class to start along with other people I heard Satan talking to me in my mind.

"Look at you! What a joke to see you sitting here to be a mentor! Who do you think you are? Do you think you are qualified to do this? This is not the place for you. You are supposed to be sitting at one of the AA meetings and tell people how drunken and miserable of a crazy life you lived in the past. Aren't you ashamed of sitting here? You want to be a mentor? What a joke!"

At the very moment, I rebuked Satan. "Get away from me, Satan! I am not going to listen to you anymore. You are not going to control me. My Lord is Jesus Christ, not you. I command you to get out of my mind in the name of Jesus Christ!"

> "Jesus said to him "Away from me, Satan! For it is written: Worship the Lord your God, and serve him only."
>
> — Matthew 4:10

I completed the orientation and was matched up with

a student, finally. I was a little bit nervous at the beginning because I was self-conscious with my English speaking ability but it didn't matter. Our relationship had been great! We shared our experiences, listened to each other and encouraged each other for our spiritual growth in God. We also became prayer partners and promised that we would start our days by kneeling down and pray to God every morning for 100 days. Our goal was making it as our habit for the rest of our lives. Sometimes I asked myself if I was my student's mentor or if she was my mentor because we became so bonded and the title of being a mentor or a mentee meant little to us. We were just real good friends and gave thanks to God for the wonderful friendship that we found in Jesus.

God's Invitation

Since I started mentoring, God put a strong desire in my heart that I wanted to do something for people who needed a second chance. I realized that my attempts to get a new job or change a career in a different business was not something God had in His mind. I wanted to know more about what He exactly wanted me to do. I knew that I was born in this world with a mission but I had been wondering to figure out what it was for such a long time.

I always asked God, "What should I do? I know I should do something but I don't know what it is. God, what do you want me to do??"

On Tuesday May 15, 2012 when I was in the middle of the thought again on what I should do in my life, I felt the Holy Spirit was telling me, "Write a book."

I thought it was one of my crazy thoughts that didn't make any sense and questioned myself, "Write a book? Is this my own thought or am I hearing God's voice?"

Then the thought came back again. "Write a book."

How in the world can I write a book? I am not a writer. This crazy wild thought will disappear eventually. I should think of something else. But the voice kept coming repeatedly.

"Write a book. Write a book."

I started feeling a heavy burden. *Among everything in the world why did I choose this thought of something I am not capable. I should think something else; something that I could handle.* But the thought did not go away. Instead it came back again and again as if someone was chanting to my ear; write a book, write a book, write a book...

I said, "OK. God. If I have to write a book, what should I write about?"

"Your life."

"My life? Who's going to read it? You know I have been trying to forget my painful memories but now I have to remember them all? Uhhhh…."

Then I asked again "You can use my hands because I am not a writer but what language? I know Korean will be much easier than English."

"English."

How in the world am I going to write a book in English??? This must be my own crazy thought, definitely not God.

I still struggled with English once in a while. Matt was used to my broken English and he understood what I meant exactly. My job at work didn't require much in speaking or writing because I worked on a computer for creating and fixing digital files. I would probably speak broken English for the rest of my life. I doubted and hoped the random thoughts would disappear the next morning.

I woke up the next morning and the first thing that I remembered was writing a book about my life in English. The heavy burden did not go away!!! Even though I was nervous I also felt that I was strangely getting excited at the same time. I had half doubt and half trust. I was not quite sure. Then I opened the Bible to seek for God's answer as I always did whenever I needed His guidance. I needed to know to make sure that I was not confused by my own random thoughts. I didn't know why but I felt like reading the book of 1 John.

I asked myself, "What's in the book of First John?"

Good words for sure but I didn't remember any particular

scripture in the book.

"If we confess our sins, He is faithful and just and will forgive us our sins and purify us from all unrighteousness."

— 1 John 1:9

Oh, I liked that scripture very much. I was curious what the next verse was and expected to read some encouraging ones before I left for work that would say that therefore God would bless us abundantly after we return to Him. I kept reading the book then I rubbed my eyes and re-read what I just saw because I felt something unexpected as if God was telling me in person.

"My dear children, I write this to you so that you will not sin."

— 1 John 2:1

"I write to you, dear children, because your sins have been forgiven on account of his name."

"I write to you, fathers, because you have known him who is from the beginning."

"I write to you, young men, because you have overcome the evil one."

"I write to you, dear children, because you have known the Father."

— 1 John 2:12-13

I felt the "I" in the scriptures was me. The scriptures also showed me the reasons why I should write too. I always wanted to help other people who needed a second chance. I wanted to let them know that there was a way to be forgiven. I wanted to encourage them that they could do better. Perhaps these reflections on my own past will keep sin from entering into my life.

Satan also came to me as he always had been in order to stop me from doing a good thing. I knew he was really good at his work. Satan, one by one, reminded me of my sins in the past, the girls who gossiped behind my back at work and the Christian people who accused and blamed me when I didn't do their ways. Satan questioned how they were going to gossip about me when the book finally came out. The evil Satan said that my book would become a mockery in the world and I would embarrass my entire family. However, God showed me this when I was reading His words in my quiet time.

"Forget the former things; do not dwell on the past, See, I am doing a new thing! Now it springs up; do you not perceive it?"

"I am making a way in the desert and streams in the wasteland."

— Isaiah 43:18-19

I went to the church in downtown again during my lunch break and cried out to God to guide me. *If writing a book is not Your purpose for me then please remove the heavy burden from my heart.* Besides, how could I get the money to print and publish the book? And how could I distribute the books? Am I going to end up putting a thousand copies of the books in my basement?

I felt absolutely helpless. I wondered why God wanted to use me, who had no ability and no capability of writing whatsoever. Writing a book about my life in English didn't seem to go anywhere.

I kept praying, "My Lord, I am nobody and I have nothing. What do You want from me? If this is not Your will, please do not allow me to have this burden." I just sat there cried and cried. The more I cried and prayed the more promises He showed me and encouraged me.

"He said to me, you are my servant, Israel, in whom I will display my splendor."

— Isaiah 49:3

"Trust in the Lord with all your heart and lean not on your own understanding; in all your ways acknowledge Him, and He will make your paths straight."

— Proverbs 3:5-6

I decided to give God 100 days of fasting, sort of. I quit drinking coffee and anything that had caffeine in it. Water was made by God but all drinks with caffeine were made by man. I used to drink coffee in unlimited quantities all day long. I tried to quit it several times but soon I found myself drinking it again after two or three days. This time it was different though. I wanted to be closer to God by giving up something I was obsessed with. I decided to focus on God's words and meditate on them.

I started getting up early in the morning which was almost impossible to do in the past because of a hangover or the lack of sleep from drinking coffee too much. I knelt down in a quiet room alone and started praying to God. I wanted to listen to His voice and communicate with Him. I wanted to know that He was there with me and feel His presence. At the beginning I couldn't help but crying not because I was sad but because I was so thankful for what He had done for me. God had seen me wandering around and becoming lost in the crowd. He had to do something in order to bring me back. So He himself came down to this world and died on the cross for my sins. I saw Jesus hanging on the cross on behalf of me. A bright light shined upon my dark heart like a search light and I confessed all my sins.

"Even if you have been banished to the most distant land under the heavens, from there the Lord your God will gather you and bring you back."

— Deuteronomy 30:4

"I am the way and the truth and the life. No one comes to the Father except through me."

— John 14:6

A full time job, a toddler to look after, and house chores didn't give me much quiet time to write a book. Sometimes I didn't know where to start but whenever I had a hard time I just prayed to God to help me. I knew that writing a book without His guidance would be a meaningless process and I didn't want to do that. I prayed and studied His words then I went back to my computer to keep writing. But I never thought of quitting. Once I started I did not want to excuse myself. No matter what, I wanted to finish. I learned that from my pilot training. If this book ever gets printed and read by someone it will be a true miracle because without God's help this project was impossible to begin with.

"Jesus looked at them and said, "With man this is impossible, but with God all things are possible."

— Matthew 19:26

I believe the trials in my past were the training that God permitted specifically for me and He sent my personal trainer, Jesus Christ. There were numerous times that I felt that God didn't listen to my prayers but to the prayers of others. I felt so many times that God was too slow to do His work for me. However, when I thought that He was too slow there were much more invaluable lessons that I learned and He molded me in the fire. When He had to work fast He never wasted any minute and never stopped amazing me with the miracles caused by His own ways far beyond my imagination. He gave me the first work visa after six months of the spiritual training but He gave me the new passport in less than eight hours when I was in a state of haste and urgency in Canada. He called me back to Korea with an unthinkable family emergency and had me get the surgeries so that I could conceive and have a baby, finally. He sent me all the angels each time I needed help. I truly experienced His miracles one after another.

"Even though you do not believe me, believe the miracles, that you may know and understand that the Father is in me, and I in the Father."

— John 10:38

I consider the first half of my life was training at God's boot camp. Now I am living the second half of my life. I don't want to repeat the same mistakes that I made before. I am out of the boot camp and I want to enter into the Promised Land as a mustard seed. I used to question God what I could do since I had nothing to share and I was nobody. He gave me this thought that He would not plant a big tree with no fruit underground but rather plant a mustard seed instead, and grow.

"It is like a mustard seed, which is the smallest seed you plant in the ground. Yet when planted, it grows and becomes the largest of all garden plants, with such big branches that the birds of the air can perch in its shade."

— Mark 4:31-32

—The new beginning starts right here—